The Evolution of Path Dependence

NEW HORIZONS IN INSTITUTIONAL AND EVOLUTIONARY
ECONOMICS

Series Editor: Geoffrey M. Hodgson
Research Professor, University of Hertfordshire Business School, UK

Economics today is at a crossroads. New ideas and approaches are challenging
the largely static and equilibrium-oriented models that used to dominate
mainstream economics. The study of economic institutions – long neglected in the
economics textbooks – has returned to the forefront of theoretical and empirical
investigation.

This challenging and interdisciplinary series publishes leading works at the
forefront of institutional and evolutionary theory and focuses on cutting-edge
analyses of modern socio-economic systems. The aim is to understand both the
institutional structures of modern economies and the processes of economic
evolution and development. Contributions will be from all forms of evolutionary
and institutional economics, as well as from Post-Keynesian, Austrian and other
schools. The overriding aim is to understand the processes of institutional
transformation and economic change.

Titles in the series include:

Institutions, Money and Entrepreneurship
Hayek's Theory of Cultural Evolution
Edited by Jürgen G. Backhaus

Productivity, Competitiveness and Incomes in Asia
An Evolutionary Theory of International Trade
Hans-Peter Brunner and Peter M. Allen

The Hardship of Nations
Exploring the Paths of Modern Capitalism
Edited by Benjamin Coriat, Pascal Petit and Geneviève Schméder

An Economic Analysis of Innovation
Extending the Concept of National Innovation Systems
Markus Balzat

Evolutionary Economics and Environmental Policy
Survival of the Greenest
*Jeroen C.J.M. van den Bergh, Albert Faber, Annemarth M. Idenburg and
Frans H. Oosterhuis*

Property Rights, Consumption and the Market Process
David Emanuel Andersson

The Evolution of Path Dependence
Edited by Lars Magnusson and Jan Ottosson

The Evolution of Path Dependence

Edited by

Lars Magnusson

Professor of Economic History, Department of Economic History, Uppsala University, Sweden

and

Jan Ottosson

Associate Professor, Department of Economic History, Uppsala University, Sweden

NEW HORIZONS IN INSTITUTIONAL AND EVOLUTIONARY ECONOMICS

Edward Elgar
Cheltenham, UK • Northampton, MA, USA

Published by
Edward Elgar Publishing Limited
The Lypiatts
15 Lansdown Road
Cheltenham
Glos GL50 2JA
UK

Edward Elgar Publishing, Inc.
William Pratt House
9 Dewey Court
Northampton
Massachusetts 01060
USA

A catalogue record for this book
is available from the British Library

Library of Congress Control Number: 2009928591

Mixed Sources
Product group from well-managed
forests and other controlled source:
www.fsc.org Cert no. SA-COC-156!
© 1996 Forest Stewardship Council

FSC

ISBN 978 1 84376 137 2

Printed and bound by MPG Books Group, UK

Contents

List of figures   vii
List of tables and boxes   viii
List of contributors   ix
Acknowledgements   x

Path dependence: some introductory remarks   1
Lars Magnusson and Jan Ottosson

1   Path dependence versus path-breaking crises: an alternative view   19
    Bo Stråth

2   Second-degree path dependence: information costs, political
    objectives, and inappropriate small-farm settlement of the
    North American Great Plains   43
    Gary D. Libecap

3   Revisiting railway history: the case of institutional change and
    path dependence   70
    Lena Andersson-Skog

4   Path dependence in economic geography   87
    Magnus Lagerholm and Anders Malmberg

5   The deceptive juncture: the temptation of attractive
    explanations and the reality of political life   108
    PerOla Öberg and Kajsa Hallberg Adu

6   The role of institutions and organizations in shaping radical
    scientific innovations   139
    Rogers Hollingsworth

7   Path dependence and public policy: lessons from economics   166
    Stephen E. Margolis

8   Can path dependence explain institutional change? Two
    approaches applied to welfare state reform   191
    Bernhard Ebbinghaus

Index   219

v

Figures

2.1	The Great Plains	49
2.2	Montana annual precipitation	52
2.3	Federal aid per capita in the Great Plains, 1933–36	57
2.4	Net migration in the Great Plains, 1930–35	59
2.5	Farm size adjustment: the Great Plains, the Midwest and New South Wales	60
2.6	Great Plains soil erosion, 1934	64
5.1	The time horizons of different causal accounts	117
6.1	The relationships among scientific diversity, communication/integration and making major discoveries	150
6.2	Multi-level analysis of major discoveries, panel one	158
6.3	Multi-level analysis of major discoveries, panel two	159
6.4	Multi-level analysis of major discoveries, panel three	160
8.1	Path dependence I: trodden path	194
8.2	Example of path dependence I: early retirement	197
8.3	Path dependence II: branching pathways	201
8.4	Path dependence II: pension reform	204
8.5	Mechanisms of self-reinforcement	206

Tables and boxes

TABLES

2.1	Small farms on the Great Plains	50
2.2	Great Plains farmers with relief and rehabilitation grants and advances, 1935	58
2.3	Family emigration, Great Plains states, 1930	58
2.4	Farm size change 1930 to 1970 in Great Plains counties	60
7.1	Adoption payoffs	176
8.1	Two models of path dependence	211

BOXES

6.1	Indicators of major discoveries	148
6.2	Organizational contexts facilitating the making of major discoveries	149
6.3	Organizational contexts constraining the making of major discoveries	153

Contributors

Lena Andersson-Skog, Professor, Department of Economic History, Umeå University, Sweden.

Bernhard Ebbinghaus, Professor of Macrosociology and Director of Mannheim Centre for European Social Research (MZES), University of Mannheim, Germany.

Kajsa Hallberg Adu, Research Assistant, MA, Department of Government, Uppsala University, Sweden.

Rogers Hollingsworth, Professor, University of Wisconsin–Madison, USA.

Magnus Lagerholm, PhD, Department of Social and Economic Geography and Centre for Research on Innovation and Industrial Dynamics, Uppsala University, Sweden.

Gary D. Libecap, Professor, Donald Bren School of Environmental Science and Management, University of California, Santa Barbara and National Bureau of Economic Research, USA.

Lars Magnusson, Professor, Department of Economic History, Uppsala University, Sweden.

Anders Malmberg, Professor, Department of Social and Economic Geography and Centre for Research on Innovation and Industrial Dynamics, Uppsala University, Sweden.

Stephen E. Margolis, Professor, North Carolina State University, Raleigh, USA.

PerOla Öberg, Associate Professor, Department of Government, Uppsala University, Sweden.

Jan Ottosson, Associate Professor, Department of Economic History, Uppsala University, Sweden.

Bo Stråth, Professor, Helsinki University, Finland.

Acknowledgements

This volume was made possible by financial support from the former National Institute for Working Life, Sweden. We would like to thank Mrs Helle Stensen for administrative support. In the process of preparing the manuscript, we had good discussions with the authors in this volume at a workshop held in Visby, Sweden. We would especially like to thank the participants for their patience and insightful comments.

Path dependence: some introductory remarks[1]

Lars Magnusson and Jan Ottosson

I

The notion of path dependence has been discussed and utilized in various social sciences during the past two decades. The increasing interest in institutions and economic growth has certainly been important in this respect. Also, the role of technology as well as the discussion of various heterodox aspects of economic evolution might also be mentioned. More specifically, the rise of historical institutionalism and the interest in institutionalism in several social sciences has led to a number of applications of path dependence in various social sciences. As Gartland (2005, p. 687) rightly observes, there seem to be several applications of path dependence in various social sciences outside economics, but relatively few references among economists towards other social science's application of this concept. We can see two dangers with this development. First, the rising number of empirical applications might lead to an uncritical use of the notion of path dependence. Second, we agree with Gartland that the ignorance among some economists to acknowledge important research regarding path dependence in other social sciences might lead to two parallel discussions.

In relation to Hodgson's argument (1993) regarding the risk of economic imperialism into other social sciences, we believe that all social sciences – including economics – might gain from current discussions of path dependence broadly illuminated from various angles. Therefore it seems appropriate to further discuss the topic of path dependence from various aspects in this Edward Elgar Companion on path dependence. The aim of this volume is therefore to illustrate how various disciplines have used the concept of path dependence and to illuminate studies within these fields. Also, one further aim is to discuss the often used concept of path dependency and analyse the possibilities as well as the limitations of its applications.

The term of path dependence has been attributed to several older economists. Gartland (2005) suggest that Schumpeter was an innovative researcher in this respect when arguing that history was one important aspect when studying economics. This was later acknowledged by Rosenberg (1994) when he argued for using path dependence as a tool of such a method. Also, recent research has identified scholars such as Menger and Veblen (1915), among others, who were associated with an early use of path dependence even though they did not use the concept (Martin and Sunely, 2006, p. 397). Arrow's important discussion of the historiographic records of path dependence also points to the works of Cournot in the 1830s in terms of increasing returns, also acknowledging Veblen's work regarding path dependence (Arrow, 2000, pp. 173, 175). Douglas Puffert also listed Veblen (1915), Frankel (1955), Kindleberger (1964) and David (1975) as especially important scholars in terms of emphasizing early aspects of path dependence, especially interrelatedness of the technology and economic history (Puffert, 2003; see also Hodgson, 1998, on the early influences on path dependence).

Within the field of technology of history, path dependence has been used as a tool of understanding processes of lock-in and changing technologies. Initially, this was used as alternative explanations of choices of technology which differed from standard neoclassical explanations. Nathan Rosenberg, being immensely influential within this field, argued in the volume *Exploring the Black Box*, published in 1994, that ongoing technological progress must be understood against earlier technological experiences. Magnusson (2001) has elsewhere interpreted this as containing elements of path dependence, since earlier technological breakthroughs at least to some extent may limit choices available for actors. According to this tradition of thought, historical paths influence and limit the scope of actors involved in emerging technologies. Some well-known stylized examples of this have been gas engines and railway gauges. In a recent application of path dependence in economic history, Peter Scott (2001; 2006) has argued that the decline of the British coal industry was closely related to the lock-in effect of suboptimal technology.

Further, Magnusson argued that two types of notions of path dependence within the history of technology have emerged. If the Rosenberg interpretation might be called a 'weak' version of path dependence, 'strong' versions of path dependence can be found among scholars such as Bijker, Hughes and Latour within the systems of technology approach. They argue not only that the actual choices available are limited owing to earlier historical experiences, but that the cognitive search progress is influenced by these earlier historical events. The notion of large technical systems can be seen as one of the most influential schools of thought within this 'strong version' field, where Thomas Hughes and Bijker are among the most influential scholars.

II

The Contributions of Paul David

There is, however, no doubt about the pioneering role of Paul David and Brian Arthur, who were the first to initiate a discussion of the relevance of path dependency, in the 1980s and 1990s. They used path dependence in their original works as a description of lock-in effects in terms of technology. Arrow also points to the early work of Paul David from 1971, along with Atkinson and Stiglitz's work on technology from 1969 (Arrow, 2000, p. 175). One key factor was the recognition of non-ergodic systems, emphasizing that it was hard to shake off earlier history, as discussed by Martin and Sunley (2006). Paul David (1985) used the example of the QWERTY keyboard to illustrate how choices of new technology were influenced by forces other than mere optimal choices on a perfect market. The basic argument of this influential article was that the organization of the letters on the keyboard was a result of small chance events, thus giving rise to a standard despite the competitor Dvorak keyboard layout being more optimal, according to David. This argument was further elaborated in several publications by David (David, 1990, 1994; and David and Thomas, 2003) to follow.

In general terms, David has argued that it is not possible to understand why certain technologies have been chosen without analysing earlier events and their impact on existing technology choices. This has been discussed in terms of 'history matters'. David discusses three reasons why such dependencies occurred. First, cognitive selections developed over time can be seen as shaping a collective memory, being one part of reducing choices for actors due to historical reasons. Second, firm-specific investments might also be a part of such path dependence, sensitive to earlier historical events. The third reason relates to strong interrelatedness in complex organizations, which also would include technological interrelatedness (Magnusson, 2001; Martin and Sunley, 2006). As Magnusson has argued, this is certainly a version of path dependence which can be seen as more closely linked to the 'strong' notion of path dependence.

Also, it is indeed a far more general definition compared with Rosenberg's interpretation regarding technical systems and their process of transformation. Path dependence in this interpretation can be regarded as being sensitive to random choices at the beginning of a process, and where these random small steps will be reinforced even further. Also, in an important article by Antonelli (2006), the role of path dependence and localized technical change and innovations is discussed in terms of a framework, or a tool, for explaining economic dynamics by going beyond the static analysis of general equilibrium.

In an influential article from 2001 (also republished in 2007), David discussed the heated debate concerning path dependence, as well as the various applications. It is worth noticing that Hodgson suggest that this is one of the most important articles regarding path dependence (Hodgson, 2007, p. 14). David suggests the following definition:

> *Path-dependence*, as I wish to use the term, refers to a dynamic property of allocative processes. It may be defined either with regard to the relationship between the process dynamics and the outcome(s) to which it converges, or the limiting probability distribution of the stochastic process under consideration. (David, 2007, p. 123; original emphasis)

Also, David argues that a positive definition of path dependence might be formulated in the following way: 'A positive definition: A path dependent stochastic process is one whose asymptotic distribution evolves as a consequence (function of) the process's own history' (David, 2007, p. 125). By giving path dependence a more general definition, this also had important implications for the role of lock-in effects, as further noted by David.

> Path dependent systems – which have a multiplicity of possible equilibria among which event-contingent selections can occur – may thus become locked in to attractors that are optimal, or that are just as good as any others in the feasible set, or that take paths leading to places everyone would wish to have been able to avoid, once they have arrived there. (David, 2007, p. 131)

In line with the above stated definitions, David and Thomas have argued that path dependence should be considered as a systematic feature. They especially emphasize the role of path dependence in a dynamic system: 'of a system whose motion remains under the influence of conditions that are themselves the contingent legacies of events and actions in its history' (David and Thomas, 2003, p. 15). In this interpretation of path dependence it is not useful to analyse all economic phenomena in a path-dependence influenced analysis. They suggest that several problems can rather be better analysed by a traditional demand and supply analysis. However, David and Thomas suggest that to what extent path dependence occurs in economic life is an empirical problem. They argue strongly against the idea of path dependence as a theory. Rather, it should be seen 'as a label that refers to particular dynamic properties that characterise some but not all resource allocation processes' (David and Thomas, 2003, p. 17). They further mention that it can be defined as a process associated with the dynamic processes and the outcome or the limitation of possible actions available within a dynamic system.

Thus, a dynamic system could be characterized by being a path-independent system, where the initial conditions will not hamper future development. The case of path-dependent systems could rather be defined as: 'a path-dependent stochastic system is one in which the system's asymptotic distribution evolves as a consequence (function of) the process's own history' (David and Thomas, 2003, p. 18).

The authors also argue that path-dependent processes are not only a matter of identifying suboptimal choices, due to static inefficiencies. They see, for example, markets with strong network externalities as particularly sensitive to initial historical shaping events, but they also emphasize that in some instances, path dependence might also be a mechanism that can be important in promoting dynamic efficiency. The analysis of positive feedback phenomena are at the centre of both such approaches (David and Thomas, 2003, p. 26).

To sum up, this interpretation of path dependence suggests that only some economic issues are suitable for this label. Traditional demand-supply explanations are in fact more useful in explaining several economic phenomena. On the other hand, for specific empirical problems, for example, in industries with network externalities, path dependence can be used as a label or tool to study positive feedback phenomena. Such phenomena can be both negative to its character – hampering economic dynamics – or positive – by enhancing successful economic development even further.

According to our view, this new development of the concept of path dependence may intuitively be promising, since the issue of institutional change might be included in such a definition. However, there might be a risk of adding little explanatory value with this broad concept of path dependency, owing to the obvious risk of explaining every dynamic process – successful or not – as a path-dependent process. This opens up path dependency to types of explanations that are very general.

Brian Arthur and Increasing Returns

Brian Arthur discussed, with regard to the technology interpretation, the mechanisms that created path dependence and the interrelationship with positive feedbacks in the economy in terms of increasing returns. The notion of increasing returns was especially important within knowledge-based industries, according to Arthur. In contrast to diminishing returns, increasing returns made it possible to reach several equilibria. This made it possible to better understand why the market choice was not necessarily the only optimal solution. The importance of initial random effects, 'small effects' as Arthur put it in a seminal article in 1989, and the locked-in path once chosen, were essential in Arthur's discussion of path dependence and increasing returns.

Important factors behind these mechanisms were positive learning effects (on the supply side, according to Puffert), large initial investments, economies of scope, externalities (demand side – Puffert, 2003; see also Katz and Shapiro, 1994), and regional external economies. The last factor was emphasized by Arthur, where the initial location decision was crucial for the future lock-in effects in terms of agglomerative effects (Magnusson, 2001, p. 110). Another empirical example used by Arthur, widely cited, criticized and discussed afterwards, was the choice between the videocassette recorder (VCR) systems – VHS and Betamax.

Both David and Arthur emphasized the case of technology, and the importance of chance or initial events. Also, both authors claimed that the notion of path dependence was indeed important with respect not only regarding the technology in itself, but also the whole economy. However, one difference between the two authors which Puffert (2003) points out is that David can be seen as one representative of a long tradition of technological interrelatedness, while Arthur in the early articles on path dependence is influenced by mathematical economics.

The Liebowitz–Margolis Criticism of Path Dependence

In several highly critical articles and books, Liebowitz and Margolis (for example, 1995) have forcefully argued that most of these phenomena discussed within the path dependence discussion could be analysed by standard neoclassical economics. In one important work they discuss three types of path dependence, where the difference between these types is the information available for the agent. Within the first degree of path dependence a second-rate choice might be rational and optimal owing to the fact that the agent is aware of the costs attained when abandoning an earlier path. The second degree of path dependence can be seen as a higher degree of incomplete information in a choice situation. An economic agent can later be aware of the incomplete information at the time of the earlier choice.

However, according to Liebowitz and Margolis, that is not a case of inefficient solution owing to the actual loss of relevant information. The third case of path dependence is where the economic actor is well aware of more optimal choices, but still prefers the path-dependent choice. The authors thus conclude that the two first mentioned cases of path dependence can be seen as rational choices, best analysed with standard neoclassical tools. The third option was seen as being very rare and not worthwhile concentrating on.

We have in earlier works (Magnusson and Ottosson, 1996) discussed these three degrees of path dependence and argued it may not be entirely clear that the first two degrees of path dependence might be analysed properly within the framework of neoclassical economics, since it may not be clear what the actual cost of abandoning earlier paths of choice might be for the agent. Also, in a situation with radical uncertainty, arguments regarding rule-following might still be more fruitful. Another point of discussion that we highlighted was the possibility that the rule-following process and the process of obtaining and processing information might be socially influenced, thereby restricting actual choices, thus creating path-dependent choices. This argument in terms of genuine rule-following was developed by Vanberg (1988) and further extended by Rutherford (1994). This can be seen as a reference to the earlier mentioned 'strong' view of path dependence.

On the other hand, we pointed out the risks of totally denying the forceful criticism of Liebowitz and Margolis, also acknowledging the need for an ongoing discussion of the concept of path dependence. The ongoing discussion during this decade on these issues has developed in various directions. The answers to this criticism from Arthur and David have been extensive.

The second part of Liebowitz and Margolis's main criticisms on path dependence was built upon through empirical studies on the most cited empirical examples emphasized by David and Arthur. The case of QWERTY was heavily criticized as being misinterpreted. The choice of the QWERTY keyboard was, according to Liebowitz and Margolis, the most efficient choice, since the Dvorak keyboard represented underperforming technology. Also, the case of the VCR was also seen as an example of how efficient markets could adopt the most efficient technology. As noted earlier, Paul David answered this criticism in an important article in 2001.

A third position in this debate has been launched by Martin and Sunley (2006), concluding that both David's argument with regard to Liebowitz and Margolis as well as the interpretation by these authors of path dependence might be considered somewhat ambiguous. Several authors have recognized the different meanings of path dependence and lock-in when further interpreted by David and Arthur (Lawson, 1997). According to Martin and Sunley there is a difference between evolutionary economic systems and path dependence. In line with Witt (2003a; 2003b), they argue that an evolutionary economic system might be interpreted in much broader terms compared with the narrow concept of path dependence, despite the fact that some authors suggest that path dependence is the first-order concept in evolutionary economics. Indeed, Vromen (1995), as noted by Martin and Sunley, suggests that path dependence is only one aspect of selection as well as adaptive learning.

The third position in this debate points to the increasing literature on the role of choice, where rational choice and rule-following arguments have been among the most discussed topics, the path dependency discussion points to the importance of increasing our understanding of such processes of agent's choice (Ramstad, 1994; Rutherford, 1994; Vanberg, 1994). Within the tradition of Nelson and Winter (1982), several authors have emphasized that rule-following exists (Rutherford, 1994, p. 54). Also, such routines can be of importance during long periods of time, as discussed by Nelson and Winter. The role of uncertainty and the consequences for the economic actor's behaviour in terms of rule-following has been illuminated by Heiner (1983), North (1990; 2005) and Denzau and North (1994).

Institutional Theory: North versus Anti-Determinism

The debate regarding the role of history, lock-in effects and the acknowledgement of increasing returns also made clear that institutions and history did play an important role in terms of general economics, the initial articles by David and Arthur became important analytical component in Douglass North's work (1990; 2005). Why some nations were stuck in poverty while others prospered was seen as one important example of the existence of suboptimal behaviour directly affecting economic growth between various nations. Positive transaction costs, uncertainty, and actors forming organizations and institutions as rules of the game, made it possible to more directly explain the mechanisms behind different paths of economic growth. North (1990, p. 95) suggests that path dependence can only occur in certain situations when increasing returns and imperfect markets are at hand. North (2005) has further emphasized the role of culture in influencing choices made by economic agents.

The debate regarding the lock-in effect and the mechanisms that constitute paths chosen has also pointed to the notion of path dependence and change. Earlier studies by Thelen and Steinmo, Gersick and Setterfield discussed two types of processes of change. The first process was discussed in terms of punctuated equilibrium, where a sudden dramatic change radically broke earlier patterns of path dependence. A strong version of this explanation is preferred by Mahoney (2000), who argues that only a precise definition of path dependence is useful when understanding certain event chains with 'deterministic properties' (quoted from Streeck and Thelen, 2005; Mahoney, 2000, p. 507). Another example of scholars wanting a more precise definition of path dependence in this respect are Martin and Sunley (2006; 2007), who have raised the issue that path dependence as an explanation might be lacking a more precise meaning within the field of economic geography. Similar argument has been raised by Page (2006).

The second process was discussed in terms of a slow continuous process of change, where attention was focused on incremental changes and learning in relation to adaption, see for example, North (1990), where he explains the latter as the most common one. In a more recent contribution Streeck and Thelen note 'the impoverished state of theorizing on issues of institutional change' (Streeck and Thelen, 2005, p. 1). They criticize the punctuated equilibrium model in its strong interpretations of drawing too heavily on exogenous shock types of explanations for not being able to explain processes of gradual change. On the other hand, they continue, recent approaches within the field of variety of capitalism type of explanations (Hall and Soskice) tend to emphasize institutional resiliency. However, according to Streeck and Thelen, such explanations seem to neglect possible explanations of institutional change. Rather, these theories 'regard . . . almost all feedback within a system as positive and operating to maintain traditional structures' (Streeck and Thelen, 2005, p. 5). Also, scholars like Amable (2000) and Boyer (2005) have, inspired by the variety of capitalism literature, discussed institutional complementarities in terms of alternative approaches towards initial path-dependent conditions (see also Aoki, 2000, in this respect). Boyer, for example, discusses how such complementaries might be of special interest regarding the convergence–divergence debate (Boyer, 2005).

Paul Pierson's (2000; 2004) discussion of institutions and path dependence as a tool of understanding the welfare state is seen as one example of a theory more helpful in explaining institutional resilience, but not satisfactory in understanding institutional change. Rather, Streeck and Thelen suggest that a more complex theory might give room for explanations open to processes of 'incremental change with transformative results' (Streeck and Thelen, 2005, p. 9). Especially important engines of institutional changes are the difference between design processes of institutions and their implementation, respectively. Five models of gradual change of formal institutions (which differ from North's latest emphasis on informal institutions) are discussed, all examples of gradual change (see also Crouch and Farrell, 2004).

Close to development within political science and the role of path dependence, similar patterns of thought have emerged in political economy and transaction costs, as we have discussed elsewhere (see Magnusson and Ottosson, 2001). One of these lines of analysis, the notion of political transaction costs, is especially relevant in this context. Political transaction costs deal with actors trying to make decisions in complex and uncertain political spheres. The actors are seen as acting in the field of bounded rationality. Transaction costs are transferred from the element of real-world economics to the field of policy (Dixit, 1996; Olson, 2000; Williamson, 1996). Based on an extension of Williamson's model of transaction cost economics, Dixit suggested that the complexity, uncertainty, information impactedness, opportunism and asset specificity in a dynamic environment might be applied within the political world (Dixit, 1996;

Dugger, 1993, might also be mentioned in this context). Owing to the incompleteness of contracts a difference emerges between policy outcomes and policy aims.

The main reason, according to Dixit, is the complexity of political contracts, since such contracts are even more incomplete. This results in higher transaction costs, but the consequences of these transaction costs are more problematic compared with the economic sphere, owing to the longer term involved in constitutional arrangements. Incomplete contracts within the field of constitution leave room for actors' opportunistic behaviour (Dixit, 1996, pp. 20–21). Dixit further argues that within the field of policy decisions, monitoring and incentives are more complex compared with the marketplace, since the costs of enforcement are higher. Further, the complexity of the principal–agent dilemma is illustrated through the existence of multilateral principal–agent relations within public administration. Within this tradition, the paths of implementation are also acknowledged as important, with government agencies as key actors owing to incomplete contracts, and multiple principal–agent relationships (Dixit, 1996, p. 56; Wilson, 1989, ch. 17).

As we have argued elsewhere (Magnusson and Ottosson, 2001), this can be discussed in light of the findings by Krueger (1996, pp. 169–218) regarding regulatory systems and the role of history in understanding regulated economies (Goldin and Libecap, 1994). The role of history might be better illuminated in understanding processes of policy outcomes in regulation of the economy, due to path-dependent patterns influencing implementation in such policy processes.

There are limits to applying political transaction costs in neoclassical designs (Magnusson and Ottosson, 1996; 2001). Instead, we have suggested elsewhere that it might be more fruitful to discuss such an approach within a more historically grounded framework with more specific path-dependent factors included in explaining dynamic types of processes available (Magnusson and Ottosson, 1996, p. 353).

III

To what extent is path dependence a useful concept in economics? As we have seen, there is no general agreement among scholars on this point. For example Liebowitz and Margolis (1995) argue that 'real' path dependence occurs extremely seldom in economic life and, consequently, the phenomenon might very well be discarded altogether. Irrational behaviour – to the extent it occurs – has no place in economics. Rather, the task of economics is to explain economic behaviour given a certain set of conditions (including the information available) which 'bounds' the individual to make specific choices in an economic world of more or less uncertainty. Hence, what in general seems to be 'irrational' behaviour must be understood in such a context of cognitive boundedness and lack of full information. Certainly, with such a strict definition of rationality it seems unlikely that much economic behaviour falls outside. To follow a 'path' or to stick to rule behaviour according to tradition is thus best understood as a consequence of high levels of uncertainty; the cost of breaking off from the traditional path can in some circumstances be too high. Hence, something we might call 'path dependence' or 'rule-following' of course occurs frequently in economic life (Rutherford, 1994). Moreover, it can be explained in a customary way from the maximizing and rational behaviour of the individual.

However, this does not exclude, of course, that path dependence of the first and second order (according to Liebowitz and Margolis's vocabulary) is an interesting phenomenon in the economic world. The high cost of information as well as high sunken costs of different kinds can make it very expensive indeed (and highly risky) to change one's behaviour. Moreover, such costs also create barriers of entry for those who seek to compete. In such an economic realm increasing returns of scale often occur, which also propel strong forces in favour of path dependence. Hence, the conclusion must be that 'path dependence' is still an interesting phenomenon and to understand how it is created must be of utmost important for economic science. Under which institutional constraints are path dependence (or rule-following) likely to occur? At which levels of cost? In which context of uncertainty can we expect path dependence to appear? What is the price for breaking with a path? Without doubt these are pertinent questions if one is to be able to understand economic behaviour and change (or perhaps, rather, the lack of it). Only a small proportion of our behaviour, for example, on the market can be explained as rational choices in a situation of perfect information (lemons). Not least the insistence by economists such as Stigler and Akerlof on how common situations of assymetrical information appear in a specific market has further emphasized this point. Rather, in many instances we follow the tradition and stick to a certain set of rules which seems to have served us well previously. We are not willing to undertake the cost – or are too lazy even to count the cost involved – to change our behaviour.

Economic institutions, according to North and others, can be regarded as rules (formal and informal). They are set to work by rational actors in circumstances where public choices have to be made. There are reasons to believe that the institutions we choose in order to solve such conflicts are to some extent determined by past experiences, the choices we have made in the past and given our (without doubt highly restrictive) knowledge of institutional alternatives and how they work in practice. This might help to explain institutional inertia as a general phenomenon, but also why we so often seem to acknowledge different institutional 'styles' or modes of governance, for example, varying among different countries. Without doubt there are different national systems or regulations which can only be understood in a context of path dependence. We recognize different 'varieties of capitalism', different models of welfare and labour market regulations, and so on. Hence the rules that define different institutions are historically created according to choices that are highly path dependent. We should then not be surprised to find specific and long trajectories of regulations with regard to specific goods and markets, for example, the American sugar (Krueger, 1996) or the European aeroplane industry (Ottosson, 2001).

However, individual choices are highly influenced by rule-following and path-dependent behaviour. As consumers we are often prone to follow certain rules of thumb when we feel that calculations are too costly or the outcome highly ambiguous. Also firms follow certain rules, or what Richard Nelson and Sidney Winter (1982) have called 'routines'. Past experience creates a pool of useful knowledge which can be used when individuals or firms confront a specific problem or are forced to make choices. Without doubt, behaviour on such a basis can very well be defined as 'path dependent'.

Growth processes occurring over time include path-determined aspects. Hence, increasing returns often help to create growth processes in certain sectors of the economy or with specific regional attributes which are stable over long periods of time. Past and sunken investments also contribute to such a process of 'first- and second-order' path dependence (once again according to Leibowitz and Margolis, 1995). Certain patterns of economic growth also lead to specific collective problems of choice which, in turn, lead to specific institutional solutions. These, in turn, probably even further enforce specific growth processes over time, including such spirals over positive and negative economic development which Douglass North speaks of (North, 1990). As such institutions give opportunity to diffuse different incentives among actors this even further enforces such spirals of 'good' or 'negative' development or specific part-determined growth processes.

It seems clear that path dependence can be a useful concept for economists when applied in such an open way. It can be a useful label in order to describe different forms of rule-following and when a given path is chosen instead of other or new alternatives. The next step is to analyse the specific circumstances and causes of why rule-following and path dependence occurred in the specific context. It can shed light both on why repetition and inertia is so common in human social and economic affairs, but also in which circumstances changes occur. When new information appears or when its price radically shifts downwards, a long historical path can suddenly be deserted. Big events and shocks from outside often force us to carry out calculations and make new choices. However, small incremental changes can also suddenly change the cost and price structure in a fashion which make new choices feasible and necessary. Hence, so-called punctuated equilibria as a consequence of shocks from outside are not the only way to understand and explain change. But there is no doubt that big events often stimulate people to think in new ways and make radically new choices. For all this, the concept of path dependence can be a useful tool for further analysis. However, it is not – perhaps to the disappointment of some radicals – an alternative to mainstream economic theory. Rather, in our view, it can be seen as a complement to the general economic analysis of phenomena such as choice and market behaviour. However, its radical implication is that it challenges the economists to pay more attention to the role of institutions and historical development. Hence, as the great economic historian John Clapham emphasized long ago, there is perhaps nothing genuinely wrong with analytical economics. However, its empty boxes must be filled with content in order to become really relevant as a social science.

IV

The application of path dependence has been widespread, which we have illustrated above, with examples from the history of technology, the rise of the welfare state as interpreted by Pierson (2000), and the use of path dependence in political economy. (See also Page, 2006, as well as Alexander, 2001.) Various applications can be found in several social sciences besides the above-mentioned cases: from economic geography, industrial relations (Howell, 2005), studies of Russia and the transition economies (Hedlund, 2005; see also Chavance and Magnin, 2002), within the field of business studies (see examples mentioned by Ebbinghaus in this volume), and financial economics, to economic history and detailed studies of coal mines in England, to medieval trade (Greif, 2006) and railway gauge (Puffert, 2002; see also Cowan, 1990, 1996). Also, one example from sociology is found in Goldstone (1998), as well as several examples from within the field of innovation studies (Langlois and Savage, 2001; Redding, 2002). In this volume we give some further insights into how various applications of path dependence have been used. The contributions in this volume suggest that there has been a development from applications of path dependence in the history of technology towards other fields of social science. The discussion has focused upon various types of definitions of path dependence (strong or weak type of definitions). Also, the application of the notion of path dependence has been discussed widely within some parts of social sciences. One further important aspect deals with various types of institutional stagnation versus institutional change. Such phenomena are discussed in the chapters that follow.

In Chapter 1 historian Bo Stråth critically examines the concept of path dependence from the viewpoint of scepticism towards structural explanations in understanding historical processes. In the second chapter economic historian Gary Libecap discusses path dependence from the viewpoint of political economy, political action by the state in land use and property right, with long-term implications for the farmers in the USA. Economic historian Lena Andersson-Skog discusses various applications of path dependence with reference to the example of the railway sector. From the viewpoint of economic geography, the important contributions, for example, by Krugman in relation to various explanations of economic agglomerations are discussed by Lagerholm and Malmberg. Examples from the political field of applications are presented by Öberg and Hallberg Adu, who argue that there is a need to further improve theories of evolution, while looking at stability and change within the same analytical frame. They especially discuss how various country patterns of polity and industrial relations can be interpreted by path dependence. Within the field of economic growth, and the interaction between science, technology and innovations, historian Hollingsworth discusses interaction processes against such a background with references to the French regulation school of thought together with historical institutionalism. Further, Hollingsworth discusses in detail how institutional environments influence organizations' innovativeness by studying major innovations in biomedical science, pointing to the role of organizational culture in this respect. Margolis discusses from the viewpoint as one of the leading critics against earlier interpretations of path dependence, but discusses other potential areas of using path dependence, as one part of analysing policy processes. In the final chapter Ebbinghaus interprets labour markets and the welfare state as especially interesting in using path dependence. Ebbinghaus also discusses institutional change in relation to path dependence and discusses the limits of path dependence in this respect.

The chapters presented in this volume illustrate the various interpretations of path dependence as one important common ground. Ranging from a principal and critical discussion of use of structural type of explanations towards more positive views of the potential of path dependence in new areas, such as the political economy and economic geography, there are some particular points of interest. First, one of the most forceful critics of path dependence within the field of technology suggest that path dependence might be potentially important within the field of political economy, owing to the differences between market and policy. In order to better explain economic policy outcomes, path dependence might be useful.

Second, several authors comment upon the interrelation between stability and change, and how path-dependent types of explanations need to be further developed towards explaining patterns of change. Also, various levels of analysis in relation to path dependence have been raised as a point of particular interest, where not only micro- or macro-levels have been addressed, but also various middle-range theories. Third, the interaction between actor and structure in relation to the path dependence discussion has been addressed in various parts of this volume. As we have argued in this chapter, it is crucial to further discuss more precisely what type of notion of path dependence various applications are using. If the concept is not carefully defined from the viewpoint of a new area of application, the risk is obvious that the explanatory value of path dependence might be in danger. Instead, it is certain that there is a range of empirical fields which we can only address properly by using a clearly defined path-dependence type of explanations. The discussions in this volume also make it clear that using path dependence uncritically in various empirical areas may not achieve such a development.

NOTE

1. We would especially like to thank Geoffrey Hodgson for most valuable comments on an earlier version of this chapter.

REFERENCES

Alexander, G. (2001), 'Institutions, path dependence and democratic consolidation', *Journal of Theoretical Politics*, **13** (3), 249–270.

Amable, B. (2000), 'Institutional complementarity and diversity of social systems of innovation and production', *Review of International Political Economy*, **7**, 645–87.

Antonelli, C. (2006), 'Path dependence, localised technological change, and the quest for dynamic effiency', in C. Antonelli, D. Foray, B.H. Hall and W.E. Steinmueller (eds), *New Frontiers in the Economics of Innovation and New Technology: Essays in Honour of Paul A. David*, Cheltenham, UK and Northampton, MA, USA: Edward Elgar, pp. 51–69.

Aoki, M. (2000), *Information, Corporate Governance, and Institutional Diversity: Competitiveness in Japan, the USA, and the Transitional Economies*, Oxford: Oxford University Press.

Arrow, K. (2000), 'Increasing returns: historiographic issues and path dependence', *European Journal of History of Economic Thought*, **7** (2), 171–80.

Arthur, B. (1989), 'Competing technologies, increasing returns, and lock-in by historical events', *Economic Journal*, **99**, 116–31.

Boyer, R. (2005), 'Coherence, diversity, and the evolution of capitalisms: the institutional complementarity hypothesis', *Evolutionary and Institutional Economic Review*, **2** (1), 43–80.

Chavance, B. and E. Magnin (2002), 'Emergence of path-dependent mixed economies in central Europe', in G. Hodgson (ed.), *A Modern Reader in Institutional and Evolutionary Economics*, Cheltenham: European Association of Evolutionary Political Economy, pp. 168–200.

Cowan, R. (1990), 'Nuclear power reactors: a study in technological lock-in', *Journal of Economic History*, **50**, 541–67.

Cowan, R. (1996), 'Sprayed to death: path dependence, lock-in and pest-control strategies', *Economic Journal*, **106**, 521–42.

Crouch, C. and H. Farrell (2004), 'Breaking the path of institutional development? Alternatives to the new determinism', *Rationality and Society*, **16** (1), 5–43.

David, P.A. (1975), *Technical Choice, Innovation and Economic Growth: Essays on American and British Experience in the Nineteenth Century*, Cambridge: Cambridge University Press.

David, P.A. (1985), 'Clio and the economics of Qwerty', *American Economic Review*, **75**, 332–37.

David, P.A., (2001; 2007), 'Path dependence, its critics and the quest for "Historical Economics"', in P. Garrouste (ed.), *Evolution and Path Dependence in Economic Ideas*, Cheltenham, UK and Northampton, MA, USA: Edward Elgar. Also published in Hodgson, Geoffrey M. (ed.) (2007), *The Evolution of Economic Institutions: A Critical Reader*, Cheltenham, UK and Northampton, MA, USA: Edward Elgar, pp. 120–42.

David, P.A. (1990) 'Heroes, herds and hysteresis in technological history: Thomas Edison and the "Battle of the Systems" reconsidered', *Journal of Industrial and Corporate Change*, **1**, 129–80.

David, P.A. (1994), 'Why are institutions the "carriers of history"? Path dependence and the evolution of conventions, organizations and institutions', *Structural Change and Economic Dynamics*, **5**, pp. 205–20.

David, P.A. and M. Thomas (eds) (2003), *The Economic Future in Historical Perspective*, Oxford: Oxford University Press.

Denzau, A.T. and D.C. North (1994), 'Shared mental models: ideologies and institutions', *Kyklos*, **47** (1), 3–31.

Dixit, A.K. (1996), *The Making of Economic Policy: A Transaction-Cost Politics Perspective*, Cambridge, MA: MIT Press.

Dugger, W.M. (1993), 'Transaction cost economics and the state', in C. Pitelis (ed.), *Transaction Costs, Markets and Hierarchies*, Oxford: Basil Blackwell, pp. 188–216.

Frankel, M. (1955), 'Obsolescence and technological change in a maturing economy', *American Economic Review*, **45**, 296–319.

Gartland M.P. (2005), 'Interdisciplinary views of sub-optimal outcomes: path dependence in the social and management sciences', *The Journal of Socio-Economics*, **34**, 686–702.

Goldin, C. and G.D. Libecap (eds) (1994), *The Regulated Economy: A Historical Approach to Political Economy*, Chicago: University of Chicago Press.

Goldstone, J. (1998), 'Initial conditions, general laws, path dependence, and explanations in historical sociology', *American Journal of Sociology*, **104** (3), 829–45.

Greif, A. (2006), *Institutions and the Path to The Modern Economy: Lessons from Medieval Trade*, New York: Cambridge University Press.

Hedlund, S. (2005), *Russian Path Dependence*, London: Routledge.

Heiner, R.A. (1983), 'The origin of predictable behavior', *American Economic Review*, **73**, 560–95.

Hodgson, G.M. (1993), *Economics and Evolution: Bringing Life Back into Economics*, Cambridge: Polity Press.

Hodgson, G.M. (ed.) (1998), *The Foundations of Evolutionary Economics, 1890–1973*, Cheltenham, UK and Northampton, MA, USA: Edward Elgar.

Hodgson, G.M. (2007), *The Evolution of Economic Institutions: A Critical Reader*, Cheltenham, UK and Northampton, MA, USA: Edward Elgar.

Howell, C. (2005), *Trade Unions and the State: The Construction of Industrial Relations Institutions in Britain, 1890–2000*, Princeton, NJ: Princeton University Press.

Katz, M.L. and C. Shapiro (1994), 'Systems competition and network effects', *Journal of Economic Perspectives*, **8**, 93–115.

Kindleberger, C.P. (1964), *Economic Growth in France and Britain, 1851–1950*, Cambridge, MA: Harvard University Press.

Krueger, A. (1996), 'The political economy of controls: American sugar', in L. Alston and T. Eggertsson (eds), *Empirical Studies in Institutional Change*, Cambridge: Cambridge University Press, pp. 125–53.

Langlois, R.N. and D.A. Savage (2001), 'Standards, modularity and innovation', in R. Garud and P. Karnoe (eds), *Path Dependence and Creation*, London: Lawrence Erlbaum Associates, pp. 149–68.

Lawson, T. (1997), *Economics and Reality*, London: Routledge.

Liebowitz, S.J. and S.E. Margolis (1995), 'Path dependence, lock-in, and history', *The Journal of Law, Economics and Organisation*, **11** (1), 205–26.

Magnusson, L. and J. Ottosson (1996), 'Transaction costs and institutional change: a case of the survival of the fittest?', in J. Groenewegen (ed.), *Transaction Costs and Beyond*, Boston, MA: Kluwer Academic Press, pp. 351–64.

Magnusson, L. (2001), 'The role of path dependence in the history of regulation', in L. Magnusson and J. Ottosson (eds), *The State, Regulation and the Economy: An Historical Perspective*, Cheltenham, UK and Northampton, MA, USA: Edward Elgar, pp. 107–19.

Magnusson, L. and J. Ottosson (eds) (2001), *The State, Regulation, and the Economy: an Historical Perspective*, Cheltenham, UK and Northampton, MA, USA: Edward Elgar.

Mahoney, J. (2000), 'Path dependence in historical sociology', *Theory and Society*, **29**, 507–48.

Martin R. and P. Sunley (2006), 'Path dependence and regional economic evolution', *Journal of Economic Geography*, **6**, 395–437.

Martin, R. and P. Sunley (2007), 'Complexity thinking and evolutionary economic geography', *Journal of Economic Geography*, **7** (5), 573–601.

Nelson, R.R. and S.G. Winter (1982), *An Evolutionary Theory of Economic Change*, Cambridge, MA: Belknap Press of Harvard University Press.

North, D.C. (1990), *Institutions, Institutional Change and Economic Performance*, Cambridge: Cambridge University Press.

North, D.C. (2005), *Understanding the Process of Economic Change*, Princeton, NJ: Princeton University Press.

Olson, M. (2000), *Power and Prosperity: Outgrowing Communist and Capitalist Dictatorships*, New York: Basic Books.

Ottosson, J. (2001), 'The state and regulatory orders in early European civil aviation', in L. Magnusson and J. Ottosson (eds), *The State, Regulation and the Economy: An Historical Perspective*, Cheltenham, UK and Northampton, MA, USA: Edward Elgar, pp. 148–66.

Page, S. (2006), 'Essay: path dependence', *Quarterly Journal of Political Science*, **1**, 87–115.

Pierson, P. (2000), 'Increasing returns, path dependence, and the study of politics', *American Political Science Review*, **94** (2), 251–67.

Pierson, P. (2004), *Politics in Time: History, Institutions, and Social Analysis*, Princeton, NJ: Princeton University Press.

Puffert, D.J. (2002), 'Path dependence in spatial networks: the standardization of railway track gauge', *Explorations in Economic History*, **39** (3), 282–314.

Puffert, D.J. (2003), 'Path dependence', *EH.Net Encyclopedia*, ed. Robert Whaples, 10 June, http://eh.net/encyclopedia/article/puffert.path.dependence, accessed 11 March 2008.

Ramstad, Y. (1994), 'On the nature of economic evolution: John R. Commons and the metaphor of artificial selection', in L. Magnusson (ed.), *Evolutionary and Neo-Schumpeterian Approaches to Economics*, Boston, MA, Dordrecht and London: Kluwer Academic Publishers, pp. 65–122.

Redding, S. (2002), 'Path dependence, endogenous innovation, and growth', *International Economic Review*, **43** (4), 1215–48.

Rosenberg, C. (1994), *Exploring the Black Box*, Cambridge: Cambridge University Press.

Rutherford, M. (1994), *Institutions in Economics: The Old and the New Institutionalism*, Cambridge: Cambridge University Press.

Scott, P. (2001), 'Path dependence and Britain's "Coal Wagon Problem" and the slow diffusion of high throughput technologies in inter-war British coal', *Explorations in Economic History*, **38**, 366–85.

Scott, P. (2006) 'Path dependence, fragmented property rights mining', *Business History*, **48** (1), 20–42.

Streeck, W. and K.A. Thelen (eds) (2005), *Beyond Continuity: Institutional Change in Advanced Political Economies*, New York: Oxford University Press.

Vanberg, V. (1988), 'Rules and choice in economics and sociology', in E. Böttcher, P. Herder-Dorneich and K.-E. Schenk (eds), *Jahrbuch für Neue Politische Ökonomie*, vol. 7, Tübingen: Mohr Siebeck, pp. 146–67.

Vanberg, V. (1994), *Rules and Choice in Economics: Essays in Constitutional Political Economy*, London: Routledge.

Veblen, T. (1915), *Imperial Germany and the Industrial Revolution*, New York and London: Macmillan.

Vromen, J.J. (1995), *Economic Evaluation: An Inquiry into the Foundation of New Institutional Economics*, London: Routledge.

Williamson, O.E. (1996), *The Mechanisms of Governance*, New York: Oxford University Press.

Wilson, J.Q. (1989), *Bureaucracy: What Government Agencies Do and Why They Do It*, New York: Basic Books.

Witt, U. (2003a), *The Evolutionary Perspective on Organizational Change and the Theory of the Firm*, Jena: Max-Planck-Institute for Research into Economic Systems.

Witt, U. (2003b), *The Evolving Economy: Essays on the Evolutionary Approach to Economics*, Cheltenham, UK and Northampton, MA, USA: Edward Elgar.

1. Path dependence versus path-breaking crises: an alternative view

Bo Stråth

THE ANGEL OF HISTORY

There is a famous interpretation by Walter Benjamin of Paul Klee's painting of *Angelus Novus* or *The Angel of History* as Benjamin conceptualizes him. The Angel gazes with a wide-open mouth and extended wings on the heap of the ruins of History. A strong wind blows from Paradise and prevents the Angel from closing its wings, or from coming closer to the past at which it gazes. The wind drives the Angel unceasingly, with its back towards the future. According to Benjamin, this wind, which began in Eden, is what we call progress. Klee's painting and Benjamin's interpretation have provoked many comments (cf. Niethammer, 1989; Stråth, 1991, pp. 132–3).

The landscape that the Angel sees, driven into the future with its back ahead, changes continuously. Can the journey of the Angel through this landscape be conceptualized as path dependency? In a certain sense yes, because there is no way it can escape its connection to the past. However, the question is whether the ruins of History constitute a path. Is there a pattern or some organizing principle in the landscape? Or is all in a chaotic heap of ruins?

These questions have occupied historians since the Enlightenment. The Enlightenment philosophers believed in rationality and in the progress of History conforming to law. Few were on this point more consequent than Hegel when he mapped the movement of Reason through history. Hegel's influence on Marx is well known. The issue at stake was the discovery of the laws, on the basis of which historical processes on principle were predictable. Historians of the nineteenth century increasingly questioned and rejected the idea of history conforming to law and emphasized the uniqueness of every moment along the time axis. A distinction between historical and social sciences ensued.

The emphasis on the singularity and individuality of the historical events and epochs was particularly evident in Germany and interlaced with Romanticism. The idealistic organic view on past developments was called historism and had the aim to re-create reality 'as it really had been' in the past.[1] This cumulative mapping of the past emphasized political leaders and states in opposition to the 'speculative philosophy' of Hegel. On the basis of historism the historical school criticized the classical economists like Adam Smith and David Ricardo for having separated economic phenomena from their concrete historical contexts and described economic life as subject to (natural) laws. The investigation of the historical development was the only basis on which economic theories could be built. Political economy was a kind of parade discipline in the academic Enlightenment reflection. With the ever more obvious social problems in the wake of capitalist expansion and industrialization in the nineteenth century, its arguments about the long-term automatic harmonizing effects of the market to the benefit of everybody came under pressure. The emerging social issue was too obvious to ignore. Theories about marginal utility, based on the vision of *homus oeconomicus*, the rationally calculating individual in free market exchange with other rational individuals, tried to solve the crisis of the theories of classical economy. The emerging neoclassical theory was one step further in a de-historicizing direction. The methodological confrontation between Gustav Schmoller and other adherents of the historical school, and Carl Menger with his marginal utility theory at the end of the nineteenth century, is well known. However, at the same time the idiographic view of historical method was also challenged by more nomothetic perspectives among the historians. Karl Lamprecht tried to develop a total cultural history with nomothetic ambitions. This triggered the vehement *Methodenstreit* in Germany. Lamprecht was a source of inspiration for the French Annales school.

The tension between singularity and uniqueness on the one side, and universality on the other, in the views on society and social change has since the Enlightenment resulted in a complex pattern of confrontation and compromise between the extreme positions. Social sciences and history became, in the nineteenth century, separate academic disciplines with a varying and ambiguous interest in interdisciplinary dialogue. Several attempts have been undertaken to bridge the division, most recently in the 1960s and 1970s, among historians through the connection of historical observations to a reflection on more general patterns in the social relations, and in social sciences through the introduction of an explicit historical dimension in the theories on society. Historical sociology can be seen as a culmination of such bridging efforts.

At the moment when historical sociology peaked in the 1970s and 1980s it came under ever more fire from a theoretical and epistemological perspective that argued that developments were not dependent on the (predictable) operations of socio-economic structures but on the potential of the language. The professional task of the historians became less to discover causative explanatory mechanisms and more to construct inter-pretative frameworks. The methodological focus of this 'linguistic turn' moved from source criticism towards a critical approach to the narrative structures ('emplotment') in which the historical events and facts were brought together.

This long methodological debate since the Enlightenment between idiographic and nomothetic, explanatory and heuristic ideals provides the framework in which the question of path dependency must be dis-cussed. The historical dimension appears to constitute a core aspect of path dependence theories. Nevertheless, the question is what that his-torical dimension really means. This is the question of what 'The Angel of History' really saw.

THE CRITIQUE

The concept of path dependency is not very clear. Generally it assumes that polities and cultures follow certain paths of development. They are for some reason bound to a specific developmental trajectory, which they cannot easily abandon. The reason for this constraint varies. The paths are argued to follow from some social and/or economic structure and/or some specific historical or cultural heritage. Implicitly a prognostic value is inscribed in the concept. The term 'path dependency' connotes linear teleology. There is in the path-dependency concept a tension between a historical idiographic ideal emphasizing the uniqueness of each historical moment and social scientific nomothetic ideals emphasizing theoretical generalization. This is the century-old tension between the perspectives of Schmoller and Menger, which is still with us.

The case in point is the German *Sonderweg* thesis developed by the social historians in Bielefeld in the 1970s and 1980s (Kocka, 1988b; Wehler, 1975; 1988). In an innovative way they began from new perspectives to critically question the German development leading up to 1933. Instead of looking for the answer to how and why the German catastrophe could occur at the political level of the elites, they were interested in broader social struc-tures. What was wrong in German society before the 1930s? With that question the focus was directed towards the lack of liberalism, the roles of the land-owning aristocracy (the Prussian *Junker*), the peasants and the capitalist industry owners, banks and employers. An intensive academic debate emerged over the question whether the German derailment began with the failed revolution in 1848, earlier (*Vormärz*) or only later after the establishment of the *Kaiserreich* in 1871. In contrast to the unique German trajectory a Western standard development towards democracy was outlined, in a revolutionary version represented by France, and in a non-revolutionary version represented by Britain and the USA. The big question was why Germany came to deviate at all from that standard.

The heated debate on the *Sonderweg* thesis led to ever closer comparisons of the cases of standard and deviation. The closer the comparisons went and the richer the details became, the more difficult it was to maintain the simple contrast design in black and white. The conclusion from Jürgen Kocka's big *Bürgertum* project at the end of the 1980s was, rather, that there is no standard development and that all developments represent unique trajectories (Kocka, 1988a).

The German *Sonderweg* debate could draw on the path-breaking work by the historical sociologist Barrington Moore. He compared different national development trajectories in *Social Origins of Dictatorship and Democracy* (Moore, 1967).[2] His aim was to explain what structural and historical features distinguish breakdown cases of democracy in the interwar period from societies that remained democratic. The breakdown cases (Germany and Japan) were characterized by an authoritarian coalition of landed aristocracy, the state and the bourgeoisie, with the landlords in the decisive role. The landlords who had previously cemented an alliance with the state, exercised a political and ideological hegemony over the rising bourgeoisie, which did not find the ideological leadership of the landlords incompatible with its own interests, owing to the state support available for industrialization. Only in states where there was a bourgeoisie-led break with the aristocratic past was there democratic development. This conclusion comes close to the argument in the German *Sonderweg* debate about the lack of liberalism.

In the debate that followed Moore's thesis, the earlier sharp line of demarcation in historical sociology between class conflict and bureaucratization (that is, between Karl Marx and Max Weber) as the prime mover in social change was certainly transgressed. The more or less implicit assumption was some kind of 'normalcy' with deviating development patterns. The 'normal' standard development was called modernization, and the deviations were, as a rule, explained with reference to socio-economic structures, which were reflected in the political and ideological developments towards democracy and dictatorship. Moore only discussed the role of culture in his short epilogue where his point of departure was an assumed relationship between social movements and culture. Although Moore was open to complexity, he still desired a solution in which the cultural factor could be derived from specific interests and socio-economic structures, an explanatory power, which assumed predictability in principle.

The framework of the debate was the Cold War where the issue of democracy and dictatorship was quite clearly on the agenda and needed historical derivation. With growing welfare production the Western bloc emerged as an assembly of national communities of destiny, which at least after 1945 all followed the modernization standard. The events of 1989 through to 1991 took everybody by surprise, but quickly the image of the Western standard as *the* standard emerged. In the long run all would emulate this. The image was underpinned by hopes in the transfer to market economy in the countries of the former Eastern bloc. The lack of a democratic culture certainly represented a ballast, but in the long run it could not prevent the victory of democracy. The path was also set for the newcomers.

Historical sociology can be seen as an attempt to merge the idiographic and nomothetic ideals. The consequence was a very structural view on historical developments. Historians and sociologists discerned highways – rather than paths – in the landscape of the Angel of History. Their mistake was that they believed that the highways really existed 'out there' in the past landscape and that they were about to discover and lay them bare.

The political developments in the 1980s undermined this structural perspective with predictable ambitions. The linguistic school argued that the highways were an *ex post* mental construction in a retrospect view of the past, in order to understanding the present through coming to terms with the past. The socio-economic structures which determined development in the historical sociology was nothing but a discourse and a narrative about such structures.

The historical sociological approach was not only undermined by academic methodological and epistemological challenges but also by political developments. After the dramatic shift in a few years in the 1990s, from Fukuyama's theory of the end of history to Huntington's perspective of clash of civilizations, the future has become much more open (Fukuyama, 1992; Huntington, 1993). The historical sociology operated with implicit or explicit assumptions that the developments followed certain patterns which on principle were more or less predictable. It is, since the political developments of 1989, more difficult to think in terms of linear teleology.

However, despite the new attention given to openness towards the future, teleology in the form of a master narrative with a clear direction survives. After the earlier master narratives about rationalization in the 1920s and modernization in the 1950s and 1960s, which broke down in the 1930s and the 1970s respectively, the new master story emerged in the 1990s: globalization. All three could probably be translated to, and subsumed under, the concept of Americanization.

The argument in this chapter is that the concept of path dependency is very much inscribed in a long tradition of nomothetic teleology with ideals of predictability based on a structural view of history where socio-economic factors ('reality') inherently determine the development. The problem is the implicit or explicit prognostic ambition invested in the term. This is what could be called the 'hard path-dependency' view.

The term 'path dependency' would function better in a retrospective exercise where the aim is to better understand the developments that led up to the present situation. Such a view would emphasize the narrative and constructed dimension and that the outlined path is a preliminary mental projection to provide temporary orientation in a constantly changing present. We unavoidably need historical orientation in order to reflect on why and how we came to where we are. A path is laid down towards the past. This is what could be called a 'soft path dependency'.

However, there is a problem with the concept of this soft version: it has a tendency to obscure the fact that today's openness towards the future was also the precondition under which past futures were experienced. Therefore, the aim of this chapter is to look for an alternative conceptualization, which emphasizes openness towards the future, in the past as well as in the present, and the principle lack of a standard development. The term that is suggested for such an alternative view is crisis. The emergence of crisis might be dependent on a specific development, but the *response* to crisis is, at least potentially, path breaking rather than path dependent, where the analysis focuses on how developments are shunted into new directions rather than on confirming old ones.

THE CONCEPT OF CRISIS

In his path-breaking *Kritik und Krise* Reinhart Koselleck developed a view of modernity as a permanent tension between critique and crisis (Koselleck, 1988 [1954]). The public debate in the wake of the Enlightenment meant social critique of a new kind. Critique provoked, in situations where it won general attraction and became massively mobilizing, feelings of crisis, which, in turn, provoked political action to escape crisis through integration or rejection of critique. At these points of crisis social change was particularly great, potentially dramatic, where developments were shunted onto new tracks. Critique emerged as expectations based on interpretation of experiences. Experiences as interpretations of the past provoked the projections of future expectations. Modernity took shape in the field of tension between experiences and expectations. Koselleck illustrates his thesis with the concepts of freedom/liberty and equality/solidarity, which in the French Revolution were kept together in one *Denkfigur* but after 1848 began to split into two future-oriented diametrically opposing principles, which in the 1950s, when he developed his theory, in the form of Western liberalism and Soviet socialism, had brought the world to the edge of the precipice. Through changing communication technology information grew exponentially, this multiplied the expressions of critique and the experiences of crisis. The scope between experiences and expectations narrows; we perceive this as the acceleration of time. The experiences get ever more difficult to interpret and translate into horizons of expectations. This acceleration of time is the core of modernity. The term 'future shock' has been launched to describe this scenario.

Koselleck's perspective is basically pessimistic: the experiences accumulated over time lead to a loss of capacity to translate experiences into mobilizing expectations and future horizons under democratic conditions. Rather than triggering permanent critical self-reflection the successful critique had a tendency to become petrified into hypocrisy when the critics established themselves as new powers. The dynamics between critique and crisis, which triggered the French Revolution, and became a crucial dimension of modernity, brought after the victory of the revolutionaries, dislike of continued critique. Instead of continuous self-critique, in the view of Reinhart Koselleck, smugness and hypocrisy followed the revolution. The revolutionary rhetoric became hardened into institutional self-righteousness and a hypocritical tension between language and institutional cover emerged.

We often understand past developments in terms of causal chains. A provoked B, which provoked C, and so on. However, since development means that old and repetitive factors and circumstances emerge in ever new contexts, each point of time is always new, and we cannot talk about pure causes that can be isolated like the links of a chain. The fact that each situation contains elements of both continuity and discontinuity means that our experiences are of limited use, and again and again we must design future expectations to solve emerging problems. Instead of historical understanding through causal chains, a more reasonable and realistic perspective is one that discerns situations of problem resolution. Each such situation is marked by old experiences, which provoke new questions and responses. Each problem resolution, in turn, is replete with new unforeseen problems. The framework of the debate alters unceasingly with permanently changing problem definitions. The experiences are interpreted and translated into ever new future horizons of expectations and new political actions in the face of ever new challenges. This scenario becomes more complicated by the fact that each participant in the process of problem resolution has his or her own specific experiences as the points of departure from which their future perspectives are derived differently. Uncertainty about the future perspectives of other participants is high, even that of one's own future estimation. Moreover, there is often a lack of a superior co-ordinating force with a capacity to co-ordinate future perspectives and political action.

Situations of problem resolution with particular absence of co-ordination and distinct compatible future expectations and orientations are experienced as chaotic and can be described as crises. The concept of crisis is derived from the Greek κρινειν, *krinein*, to sift, separate, decide, to judge, which gives a meaning in the direction of distinction, discrimination, decision. It was in this sense that the historian Thucydides used the term in his accounts of the Peloponnesian War and the battles on land and sea, which had resulted in the *krinein* in the big conflict between the Greeks and the Persians. In the same way, Hippocrates, 'the father of medicine', talked about the crisis that occurs in states of illness in exactly the decisive moment when the disease either increases in intensity or begins to abate. In Thucydides' description of the plague in Athens he tells about how the crisis for those who had been hit occurs after seven to nine days.

From crisis in this, the verbal, sense vital meaning with quite different future perspectives, the Enlightenment philosophers Rousseau and Paine more than a thousand years later took over the concept and described crisis as an emancipating dissolver of the old order. From here the step was not far to Karl Marx's theory of crisis, where he described the economic depressions that had occurred since 1825 as crises which constituted an unavoidable and, in the end, lethal mechanism built into the capitalist order. From Marx the concept was developed by neoclassical economists, who saw crisis as a temporary disequilibrium in a natural state of equilibrium, where the outcome of each crisis in principle is given, like for Marx but opposite, the re-creation of equilibrium. With crisis' appropriation by Marx and the neoclassical economists it lost its original connotation of openness towards the future. Reinhart Koselleck tried to re-establish this openness in *Kritik und Krise*. History since the Enlightenment, the modern era, is characterized by social critique, which leads to crisis, and more or less successful attempts to respond to the critique, but no outcome is given. Rather than having a path-dependent capacity, the crisis concept has a path-breaking potential. However, there is also the risk of losing control over the situation and creative imagination. History is full of losers as well as winners, and the winner at one turning point might be the loser at the next. A third alternative scenario emerges in the view of Koselleck from attempts to stabilize the situation through hypocritical language. Connected to the concept of problem resolution, much more than to Marxist or neoclassical theory, crises becomes an important analytical category that offers a new perspective on the preconditions of social change and structural dictates.

In this perspective there are points which are also developed in the view on social change applied by Karl Polanyi (Polanyi, 2001 [1944]). Market expansion provokes claims for protection, either as protests from social groups exposed to market threats or from low-performing industries exposed to competition on world markets. In complex patterns of opposition, liberalism clashed with protectionism and labour with capital. In *The Great Transformation* Polanyi argued that the free market is as much a political creation as the socialist planned economy. Both planning and market exchange require a political framework. The fact that the operation of the market has a tendency to transgress this framework only means that society, in self-defence, develops new institutions reducing the deleterious effects of the market. The (market) solutions of today become, so to speak, the (political) problem of tomorrow. There are interactive dynamics between market expansion and political regulation. These dynamics cannot be understood or conceptualized in an evolutionary or neoclassical perspective. Modernity must be separated from functionalist connotations to smooth and linear evolution. Polanyi had in particular commodity and monetary markets in mind. However, his perspective can be used also for labour markets where varying degrees of strengths and interdependencies among employers, employees and political representatives are confronted in problem resolution.

HISTORICAL POINTS OF CRISIS

In the development of Western industrial societies there are several periods of particular problem accumulation, which were experienced as crises. Here I refer to three such periods: the 1890s, the 1930s and the 1970s. In empirical terms I concentrate on the 1930s to demonstrate the openness in such situations, and the potential for path-breaking developments in new directions where the response to one and the same problem can orient action very differently. The crises at these points have all dealt with the issue of social integration.

In the 1830s 'the social question' was identified as a major problem in industrializing societies. From the 1830s the social question reverberated through the industrializing world; a social sphere was invented between political regulation and economic organization based on images of the market developed in the eighteenth century; expanding markets triggered experiences of new problems and claims for new political regulation; the key issues were who was responsible for the problems and how was society to pay for the solution.

In the more general framework of the social question the concept of unemployment was invented to mediate experiences in the growing and rapidly changing labour markets. Thus, during the nineteenth century, a distinction emerged between poverty and unjust poverty, or between the 'deserving' and the 'malingering and undeserving' poor, and later, between employed and unemployed, indicating that poverty and unemployment was not necessarily the fault of the individual. The causes of destitution were through this conceptual differentiation to be sought on a different level. The rise of the social question and the concept of unemployment reflected a growing understanding that industrialization brought systemic problems that highlighted the question of social responsibility for its victims (Donzelot, 1984; Mansfield et al., 1994; Salais et al., 1986; Topalov, 1994). (For a similar theoretical perspective, see several of the contributions in Keyssar, 1986; Lepetit, 1995. For the most recent case study, see Zimmermann, 1999.)

In 1871 a founding member of the German *Verein für Sozialpolitik* argued that with the conclusion of the national question the social question had become most important for the future. We know today that he erred in the assumption that the national question had come to an end with the creation of the German Empire. Of lasting interest, however, is the linking of the national and the social questions (Wagner, 1990; Wagner and Zimmermann, 2004, p. 31). Class and nation were both competitive, excluding and overlapping categories of identity construction. Tension between the social and the national questions with the mediating role of the state were at the core of all three crisis periods. The solution to this tension was a very open question where we, in retrospect, can see how a variety of reactions emerged in the industrialized world.

The framework of the 1890s was the long economic depression beginning in the 1870s, which in the 1880s led to a massive break-up of the free-trade order established in the 1850s and 1860s and the triumph of protectionism, which was accompanied by a growing nationalistic language. Nationalism underpinned a Darwinian interpretation of survival of the fittest nation on the world market. National values acquired physical strength through military armament, which, in turn, reinforced the interpretations of a fight for survival and contributed to the recovery from the economic depression. At the same time the intensification of industrial manufacturing production, and the unionization of the rapidly growing number of workers under construction of class identities, underlined the emphasis on national values. National identity was launched as an alternative to class identity. The overall problem dealt with social cohesion and integration when class language clashed with nationalistic language under power relationships that varied widely from case to case. The outcome of these clashes and the degree of integration of the working class also varied significantly.

The 1930s brought responses to the economic crisis with mass unemployment in two directions: fascism/Nazism and social democratic liberalism with concessions to the working class, which, in the long run, created preconditions for mass consumption, which, in turn, provided the basis of mass production in a mutually reinforcing process. What was at stake everywhere in the 1930s was the social question and the responsibility for that question.

Like all attractive political concepts 'unemployment' contained both a general recognition of a problem and, at the same time, a controversy as to specific solutions and recommendations for courses of action. There was a growing general agreement that above and beyond the individual level *someone* had to take responsibility. However, before the 1930s it was difficult to discover social organs accepting this responsibility. The states, local governments, employers' associations and trade unions all strove to shift responsibility to one another.

The great issue in these bargaining processes on the social question, after areas of responsibility had been identified, was who is responsible for old-age pensions, to guarantee income in cases of sickness or disability, for unemployment insurance, and so on? Such issues distinguished and confronted different social interest groups. The precise outcome of the complex struggles of the nineteenth century varied from country to country according to specific power relationships and interpretations of historical experiences. However, in more general terms, the answer that emerged following the turmoil of the 1930s, and the experience of crisis, massively assigned social responsibility to the fiction of the state. In the wake of the collapse of labour markets, governments intervened in most countries on an unprecedented scale to quell or exploit social unrest. State intervention took very different forms: in the name of Fascism in Italy, of National Socialism in Germany; of the *front populaire* in France; of Social Democracy and red–green labour–farmer coalitions in Scandinavia; or of the New Deal in the USA. These solutions seemed in many respects much closer to each other than they later on proved to be. President Roosevelt's interest in Mussolini's response to the social issue is well known, for instance (Schivelsbusch, 2005).

The 1970s saw the return of mass unemployment and experiences of crisis after the international order had broken down (the dollar collapse in 1971 and the oil price shock in 1973). National class-based patterns of identity and solidarity eroded, and intensified identity construction around the enterprise emerged. In declining industries local management–workforce coalitions emerged in struggles for survival on the market against corresponding coalitions in competing companies. The invention of the concept of *Mitarbeiter, medarbetare,* eroded national class identities, based on the concept of worker, *Arbeiter, arbetare*. Centralized hierarchical corporatist structures broke down at the same time as business operations and financing strategies became truly global, transnational and momentaneous ('real time') by means of new computerized technology. The problem resolutions varied from case to case but they shared the fact that they transgressed the earlier focus on the state as the arena of solutions in two directions: the local and the global (Stråth 1987; 1996; 2000a).

The widely different reactions to the crisis in the 1930s *could*, of course, be seen as a confirmation of the thesis about path dependency. Just as the fact that the century-old debate beginning in the 1830s now resulted in such different answers, *could* be understood with reference to some intrinsic mechanism in each case. In the same way the fact that the breakthrough of the new *Mitarbeiter* language in response to the crisis in the 1970s was much stronger in Germany and Scandinavia than in Britain and France, where there was no conceptual innovation, could be seen as evidence of different historical paths. In order to demonstrate that this is too simplistic a view, and in order to demonstrate the path-breaking rather than path-dependent dimension in the periods of crisis, I am going to go into more detail concerning the crisis of the 1930s through a comparison of Germany and Sweden.

TWO CRISIS SOLUTIONS: GERMANY AND SWEDEN

In March 1930 the German coalition government under the Social Democrat Hermann Müller fell on the issue of how to finance unemployment. The first of the three presidential governments that paved the way for Hitler took over. The elections in September 1932 in Sweden brought the Social Democrats to government and, on the basis of their programme of an expansive unemployment insurance and support measures to the crisis-hit agriculture, they in the spring of 1933 built a parliamentary coalition with the farmers, which resulted in 40 years of almost unbroken social democratic government power. How could the response to exactly the same issue go in such totally different directions?

It has been suggested that the different social democratic responses in Germany and Sweden to the mass unemployment of the early 1930s depended on the historically stronger position of the peasants in Sweden and on feudal structures in Germany. An argument in the German *Sonderweg* debate was that the German development was shunted onto a fatal track in the late 1870s, when paths towards democratic liberalism were finally blocked as liberalism merged with an expansionistic and aggressive nationalism in response to the economic depression. Certainly, a heavy mortgage on later developments was taken in the 1870s, but what role did this mortgage really play in 1930? Did not the hesitation to devalue the Mark and to operate with budget deficits have more to do with the experiences and memories of hyperinflation a few years earlier? Was it not the experience of hyperinflation which finally determined the way in which problems could be identified and questions posed?

What role did the land-owning aristocracy play in Germany? What role did the strong social and political position of the farmers play in the modernization of Sweden? Historians like to put these kinds of questions. Their professional training has educated them to think using generic long-term concepts. They pay attention to cause rather than consequence. An older structure somehow causes a younger one.

An alternative point of departure is that actors are marked by the age in which they live and the specific identification and definition of the problems of that age. The problems of the age in which they live are much more decisive for their action orientation than their roots in an older society. Of course, the historical dimension plays a large role in problem solution, but this role is mediated through the translation of past experiences into present challenges in meaning-producing and interpretative processes. In Germany the experiences of the state financial collapse in the early 1920s blocked the way towards fiscal expansion. In Sweden the Social Democrats after an election disaster in 1928 on a politically radical programme began to look for new ways towards parliamentary power. Here the coalition with the farmers was timely. Furthermore, immediate political action in response to immediate political claims and threats is more relevant than long-term strategic or theoretical considerations. The acute pressure from the Swedish workers massively facing the threat of mass unemployment was more important than emerging theories on the connection between government expenditures and economic growth. The government did what it felt obliged to do in response to political pressure and made a bill that was attractive enough to find a parliamentary majority. In Germany the political polarization was stronger and the parliamentary interest in integrating the workers therefore smaller. Hitler carried through this integration on his election programme on expansive financial politics for a strong Germany with employment for all.

The mobilizing language oriented action in different directions in the two cases. The interpretative power rather than certain socio-economic structures shunted the developments onto different tracks. The translation and the interpretation of historical experiences were important when new future horizons emerged, but there was nothing predetermined in history itself. The language of the present determined the developments.

The response to the crisis of the early 1930s was full of alternatives, contingent on the precise perceptions of the situation, and the capacity to translate these perceptions into political actions. This is what the comparison of the crisis reaction in Germany and Sweden tells us, not that the responses were somehow predetermined.

The comparison Germany–Sweden can be taken one step further in a more historical direction in order to underpin the argument. The comparison deals with the *Volk/folk* concept. In the introduction to the 1981 edition of *The Crisis of German Ideologies*, George Mosse noted that while his book appeared to have left the impression among some readers that *völkisch* thought must inevitably lead to Nazism, this was not his intention. Not only were 'moderate', mainstream conservatives in pre-1933 Germany deeply infected with *völkisch* thoughts, but there also existed the non-authoritarian *völkische* socialism of Gustav Landauer which drew on the ideal of the *Volk* as a democratic community of equals (Mosse, 1981). Eugene Lunn has suggested that Landauer's *völkische* socialism could provide an antidote to the tendency among historians to teleologically link *völkische* romanticism with the triumph of Hitler's version of *völkische* ideology (Lunn, 1973).

Mosse contended that socialists of all countries made efforts to combine *völkisch* and socialist thought and speculated that, if such a blend had been successful, National Socialism might not have triumphed so easily. Lars Trägårdh has taken up and developed this idea in a comparison of *völkische* ideologies in two 'Germanic' countries, Sweden and Germany, taking 1933 as point of departure for the analysis. The same year as Germans voted their way to *völkische* Nazi dictatorship, in Sweden the Social Democratic government in power since 1932 built a long-term parliamentary coalition with the Farmers Party. Founded by men inspired by Lassalle, Marx, Kautsky and other luminaries of the German socialist movement, the Swedish party was in many ways modelled on the German Social Democratic Party (SPD). However, by the end of the 1920s, after the landslide defeat in the elections in 1928, the Swedish Social Democrats began to integrate *völkische* and socialists themes. They redefined their party from a workers' class-based party to a people's party, bent upon the idea of a *folkhem*, a home for the people. Class alliances replaced the class struggle as the dominant strategy for achieving the socialist dream of the classless society (Trägårdh, 1993).

The Swedish Social Democrats appropriated the political priority of interpretation of the *folk* concept after a protracted discursive struggle with the conservatives who at the turn of the twentieth century evoked the concept in a strategy that one of the protagonists in the debate on modernization, the Professor of Political Science Rudolf Kjellén, later well known for his geopolitical theories, labelled 'national socialism'.

Kjellén's concept was an ideological instrument to ward off the threats of class-struggle socialism. Rudolf Kjellén opposed class-struggle socialism as a point of departure for the political discourse. He argued from his conservative point of departure for national socialism where the country was seen as a whole which involved all the people in political work and gave them responsibility. The country was supposed to be a home for the whole people. The integrative idea of the *'folkhemmet'*, in which society was organized as a family, with the home as a metaphor, subordinated the class-struggle parole to the national welfare. When Kjellén talked about the concept of *folkhemmet*, *folk* had a different connotation from *Volk* in Germany. The Social Democrats were early on attracted by the *folkhemmet* concept, although they wanted to give it another content. The conservative version they rejected as 'the fortified poor-house' with a reference to the biased distribution between military and social state expenditures in the conservative programme. They gradually found themselves involved in a discursive struggle about the definition of the *folk* concept. When the Social Democrats appropriated the *folkhemmet* metaphor around 1930 and made it their symbol, they argued that the happiness of the lower classes, of which the working class was just one part, was based on their efforts to contribute to the *folkhemmet*. *Folk* and *folkhem* as expressions of traditional values were mobilized as linguistic instruments for modernization (Stråth, 1996).

At the end of the 1920s, during the critical debate, one might say the crisis debate, on the concepts of *folk* and class in the Social Democratic Party, after the defeat in the elections in 1928, the party leader, Per-Albin Hansson summed it up: 'Behind the words are realities. It is by no means unimportant whether we consider the party a representative of class interests or a bearer of the interests of the entire *folk*' (Stråth, 1996, p. 91; *Tiden*, 1929[3]). From its very start the party had been a *folk* party, Hansson continued, in order to legitimize the reformulation historically. When the first party congress, in 1889, made a statement on the suffrage question, the argument had been that the *folk* must be the master of the house. Kautsky's argument in Germany in the same year – it would be misleading to regard the concepts of 'people' and 'proletariat' as synonymous – had provoked protests from influential intellectuals in the Swedish party. Although the Swedish Social Democratic Party was still very much a party of the industrial working class in terms of membership composition at the turn of the twentieth century, it changed in this respect during its first two decades. In 1907 the party leader, Hjalmar Branting, argued that the party was a *'folk* party in the best sense of the word'.

The political attraction of the *folk* concept was strong by 1930. One expression of this attraction was the fact that the two Liberal parties, when they merged in 1934, chose *folkpartiet* as their new name. This did not help them much in their fight for votes, however. By 1930, the Social Democrats had clearly appropriated the concept and its interpretation.

In the nineteenth century, Germany and Sweden shared fundamental social and cultural values, which Lars Trägårdh has described as a tendency to extol the organic *Gemeinschaft* in comparison to the *Gesellschaft* of citizens – community against society in English: to take the collective rather than the individual as the basic unit from which society should be constructed. Given this tendency, Trägårdh asks whether the divergent trajectories of Swedish and German histories express varieties of an underlying Germanic ideology, embracing mutations and variations diverse enough as to include both Hitler's Third Reich and the Swedish Welfare State (Trägårdh, 1990, p. 26).

An elaboration on Trägårdh's question shows important differences between the *Gemeinschaft* and the *Gesellschaft* concepts in Germany and Sweden. There was not the same tension between the concepts in Sweden as in Germany. They were less dichotomic. The politically important concept in Sweden is *Gesellschaft*, *samhälle*, from the verb *hålla samman*, keep together. It connotes both *Gemeinschaft*, community and political organization. *Samhälle*, *Gesellschaft*, society, *societas* even became, in the twentieth century, synonymous with the state. When the Social Democrats argued for the welfare state they talked about the need for a strong society. *Samhälle* was never in opposition to the state or seen as something between market (or family: Hegel) on the one side and the state on the other. When the English and American neoliberal language was translated into Swedish in the 1980s the Anglicism *civilsamhälle* was invented and incorporated to express such opposition. On the other side, *gemenskap* was never so holistically overstretched as *Gemeinschaft* in Germany.

Trägårdh's perspective can be illustrated with still another example. While the motto of the Swedish King Gustaf V (1907–50) was 'With the people for the country', the inscription by Wilhelm II on the Reichstag building was *Dem deutschen Volk*, to the German people, that is, the parliament building was graciously given to the people by the Emperor.

The point here is that these two different formulations of the nation were never predetermined from specific social or economic structures. The trajectory can only be outlined in retrospect as a conceptual development. Nothing says that Landauer's view on the *Volk* concept could not have broken through, or that the Swedish Social Democrats had to abandon their radical socialist language after the defeat in the elections of 1928, or that they were bound to take over the interpretative power from the conservatives. *Ex post* we can see that they did it and from that observation we map out a specific trajectory which should not be mistaken for something that was necessarily bound in a causative chain. The interpretation of the situation around 1930 was important, and this proved to be a successful interpretation full of self-confirmation, but the Social Democratic leadership could not know this at the time. History is not only full of winners but also losers.

Political movements develop tactically, not logically, through improvisation in the search of support and through incorporation and adjustment of different ideas to specific goals. Political movements are a mixture of interpretations and programmes, rather than uniform intellectual orders free from contradictions. When various political movements confront each other in bargaining processes of muddling through, politics gets its shape through intuition as much as intention.

Certainly these processes occur in frameworks where rules and norms constitute a cognitive order. There is a kind of social belief, which is different for different societies in relation to, for instance, questions of employment, redundancy, productivity, and so on. This order is historically established through interpretation of accumulated experiences. Through Michel Foucault we know that such an order can have considerable inertia. However, since each situation of interpretation contains new elements to consider, the experiences are not all. New problems can provoke action orientation in new directions, particularly in situations defined as crisis where past experiences might be of limited value. A kind of mutation occurs. This is what happened in the struggle to define the nation by means of the *Volk/folk* concept in Germany and Sweden in the 1930s. There was much less continuity to the 1920s in these solutions than the concept of path dependency misleads us to believe. The 1920s in Germany did not only contain the totalitarian danger of the holistic interpretation of the *Volk* concept but also precarious expectations invested in the Weimar Republic, and in Sweden the level of the social conflict, particularly in the labour market, was much higher than the emergence of a model in the 1930s leads us to believe.

An example that illustrates the more general validity of this German–Swedish comparison, is the discourse on the concept of rationalization over the whole industrial world during the decades around the First World War. Everywhere the work process was mechanized, the labour force homogenized and enterprises bureaucratized, and the workers organized under the development of class identities. The employers responded with the development of new patterns of employer solidarity and identity whereby local and regional networks became co-ordinated at the national level. The development of national solidarity patterns among the workers promoted the national counter-organization of the employers. This epoch of 'organized capitalism' brought not only the definition and organization of interests but also of factories, where the use of scientific methods was believed to make 'rational' production possible and prevent social conflict. Science would guarantee a fair distribution without conflict. Everywhere the point of departure was the same: how can competitive capacity on world markets be improved through higher productivity? Nevertheless, the interesting thing is that the discourse of rationalization and the precise problem formulation about this basically similar problem varied from country to country. In no two countries was the solution to this problem identical. In so far as industrial Europe has a common culture, the rationalization discourse suggests that it is primarily American. However, and this is the point, one has to consider the various European revolts against, and transformations of, this Americanization. The second point is that this fact cannot be understood with reference to structural dictates but only to specific cultural idioms which set different horizons (Stråth, 1996, p. 24).

CONCLUSIONS AND PERSPECTIVES

Modernity a few decades ago meant modernization and rationalization. Through science and technology, ever higher standards of living were understood to be achievable. Western industrial societies – the USA and Europe – were the spearhead in this development, which was seen as having its own pre-programmed teleology. It was only a matter of time before the rest of the world had achieved the same standard. Japan was a good example of how a people could 'learn' from the West. The development had a direction and a goal. Today modernization in this sense is outdated, but it has a successor in the idea of globalization, which in many respects is very similar. It is mainly in such a perspective that the concept of path dependency has been used.

A more fruitful approach is to emphasize modernity – rather than modernization – as being based on 'reflexivity', 'historicity' and 'agentiality' (Wittrock, 2004). Reflexivity refers to the human and social ability to step out of the immediate present and imagine other possible worlds. Historicity means the translation of such imagination into time, where the present can be distinguished from a past that was different and a future that may be different. Agentiality refers to the belief that human action may contribute to bring a particular different future about, a belief that the world is *machbar*, 'makeable'. This view of modernity – rather than modernization – makes historical processes open without goal and directions and with no guaranteed results. This modernity cannot be translated into a single set of institutions and social structures, as the sociology of modernization has long argued. Modernity can develop a variety of interpretations, which underpin different forms of institutional arrangements (Wagner, 2000; 2001a; 2001b).

Much of cultural analysis during the nineteenth and twentieth centuries has employed a concept of culture, shared values and beliefs, which assumes the existence of well-defined and bound human communities with high cultural homogeneity (Clifford, 1988; Clifford and Marcus, 1986; cf. Friese and Wagner, 1999, for a critical comment on this view). In contrast, the perspective as outlined here sees the existence of such communities as the result of work aiming at a 'cultural construction of community' that sought to produce boundedness and internal coherence (Stråth, 2000b). As soon as we adopt a view of culture as an ongoing process of making things common, which implies a variety of scopes, from a level of personal and local attachments and interactions to a level of reflexive dialogue in a public space, we should draw consequences on the methods of research.

The argument in this chapter for the analysis of social processes in terms of path-breaking responses to crisis rather than in terms of path dependence, has a focus on institutions and the language that shapes them. Attention must be paid to questions of how particular cultural idioms and ways of thinking and talking about, for instance, work and labour markets, the nation and Europe, are or were activated in specific historical and institutional settings. They shaped opinions of what was politically possible or imperative. These specific cultural idioms are not immediately given by economic or technical developments but through interpretations of these developments, interpretations that might direct action along very different paths. The analysis of the cultural idioms implies elucidation of how authority, legitimacy and social solidarity are established from signifying elements, such as concepts, metaphors and frameworks of interpretation.

Social change is a matter of groups and classes possessing different, sometimes incompatible, political languages of widely varying provenance. This perspective entails an analysis of the conditions under which groups and discourses with very different points of departure enter into relationships of stable coexistence or even mutual reinforcement at particular moments, while elsewhere, under similar conditions, they lead to conflict and polarization. Obviously, this emergence of contrary development patterns on the basis of similar prerequisites cannot be explained by reference to any causative derivation in one direction or the other. Neither the power of language nor the direction and the strength of the cultural construction of interests and identities can ever be predetermined.

Society is not an all-embracing order but a series of diversely established unifications, coming to terms with remaining conflicts of various ranges, durations and substances. Social work is required to achieve such unifications, to interpret situations and to adapt various interpretations for one another by means of concepts, symbols and metaphors. Unifications cannot be derived from the art of conflict or from social positions. Language does not in itself cause change but establishes a particular horizon for potential experience and theory. It makes change possible, that is, it sets limits for, rather than causes, change. This is similar to Weber's view, according to which *Weltbilder* function as pointsmen, *Weichensteller*, leading developments into new trajectories. These horizons and world views are different for different societies.[4]

Language produces meaning, which is multidimensional and relationally formed. This occurs in existing discursive fields as well as in new fields that are created. Meaning is contingent. Positive definitions are dependent on negative ones and vice versa. Concepts like 'class', 'Islam' or 'Europe' are established through distinction. They are politically constructed. Therefore they must be relativized and historicized instead of being reified. Instead of being seen as objective structures *an sich*,[5] they must be seen as potential, which can be mobilized through language.

Production of meaning is not a completely fortuitous affair, but stands in some kind of relationship to social and economic processes. The different patterns of organization of production and coercion demonstrate that production of meaning is never a priori causative, but always contingent. Collective protests cannot solely be the result of changes in the economic basis of society. Nor can structural changes be expressed solely in intentional terms. The causal powers are emergent ones. As in hyperdynamic processes, where very small unforeseen changes suddenly become greatly magnified in an unpredictable way, contingency means that very little is predictable and most things are of uncertain occurrence. Nowadays one might add on the analogy of the financial markets in order to illustrate the unpredictability. The historian's reconstruction *ex post facto* means that lines of developments are drawn but these lines should not be mistaken for the *ex ante facto* perspective of the actors studied or for a priori explanative power. Only in this retrospective sense can we talk about path dependency.

When developmental trajectories are outlined through retrospection it is important to pay attention to the openness towards future, which reasonably in the past must have been the same as for us. Past futures are of the same category as the potential futures of the present.[6] Having said this, it should be added that openness is a relative concept. The degree of openness and freedom of action varies. The construction and invention of future horizons is not a totally free enterprise. Here we can refer to Foucault. Images of the past and of the future are not just a linear relation from the present but depend on the prior accumulation of such relationships and their continuous constitution and reconstitution (Olick, 2003; see also Humlebæk, 2004). The past, as well as the history of relating past and present, constitutes contingency, which cannot be freely done away with. German post-1933 history, for example, imposes a series of constraints on the way in which any German nationalism is able to manifest itself. Even if all the elements necessary for a typical nationalist discourse are available (flag, national anthem, constitution, a history), the accumulated experiences of the past set limits for how such representations can be mixed. On the other side, such limitations through experiences are not eternal but fade with the distance to the past. Societies do not only remember. They also forget.

The approach I suggest emphasizes the role of human agency but rejects a method which, in a biased way, highlights the individual as does historism. This approach opens up the path towards the social sciences where language is analysed in its capacity of parole in an ongoing communication with the social and economic world. The linguistic/cultural code operates at the very centre of economic and political processes. This is not the same as being a prime mover. The case is rather that language makes possible and sets limits. Historical horizons of expectation connect future, present and past where in retrospect development lines can be constructed. This could be seen as an argument for the soft path-dependency version. However, the problem with the term remains that it blurs the historical openness towards future. For our orientation it is necessary to draw lines of development but it is as necessary to remember how preliminary and tentative they are, and that they are nothing but a discursive narrative category. The Angel of History might be able to imagine what is coming in future behind its back, but it can never know. On the other hand, it is bound to imagine the future. Whether the imaginations are successful and path-breaking can only be judged in retrospect. On this point the metaphor of the Angel risks being overstretched. The Angel is blind towards the future and is driven by the wind of progress without really being able to influence the direction of the flight. It could be argued that the imaginative capacity of modern man is not located in the back and that the visionary power *might*, which is not the same as *must*, be creative with a capacity to change the direction of the wind. How big the scope of action in this respect really is, is a disputed and very open issue. I here only have referred to some historical examples of path-breaking innovations and in general terms to Koselleck's crisis concept and Weber's railway metaphor. The imaginations of the Angel are based on what it can see glancing to the past. The question is to what extent we can transgress the limitation of the Angel in that respect when we imagine alternative worlds. However, even if we do not recognize very different conditions from those of the Angel, the fact remains that the landscape face to face with the Angel constantly occurs in new perspectives from new positions, which means that there is a permanent need for reinterpretation of the past, irrespective of whether we discern patterns or not.

The questions raised at the beginning of this chapter remain: what is dependent on what? Is there a pattern or organizing principle in the landscape or just a chaotic heap of ruins? There is nothing intrinsic in the past as such that answers these questions but only narrative attempts to give meaning.

NOTES

1. *Historism* should be distinguished from *historicism*, historical-philosophical claims to predict future by means of deterministic development theories. Among the most prominent critics of historicism were Friedrich von Hayek and Karl Popper. Historism emphasized the idiographic dimension of the past in opposition to the nomothetic ambitions of historicism.
2. Other contributions in the same vein are Evans et al. (1985) and Rueschemeyer et al. (1992). For a critical discussion, see Stråth (1996, pp. 16–17).
3. *Tiden* was the journal of the Swedish Social Democratic Party.
4. Max Weber used a railway metaphor to illustrate how historical processes at certain points of time could be changed into new directions, when, for instance, charismatic leadership broke the general process of bureaucratization and disenchantment which characterizes modernity, and produced new magicians. Pointsmen, *Weichensteller*, shunted the train onto a new track, where the process of disenchantment continued although from a new point of departure; cf. Stråth (1996) and Wagner (1993, pp. 467–9; 1994).
5. According to Nikolaj Bucharin (*Theorie des historischen Materialismus* (1992, §54), Karl Marx coined the term in *Das Elend der Philosophie* in his distinction between the working class *für sich*, with a class conscience and a class performance, and *an sich* as a social structure (still) unaware of its political potential. However, Marx never used the term, but talked about the class as an unpropertied mass vis-à-vis capital as opposed to the class *für sich*. Bucharin's assertion has nevertheless persisted. In the Marxist teleology the progressive development was from the class *an sich* to the class *für sich*.
6. For a development of this argument, see Koselleck (1985).

REFERENCES

Clifford, J. (1988), *The Predicament of Culture. Twentieth-Century Ethnography, Literature and Art*, Cambridge, MA: Harvard University Press.

Clifford, J. and G. Marcus (eds) (1986), *Writing Culture. The Politics and Poetry of Ethnography*, Berkeley, CA: University of California Press.

Donzelot, J. (1984), *L'invention du social*. Paris: Fayard.

Evans, P.B., D. Rueschemeyer and T. Skocpol (1985), *Bringing the State Back in Again*, Cambridge: Cambridge University Press.

Friese, H. and P. Wagner (1999), 'Not all that is solid melts into air. Modernity and contingency', in M. Featherstone and S. Lash (eds), *Spaces of Culture. City/ Nation/World*, London: Sage.

Fukuyama, F. (1992), *The End of History and the Last Man*, New York: Free Press.

Humlebæk, C., (2004), 'Rethinking Spain: continuities and ruptures in national discourse after Franco', PhD thesis, European University Institute.

Huntington, S.P. (1993), 'The clash of civilisations?', *Foreign Affairs*, **72**(3), 22–49.

Keyssar, A. (1986), *Out of Work. The First Century of Unemployment in Massachusetts*, Cambridge: Cambridge University Press.

Kocka, J. (1988a), 'Bürgertum und bürgerliche Gesellschaft im 19. Jahrhundert. Europäische Entwicklungen und deutsche Eigenarten', in J. Kocka (ed.), *Bürgertum im 19. Jahrhundert*, Bd 1, Munich: dtv.

Kocka, J. (1988b), 'German history before Hitler: the debate about the German "*Sonderweg*"', *Journal of Contemporary History*, **23**, 3–16.

Koselleck, R. (1985), 'On the historical-political semantics of asymmetric counter-concepts', in R. Koselleck, *Futures Past*, Cambridge: Cambridge University Press. German original (1979), *Vergangene Zukunft. Zur Semantik geschichtlicher Zeiten*, Frankfurt/Main: Suhrkamp.

Koselleck, R. (1988), *Critique and Crisis: Enlightenment and the Pathogenesis of Modern Society*, Oxford, Berg. German original (1954 [1992]), *Kritik und Krise: Eine Studie zur Pathogenesis der bürgerlichen Welt*, Frankfurt/Main, Suhrkamp.

Lepetit, B. (ed.) (1995), *Les formes de l'experience. Une autre histoire sociale*, Paris: Albin Michel.

Lunn, E. (1973), *Prophet of Community: The Romantic Socialism of Gustav Landauer*, Berkeley, CA: California University Press.

Mansfield, M., R. Salais and N. Whiteside (1994), *Aux sources du chômage 1880– 1914*, Paris: Belin.

Moore, B. Jr (1967), *Social Origins of Dictatorship and Democracy. Lord and Peasant in the Making of the Modern World*, Boston, MA: Beacon Paperback.

Mosse, G.L. (1981), *The Crisis of German Ideology. Intellectual Origins of the Third Reich*. New York: Grosset and Dunlap. First published in 1964.

Niethammer, L. (1989), *Posthistoire. Ist die Geschichte zu Ende?* Reinbeck bei Hamburg: Rowohlt.

Olick, J.K. (ed.) (2003), *States of Memory. Continuities, Conflicts and Transformations in National Retrospection*, Durkheim: Duke University Press.

Polanyi, K. (2001 [1944]), *The Great Transformation: The Political and Economic Origins of Our Time*, Boston, MA: Beacon Press.

Rueschemeyer, D., E. Huber Stephens and J.D. Stephens (1992), *Capitalist Development and Democracy*, Chicago, IL: University of Chicago Press.

Salais, R., N. Baverez and B. Reynaud (1986), *L'invention du chomage*, Paris: PUF.

Schivelsbusch, W. (2005), *'Entfernte Verwandte'. Faschismus, Nationalsozialismus, New Deal 1933–1939*, Munich: Carl Hanser.

Stråth, B. (1987), *The Politics of Deindustrialisation. The Contracting Process of the West European Shipbuilding Industry*, London: Croom Helm.

Stråth, B. (1991), 'A conditional plea for the modern project: cultural production of meaning and social change', in K.H Jarausch, J. Rüsen and H. Schleier (eds), *Geschichtswissenschaft vor 2000. Perspektiven der Historiographiegeschichte,*

Sozial- und Kulturgeschichte. Festschrift für Georg G Iggers zum 65. Geburtstag, Hagen: Margit Rottmann Medienverlag.

Stråth, B. (1996), *The Organisation of Labour Markets. Modernity, Culture and Governance in Germany, Sweden, Britain and Japan*. London: Routledge.

Stråth, B. (ed.) (2000a), *After Full Employment. European Discourses on Work and Flexibility*, Brussels: PIE-Peter Lang.

Stråth, B. (ed.) (2000b), *Myth and Memory in the Construction of Community, Historical Patterns in Europe and Beyond*, Brussels: P.I.E.-Peter Lang.

Tiden (Stockholm) (1929), October. (*Tiden* was the journal of the Swedish Social Democratic Party.)

Topalov, C. (1994), *Naissance du chômeur 1890–1940*, Paris: Albin Michel.

Trägårdh, L. (1990), 'Varieties of volkish ideologies. Sweden and Germany 1848–1933', in B. Stråth (ed.), *Language and the Construction of Class Identities. The Struggle for Discursive Power in Social Organisation: Scandinavia and Germany after 1800*, Gothenburg: Gothenburg University.

Trägårdh, L. (1993), 'The concept of the people and the construction of popular political culture in Germany and Sweden: 1848–1933', PhD dissertation, University of Michigan.

Wagner, P. (1990), *Sozialwissenschaften und Staat. Frankreich, Italien, Deutschland 1870–1980*, Frankfurt/Main: Campus.

Wagner, P. (1993), 'Die Soziologie der Genese sozialer Institutionen. Theoretische Perspektiven der neuen Sozialwissenschaften in Frankreich', *Zeitschrift für Soziologie*, 22(6), 464–76.

Wagner, P. (1994), *A Sociology of Modernity: Liberty and Discipline*, London and New York: Routledge.

Wagner, P. (2000), 'Modernity – one or many?', in J. Blau (ed.), *Blackwell Companion to Sociology*, Oxford: Blackwell.

Wagner, P. (2001a), *A History and Theory of the Social Sciences: Not All that is Solid Melts into Air*, London: Sage.

Wagner, P. (2001b), *Theorizing Modernity: Inescapability & Attainability in Social Theory*, London and New York: Sage.

Wagner, P. and B. Zimmermann (2004), 'Citizenship and collective responsibility. On the political philosophy of the nation-based welfare state and beyond', in L. Magnusson and B. Stråth (eds), *A European Social Citizenship? Preconditions for Future Policies from a Historical Perspective*, Brussels: PIE-Peter Lang.

Wehler, H.-U. (1975), *Das deutsche Kaiserreich 1871–1918*, 2nd edn, Göttingen: V&R.

Wehler, H.-U. (1988), *Aus der Geschichte lernen?* Munich: C.H. Beck.

Wittrock, B. (2004), 'The meaning of the axial age', in J. Arnason (ed.), *Axial Transformations*, Leiden: Brill.

Zimmermann, B. (1999), *La constitution du chomage en Allemagne*, Paris: Editions de la Maison des Sciences de l'Homme.

2. Second-degree path dependence: information costs, political objectives, and inappropriate small-farm settlement of the North American Great Plains

Gary D. Libecap

Well, there isn't much rain out west. There is not enough rain to grow crops . . . The historical process which we call the westward movement shattered against these facts. Neither hope nor illusion nor desire nor Act of Congress could change them in the least. (Stegner, 1954, p. xix)

One of the most serious problems that presents itself in . . . the drought area is that too many farm families have been settled in these regions . . . One hundred prosperous farm families are far more desirable than 200 families on relief. (Frank Reinoehl, Farm Credit Administration, 1939)[1]

'You'll have to get off the land. The plows'll go through the dooryard . . .'
'But if we go, where'll we go? How'll we go? We got no money . . .'
'Why don't you go on west to California? There's work out there, and it never gets cold.' (Steinbeck, 1976, pp. 43–4)

INTRODUCTION

The distinguishing characteristic of the Great Plains is its relative aridity and fluctuating rainfall, compared with agricultural regions to the east. The region receives one-third to one-half the annual precipitation of the Midwest, and is subject to periodic droughts. The Great Plains were the last agricultural frontier, settled between 1880 and 1925, first in the southern and central plains of western Kansas and Nebraska and eastern Colorado, and than in the northern plains of the western Dakotas and eastern Montana. At the time of settlement there was no consensus as to the correct response to aridity. John Wesley Powell recommended a sharp revision in the land laws to allow for much larger units than the 160-acre

farms authorized under the Homestead Act. With an imperfect understanding of the region's climate, however, and optimistic notions that
drought would either disappear with cultivation or that its effects could be
mitigated through proper cultivation, there was no political support for
Powell's recommendations.

The need for much larger farms did not become apparent until after the
serious droughts of 1917–21 in the northern plains and throughout the
Great Plains in 1930–39. By those times, however, the region was populated by hundreds of thousands of small farmers, who were persuaded to
migrate by a generous federal land policy.

Unfortunately, the farming units prescribed by land policy were revealed
subsequently to be unsustainably small. Costly out-migration, farm consolidation and political adjustment (abandoning towns, elimination of
counties, closing school districts) were the only solutions. The population
of *two-thirds* of the counties in the Great Plains peaked in 1930 or earlier.[2]
And in the Dakotas, Nebraska and Oklahoma the figures are more dramatic with approximately *80 percent* of the counties peaking in population
in 1930 or before. By 1990, many counties had only remnants of their
former populations. For instance, Billings and Bottineau Counties, North
Dakota had their largest populations in 1910 at 10 186 and 17 295 inhabit-
ants respectively. By the 1990 census, however, Billings had 11 percent of
its 1910 population and Bottineau, 46 percent.[3]

This collapse in population that occurred throughout the region, with
its legacy of deserted homesteads and empty town sites, is testimony to
land policies that brought far too many farmers and small farms to the
Great Plains. Further, the cultivation practices of desperate small farmers
encouraged wind erosion and hampered collective action to address it. The
famous Dust Bowl, with its environmental costs and subsequent need for
soil reconstruction, was a direct result.

In this chapter, I examine the nature of path dependence associated
with US land policy in the Great Plains. I discuss the information problems regarding the region's climate and the political opposition to larger
land allocations. I then turn to estimates of farm failure, consolidation
and population out-migration. The adjustment from small homesteads
took approximately 50 years as farm size changes in the Great Plains
exceeded that which occurred in the Midwest, where small farms already
were optimal. Finally, I examine the Dust Bowl and relate its intensity
to the distribution of small farms in the Great Plains. In all, the dense
settlement of the American Great Plains and their subsequent depopulation demonstrate the importance of institutional and political path
dependence in influencing economic behavior and in determining its
costs.

AN OVERVIEW OF PATH DEPENDENCE

The notion of path dependence is a useful, if controversial, concept to describe a causal link between current economic outcomes and past decisions.[4] History, then, has an enduring influence on the economy. Choices made on the basis of transitory conditions can persist long after those conditions have changed, and as a result, understanding contemporary practices requires examination of path-dependent processes, along with consideration of current technologies, preferences, market conditions and government policies. Illustrations of the effects of path dependency include small-scale technical standards as well as large-scale institutions and patterns of economic development. Path dependence arises if there are increasing returns from adoption of certain techniques or technologies or because there are transaction costs in changing from an established practice to a different one. Examples of cases of potential path dependence are adoption of the 'QWERTY' standard typewriter (and computer) keyboard, the 'standard gauge' of railway track and VHS rather than BETA formats for videocassette recorders. More broadly, path dependence also is argued to play an important role in the differential performance of economies in the process of economic growth because superior or inferior decisions can have cumulative long-term effects across the society.

Although the notion that historical decisions matter in contemporary economic performance seems straightforward, controversy has arisen as to just how important the past might be in constraining current outcomes. That is, debate has emerged as to whether or not there are significant efficiency effects from path dependency. How costly is the 'lock-in' from the previous adoption of technologies or processes; how far have these decisions moved the economy from what otherwise would be a more efficient track?

On one side of the debate are Puffert (2000; 2002), David (1985), Arthur (1989) and Katz and Shapiro (1985) who argue that technological standards, for example, once adopted, become difficult to jettison or modify due to interrelations, scale economies and network externalities, and inappropriate standards subsequently can lead an economy down a less efficient growth path. On the other side are Liebowitz and Margolis (1995; 1998), who are skeptical of the aggregate economic impact of path dependency. They argue that if the gains from adjustment from a technology standard or practice are sufficiently high, economic agents will be motivated to make such modifications. That is, remediable inefficiency is highly unlikely to persist since there would be positive payoffs to those who made such adjustments. Accordingly, inferior outcomes from past decisions can be remedied through market activity. If what appear to be mistaken decisions were made in the past because of limited and incomplete information, however, Liebowitz and Margolis argue that it would be inappropriate to draw efficiency conclusions. The parties made the best decisions possible based on the information to hand at the time. Under this view an apparent inferior outcome is actually the most efficient one available, once all information and other transaction costs are considered. If present transaction costs prohibit a movement away from the technology or practice, then it would not be efficient to do so.

Liebowitz and Margolis develop three types of path dependence. First-degree path dependence occurs whenever there is an element of persistence or durability in a decision. There is no efficiency implication, just that current practices are influenced by past conditions even if the parties involved had properly predicted prices and other market conditions when they made their decisions. Second-degree path dependence arises when there is imperfect foresight so that *ex ante* efficient decisions turn out not to be so. There is dependence on past conditions that leads to outcomes that are regrettable and costly to change, but again, no efficiency judgments are drawn. Third-degree path dependence, however, has the strongest efficiency claims. In this case there are remediable inefficiencies that for some reason are not corrected. With third-degree path dependence there are intertemporal relationships that have durable, negative consequences for the economy. Liebowitz and Margolis challenge the likelihood of such conditions on both theoretical and empirical grounds.

Regardless of their efficiency effects, past policies and decisions can have important distributional implications. That is, the assignment of property rights inherent in the adoption of a particular practice or technology results in a specific distribution of wealth and political power. Part of the transaction costs that arise to limit adjustment to a new path is due to the actions of those who have a stake in previously established arrangements or practices. Indeed, much of political economy involves the determination of stake holders or constituencies with property rights in a certain technology, policy or institution, and the political maneuvering of existing and new constituent groups over modifications in it. There will be winners and losers in such actions, and incumbent constituents can be expected to lobby to protect their position and to demand compensation for any movement to a new arrangement. This is politics and it has its origins in path dependence.

In the case examined in this chapter there were costs to the economy from previous decisions, and political efforts to protect the wealth and political influence of those who were benefiting from those policies limited subsequent adjustments. Nevertheless, as shown below, policy decisions were made in the presence of very incomplete information and, subsequently, the transaction costs of adjustment became high for political reasons. No claims are made that path dependence resulted in remediable, but uncorrected, losses.

PATH DEPENDENCE AND THE GREAT PLAINS

Following Liebowitz and Margolis, the type of path dependence of interest here is first- or second-degree path dependence. *Ex ante*, behavior is determined by the existing stock of information and the political and economic institutions that determine individual incentives. Strong inefficiency claims that alternative arrangements were known, but ignored, leading society along a suboptimal development path are unwarranted. Rather, as described below, US land policy was molded by distributional and political goals and knowledge of northern European agriculture and eastern US climatic conditions.

As the agricultural frontier moved across North America in the nineteenth century, migrants settled and founded farms and communities based on the restrictions of federal land law. On the frontier, population density also influenced the political map. Uninhabited regions became territories and then became states based on the accumulation of settlers and settlements. Land speculators (almost all migrants), as well as aspiring politicians, depended upon the piecemeal allocation of land to attract migrants and population growth sufficient to drive up land prices and to meet the threshold for statehood. Rising land prices brought capital gains to land holders and statehood opened the doors to federal office and political influence beyond what was possible locally.

This policy worked in northern agricultural regions. As the frontier moved from the Atlantic seaboard across the Midwest, capital gains became the greatest source of wealth accumulation for the population.[5] There were no strong economies of scale in grain production so that fixed investments were made in migration to remote regions with few employment alternatives and in small grain farms. Fortunately, these investments paid off and the farms flourished. The agricultural economy expanded. Communities were founded and grew. New states were added. A workable institutional structure endured and set expectations for subsequent migrants.

United States land policy failed when the frontier passed the one-hundredth meridian in the Great Plains. In this region, small grain farms, ultimately could not survive. But at the time of settlement, there was no strong scientific evidence on the climate or on appropriate agricultural practices and farm sizes. Northern Europeans and eastern Americans had no experience with semi-arid regions and the knowledge regarding them was primitive. The dramatic adjustments called for by John Wesley Powell would have slashed settlement opportunities, expectations for higher land values, and population densities. There was no political support to do it. Costly adjustments would have been required, and they were not taken. Instead, settlement of the Great Plains occurred under the same institutional structure and generally, in the same manner, as occurred in Iowa or Wisconsin. But the outcome subsequently was quite different – widespread farm failure. Federal land policy created the conditions for path dependence. *Ex post*, the Great Plains were settled much too densely with small farms that could not succeed.

FEDERAL LAND POLICY: THE INSTITUTIONAL BASIS FOR PATH DEPENDENCE AND THE INAPPROPRIATE ALLOCATION OF PROPERTY RIGHTS TO LAND IN THE GREAT PLAINS

Throughout North America during the nineteenth and early twentieth centuries, government land was made available for private claiming and patenting in small plots.[6] The small-farm emphasis in US land policy followed Thomas Jefferson's admonishment: 'The earth is given as a common stock for man to labor and live on . . . The small landholders are the most precious part of the state.'[7] The most important American policy vehicle was the Homestead Act, first enacted in 1862, whereby any family head could claim between 40 and 160 acres, and upon five-years' continuous residence and improvement (*cultivation*), receive title. After 1862, nearly 3 million homestead claims were filed to over 510 million acres of land.[8] These small allocations were effective for northern agriculture, east of the one-hundredth meridian. As migrants moved across the frontier, they transplanted farming practices, crops and farm sizes appropriate in their places of origin.

By the 1890s, with most of the arable land claimed elsewhere, settlers turned to the Great Plains (Figure 2.1). For the first time, migrants encountered conditions that were unlike any they had experienced before in the USA or Europe. It was dry. Annual precipitation was 20 inches or less (much less in some areas). Indeed, the Great Plains had been labeled 'the Great American Desert' and thought unfit for inhabitation. In his *Report on the Lands of the Arid Region of the United States* made to Congress in 1878, John Wesley Powell warned that past methods of agricultural settlement could no longer be relied upon in semi-arid regions and called for a minimum of 2560-acre homesteads for 'pastoral regions'.[9] Two bills to change federal land policy were included in his report, but they were not considered. Powell's proposals were debated in Congress, rejected, and no

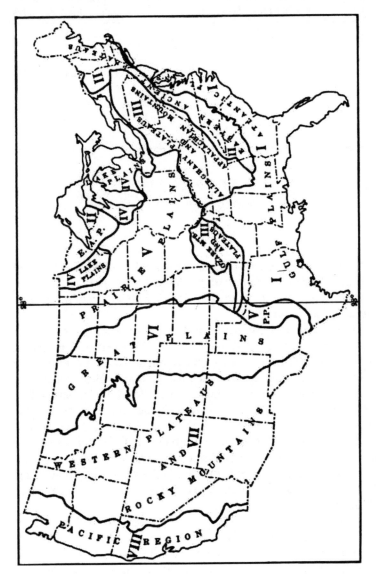

Source: Hansen and Libecap (2004a).

Figure 2.1 The Great Plains

49

Table 2.1   Small farms on the Great Plains

	Percentage of farms smaller than 180 acres	Percentage of farms smaller than 500 acres
1930	27	65
1935	30	67
1940	28	62
1945	22	54
1950	20	51
1954	18	48
1959	15	42
1964	15	39

Notes: Great Plains counties includes the 362 eastern counties of Montana, Colorado and New Mexico, all of North Dakota, those west of the ninety-seventh meridian in South Dakota, most of those west of the ninety-eighth meridian in Nebraska, Kansas and Oklahoma, and west Texas counties in the Panhandle to 32 degrees latitude.

Source: US Agricultural Census, 1930–64.

significant modifications in the land laws were made. Other than the 1909 revision in the Homestead Act to allow 360-acre claims, there were no major changes in plot size to make allowance for limited rainfall through the repeal of the law in the 1930s.

Settlers transported and transplanted Midwestern crops and farm sizes to the Great Plains. Between 1880 and 1925, 1 078 123 original homestead entries were filed to 202 298 425 acres in western Kansas, Nebraska and the Dakotas and eastern Colorado and Montana, leading to the proliferation of small, 160 to 360-acre farms throughout the region.[10] The census does not provide size categories that coincide with such homesteads, but the available data are suggestive. By 1930, as Table 2.1 reveals, nearly two-thirds of the farms on the Great Plains were less than 500 acres and over one-fourth were less than 180 acres. Although such farm sizes were viable in areas of higher and less variable rainfall, in the semi-arid Great Plains by the 1930s, agricultural economists were recommending much larger forms of 1200 acres or more.[11]

Several factors underlay the failure to change the Homestead Act in the early twentieth century to reflect more arid conditions in the West.[12] Foremost was a lack of any compelling scientific argument to do so. At the time of the debate, there was no body of scientific knowledge that supported Powell's claim. Understanding of the semi-arid climate with its highly variable precipitation and drought cycles was limited. Further, the implications that might have been drawn from the climate for farming were not obvious.[13] As it turns out, the plains were largely settled during a period of abnormal rainfall, a situation, of course, that migrants would not have known.[14] Further, there was political opposition among Great Plains politicians to any change in the land laws that would provide fewer opportunities for in-migration and settlement of the region.[15] Powell's proposed allotments were 16 times larger than those allowed by the Homestead Act. They would have drastically reduced the number of farmers that could have settled the region. Given the available body of scientific knowledge, frontier politicians were unconvinced by claims that farms had to be substantially larger in order to survive on the Great Plains.

Politicians also supported continuation of the small-homestead policy in order to maximize the number of farmers and, hence, population in their jurisdictions for political reasons. Population growth not only encouraged economic development and associated rising land values, something most frontier residents benefited from, including many politicians, but it also created political opportunities. Although there was no fixed population threshold that a territory had to meet before being admitted as a state, greater populations speeded statehood and the possibility of having two Senators and more voting members of the House, both of which opened federal political offices for local politicians. The same political rationale applied at the county level whereby apportionment in state legislatures depended upon population. Accordingly, there had to be very good reasons for changing the land laws and, until the droughts of the early 1920s and the entire 1930s, there were none.

Figure 2.2 shows the pattern of annual precipitation from 1895–1982 in the Great Plains, as represented by Montana, and the unusually wet conditions that existed during settlement. Notice that during the period of major migration to the Great Plains, from 1907 to the mid-1920s, the region had its highest mean rainfall in the century. The major test for small-farm homesteads did not come until the 1930s when precipitation fell to record lows for most of the decade.

During periods of high precipitation, the Great Plains had the characteristics of sub-humid climates, becoming superficially attractive for the kinds of agriculture more appropriate for such regions. When droughts returned, however, those agricultural practices were placed at risk.

Libecap and Hansen (2002) analyze the weather information problem for the Great Plains in the late nineteenth and early twentieth centuries. They show that the absence of knowledge about the region's climate led to the rise of folk theories to explain the weather, 'rain follows the plow', and to pseudo-scientific prescriptions for farming practices, 'dryfarming doctrine'. The former held that precipitation would increase with settlement and cultivation.[16] The latter held that even if drought occurred, its

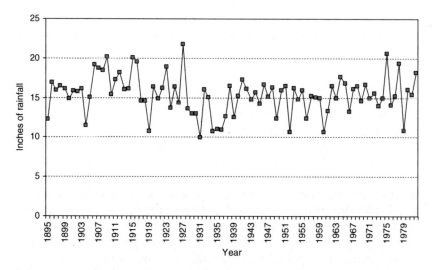

Sources: 1895–1913: Burke and Pinckney (1914); 1914–82: US Weather Bureau (n.d.).

Figure 2.2   Montana annual precipitation

effects could be mitigated through constant cultivation that would capture and store rainfall underground for later use by crops.[17] Both scenarios subsequently were found to be of little assistance in protecting small farms during drought. Nevertheless, they fueled the optimism of migrants who moved into the region.[18] Accordingly, migrants to the semi-arid Great Plains did not perceive the precarious condition of the farms they founded or of the crops they planted.

With the relatively 'wet' conditions of the early twentieth century, coupled with a lack of information about the long-term climate, the Great Plains seemed to live up to the billing of its most ardent proponents as having the country's most desirable farmland. As Representative Martin Maginnis of Montana claimed during 1879 congressional debates over Powell's recommended land law changes, the West would be 'one of the richest and greatest parts of the vast domain of the United States'.[19] Indeed, homestead farms did well when rainfall and crop yields were high. Libecap and Hansen's (2002) analysis of a sample of homesteads in Hill County, Montana, in 1916 shows that income on such farms was comparable to that earned on farms elsewhere. Homestead gross income from wheat was $2622, while farm mean gross income for the USA as a whole was $2104 in 1920. The sample data indicate why homesteading free federal land in the Great Plains was such an attractive prospect in the early part of the twentieth century.

CONSEQUENCES OF PATH DEPENDENCY 1: FARM FAILURE, SUBSIDY, OUT-MIGRATION AND FARM CONSOLIDATION

Surveys taken during the 1930s underscore the vulnerability of small homesteads to the collapse of production during drought. Halcrow's (1938) study of 503 unsuccessful farms in eastern Montana, using data for 1928–35, found that they were undiversified and small, with two-thirds below 360 acres, when at least 700 to 800 acres were deemed necessary for minimum-cost production. Cochrane's (1938) examination of 314 farms, using data for 1934–36, determined that the most productive farms (measured by net income) were twice the size of the average farm. They had approximately 1100 acres, focused on wheat cultivation with diversification into livestock production, used more machinery and were more likely to use fallow to build up soil moisture and fight wind erosion than were their less productive counterparts. With limited acreage, small farms could not afford to leave much land in fallow, and they lacked the economies of scale necessary for effective use of machinery.

Hansen and Libecap's (2004a) analysis of the characteristics of farms that failed during the 1917–21 drought in the northern plains found that size was a key factor. They used county directories from 1916 to 1930 for three counties in Montana – Cascade, Fergus and Carbon – to examine the persistence of farms over this 15-year period.[20] The directories include farmer name, farm size, address and assessed value. Matching farmer names and/ or addresses in the directories between 1916 and the post-drought years allows for the identification of survivors and non-survivors. Larger farms consistently did better. In Cascade County 37 percent of the farms listed in the directory in 1916 survived to 1923, and these farms were 17 percent larger in 1916 than were those that failed. Only 20 percent of the farms in existence in 1916 were listed in the directory in 1929, and those farms were 13 percent larger in 1916 than were those that failed. Similarly in Fergus County, 33 percent of the farms survived to 1923, and they were 20 percent larger in 1916 than were non-survivors. Farms that were larger in 1916 also were more likely to endure through 1930 than were non-survivors.

Using a logit specification to examine farm survival in those two counties, Hansen and Libecap showed that the predicted survival probability from 1916 to 1922 was 0.33 at the 1916 mean farm size of 322 acres in Fergus County, but it rose to 0.48 with farms of 1500 acres. Similarly in Cascade County, the estimated probability of survival from 1916 to 1923 was 0.37 at the mean 1916 farm size of 338 acres. Survival probability increased to 0.41 at farm sizes of 762 acres (mean + one standard deviation) and to 0.48 for farms of 1500 acres.

Carbon County, Montana, is included in the few surviving 1919 agricultural census manuscripts, and these census data provide an even clearer picture of the factors underlying the lack of durability of farming on the Great Plains. Combining county directories from 1919 to 1922 with farmer and farm characteristics found in the census, Hansen and Libecap test survival as a function of regional variables, years of farm ownership, farm size, crop acre share, value of crop sales and livestock value. They found that years of farm ownership, farm size and crop share significantly improved farm survival. Larger, more productive farms were better able to withstand the drought. Those farmers who survived drought had farms that were 28 percent larger than the farms that failed.

In the 1930s declining commodity prices, plummeting yields, and soil destruction from wind erosion adversely affected all agriculture on the Great Plains. But small farms particularly were devastated. Farm failure rates were higher in the upper Great Plains than in any other part of the US.[21] The initial reaction of the Roosevelt Administration in 1933 and 1934 was to acquire as many small farms as possible through the Resettlement Administration to facilitate farm consolidation and migration from the region. In its report to the President, the National Resources Planning Board explicitly blamed the Homestead Act for bringing about small-farm settlement that was too dense to be sustained on the Great Plains:

> The provisions of the Homestead Act, under which the region was settled, did not fit the semi-arid environment – a quarter section of land was too small a unit for successful grazing or dry-farming. Later legislation proved of little benefit. Most land holdings are still too small. Settlement without guidance. Homesteaders from humid lands in the middle and eastern interior encountered conditions in the Plains of which they had no knowledge.[22]

Soil Conservation Service geographer Warren Thornthwaite (1936, p. 243–5) suggested that the Great Plains could sustain only two-thirds of the 1930 population. He called for the slow removal of 900 000 people or 210 000 families from the region, offering numbers of 'surplus families' by state: North Dakota 7360, Montana 12 610, Colorado 2580, Texas 12 200, Oklahoma 2930, Kansas, 6100, Nebraska 4930 and South Dakota 4640.

Great Plains politicians feared such a loss in farm population and the related deterioration in local economic activity and national political influence. The number of representatives in the House was at stake, as were property values in rural communities and related investment in schools and other infrastructure. Other federal agency officials, including eventually Secretary of Agriculture Henry A. Wallace and Assistant Secretary M.L. Wilson, also opposed major population movement from the region. In its 1938 *Yearbook of Agriculture*, 'Soils and Men', the US Department of Agriculture noted the debate over whether to move farmers out of farming or to subsidize them, and sided with the latter: 'it is wise to keep a large rural population' (pp. 3–4). The department stood to lose much of its constituency in the region. Clawson et al. (1940, pp. 42–8) claimed that eliminating farms of less than 300 acres in eastern Montana would reduce the number of farms by 76 percent. But they doubted that many would be willing to accept such drastic steps. They still called for the elimination of 50 percent of the farms in the region from 1928–35 levels, and predicted it would take 30 years to do so with considerable government assistance.

A final factor in molding policy was that migrants were not received warmly in destination areas, such as California. Immigrants were viewed as competing with the local workforce for already scarce employment and as placing additional pressure on hard-pressed local governments and communities for social services. Taeuber and Taylor in their Works Progress Administration report, *The People of the Drought Area* (1937, p. 55) concluded, 'No government agency, State or Federal, will sponsor a program calling for the evacuation of a large number of families'. Accordingly, the policy focus was on relief for small farmers and subsidy for agriculture.

The Resettlement Administration was renamed and restructured as the Farm Security Administration in 1937. The Farm Security Administration assisted at least one farm family out of six in the Great Plains states. Other New Deal agencies and programs providing subsidies and relief payments included the Works Progress Administration, the Farm Credit Administration, the Agricultural Adjustment Administration (AAA), and the Federal Emergency Recovery Administration (FERA). Between September 1933 and August 1935, FERA provided $32 666 370 to Colorado, Kansas and Oklahoma for relief to farm families. The major historian of the Dust Bowl, Donald Worster (1979, pp. 131–5) estimated that three out of four farmers in the region received federal relief. A March 1935 survey indicated that up to 40 percent of farm families in the Texas panhandle, over 50 percent in southeastern Colorado and between 33 and 50 percent in southwest Kansas were dependent on government payments. The Great Plains Committee reported that per capita relief payments were as high as $200 in some Great Plains counties (1936, p. 55). The Committee credited relief payments for preventing 'extreme human suffering'.[23]

The Works Progress Administration noted that farmers on relief 'were found to be operating farms considerable smaller in size than the average farm operated by non-relief farmers' (Link, 1937, p. 37). Great Plains states had a greater portion of farmers on relief than any other section of the country (Asch and Mangus, 1937, pp. xiii, 5). Small farmers received rehabilitation loans, grants, work relief, and feed and seed loans. The range of total assistance per farm from all sources during the period 1933–37 was \$1356–\$1660 in the northern Great Plains.[24] Relief expenditures were designed to help sustain small farmers and may have slowed farm abandonment and out-migration. Larger farmers received crop adjustment payments from the AAA. These AAA payments, however, may have encouraged greater out-migration. With payments to reduce output, farmers with sharecroppers cancelled share contracts, forcing croppers off the land. The AAA payments also facilitated mechanization, which reduced agricultural labor demand, also likely encouraging out-migration.

Figure 2.3 shows the range of federal aid per capita in the Great Plains states between 1933 and 1936. As indicated, payments were greatest in the plains regions – eastern Montana, Colorado and New Mexico, and western North and South Dakota, Kansas, Oklahoma and Texas. Table 2.2 lists the ratio of farmers on relief to all farmers by Great Plains state. The northern plains states tended to have the highest ratios, but there is considerable variation, reflecting differences in rural poverty and in state eligibility rules.[25]

Even with relief payments and other forms of government support, many small-farm families were still unable to make loan and mortgage payments, pay taxes and maintain their families. They abandoned their property and migrated from the region. The US Great Plains Committee (1936, p. 8) commented: 'Excessive droughts in the Great Plains have resulted in the aimless and desperate migration of thousands of families in search of some means of livelihood . . . Many more would have been forced to leave but for public aid and relief.' The Committee (1936, p. 72) estimated that 165 000 individuals had moved from the Great Plains by 1936. By 1938, Webb and Brown (1938, p. 137) estimated that between 12 and 20 percent of migrating families left Oklahoma, Kansas, Montana and Nebraska because of farm failure, and in the Dakotas 54 percent left due to farm failure. Table 2.3 shows family emigration in 1930, at the very start of the drought, for Great Plains states.

Lebergott's (1970, pp. 845–7) data for the decade 1930–40 also show that the West North Central and West South Central states, covering most of the Great Plains, had the highest out-migration rates in the USA. Within the region, statewide, North and South Dakota, Nebraska, Kansas and Oklahoma had by far the greatest migration rates, with North Dakota's rate between two and three times that for the nearest non-Great Plains states. Gillette (1941, pp. 627–8) estimated that 120 000 people left North Dakota between 1930 and 1940, 20 000 from Montana, 92 000 from South Dakota, 278 000 from Oklahoma and 195 000 from Kansas. For North Dakota and South Dakota, this migration represented 21 percent and 16 percent of the states' rural population, respectively. It was 6 percent of Montana's rural population (8 percent of the state's Great Plains counties); 18 percent of Oklahoma's and 53 percent of its plains counties; and

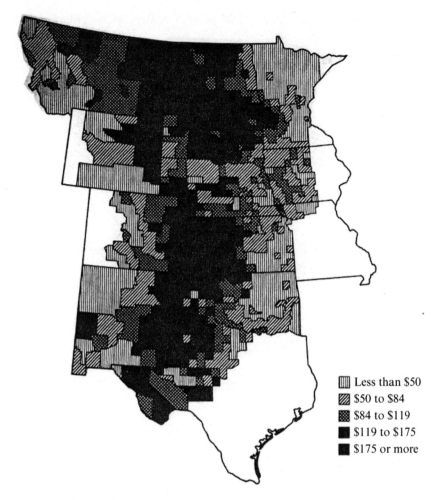

Less than $50
$50 to $84
$84 to $119
$119 to $175
$175 or more

Source: Kifer and Stewart (1938).

Figure 2.3 Federal aid per capita in the Great Plains, 1933–36

17 percent of Kansas' rural population and 43 percent of its plains counties' rural population.[26] This was a dramatic population out-migration indeed. Considering census population loss and natural increase, Gillette concluded that 982 000 people departed the Great Plains and Mountain states.[27] Figure 2.4 shows the variation in out-migration across the Great Plains.[28]

Despite all of this, the farm size adjustment process took time, requiring

Table 2.2   Great Plains farmers with relief and rehabilitation grants and
             advances, 1935

State	Ratio of farmers receiving relief to all farmers (%)
Colorado	22
Kansas	6
Montana	13
Nebraska	6
New Mexico	36
North Dakota	27
Oklahoma	27
South Dakota	33
Texas	8
US total	9

Notes: State totals, not all counties are in the Great Plains.

Source: Asch and Mangus (1937, p. 5).

Table 2.3   Family emigration, Great Plains states, 1930

State	Number of families	Families emigrating	Migrant families per 1000 families
Oklahoma	531 183	2 633	4.96
New Mexico	89 490	369	4.12
South Dakota	146 513	521	3.56
Colorado	237 936	838	3.52
Nebraska	314 957	809	2.57
Kansas	446 437	1 091	2.44
North Dakota	132 004	318	2.41
Montana	114 679	264	2.30
Texas	1 293 344	1 971	1.52

Source: Webb and Brown (1938, p. 151).

major farm size changes in the Great Plains relative to other farming
regions. The lengthy process of achieving more optimal farm sizes, in part,
was due to the availability of federal aid and other forms of support for
existing small farmers. Table 2.4 shows farm size changes from 1930 to
1970 in the Great Plains. Figure 2.5 illustrates this size adjustment and
compares it to other agricultural areas by plotting annual mean farm sizes

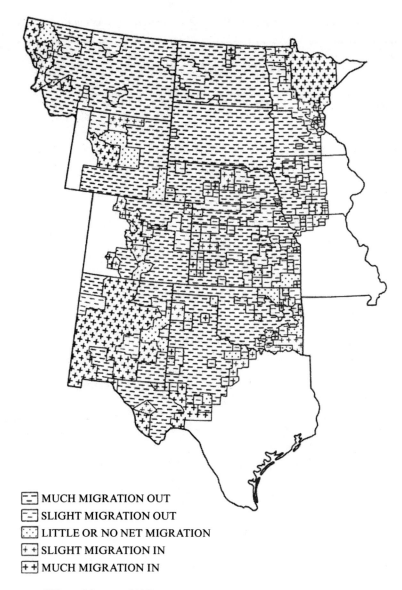

☐ MUCH MIGRATION OUT
☐ SLIGHT MIGRATION OUT
☐ LITTLE OR NO NET MIGRATION
☐ SLIGHT MIGRATION IN
☐ MUCH MIGRATION IN

Source: Kifer and Stewart (1938).

Figure 2.4   Net migration in the Great Plains, 1930–35

Table 2.4   Farm size change 1930 to 1970 in Great Plains counties

State	Average farm size 1930	Average farm size 1970	Percentage change in farm size
Kansas	558	1032	85
Nebraska	815	1652	103
North Dakota	524	1044	99
South Dakota	575	1775	209
Texas	788	1382	75
Oklahoma	335	725	116
Colorado	625	1830	193
Montana	1154	3539	207
New Mexico	1266	5150	307

Source: Calculated from census data, 1930 and 1969, as provided in the Great Plains Data Set, ICPSR.

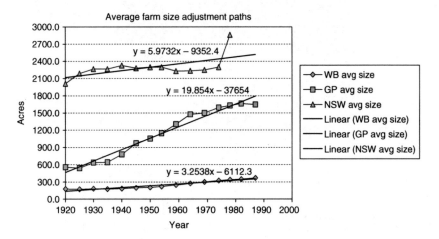

Source: Hansen and Libecap (2004a).

Figure 2.5   Farm size adjustment: the Great Plains, the Midwest and New South Wales

from 1920 through 1987, constructed from census data for the American Great Plains and the Midwest, and from Vamplew (1987, pp. 72–3) for New South Wales, Australia.[29] New South Wales accounts for approximately one-third of Australian wheat production and has semi-arid climate similar to that found in the Great Plains.

As illustrated, between 1920 and 1987 mean farm size approximately doubled from 175 acres to 371 acres in the Midwest, with the estimated annual adjustment of 3.3 acres. In the Great Plains mean farm size grew from 557 acres in 1920 to 1648 acres by 1987, a tripling in farm size, with an estimated annual increase of 19.9 acres in farm size. For New South Wales, farm size started out larger at 2010 acres in 1920 and rose to 2862 acres by 1978, the last year of available data. The major adjustment necessary in farm size in the Great Plains compared to other agricultural regions reflects the inappropriately small size of homestead allocations for that area considering its semi-arid climate. Homestead farms were too small, and 'catchup' was necessary in order to reach more optimally sized units. But the consolidation process took over 50 years.

CONSEQUENCES OF PATH DEPENDENCY 2: FAILURE OF COLLECTIVE ACTION AND THE DUST BOWL

The precipitation data for Colorado in Figure 2.2 illustrate the shortfall in precipitation that characterized the 1930s' drought. Severe wind erosion was a consequence of very dry soil and wind. Although most dust storms were local or regional, some could be huge, 600 by 400 miles, lasting 10 hours or more. The storms could be very damaging. In his book on the Dust Bowl, Vance Johnson (1946, pp. 194–5) estimated that in 1935 alone 850 million tons of topsoil had blown away from 4 340 000 acres in the southern plains. By 1938, the US Soil Conservation Service reported that 80 percent of the land in the southern plains had been subject to wind erosion, with 40 percent to a serious degree. Ten million acres had lost the upper 5 inches of topsoil, and 13 500 000 acres had lost 2.5 inches, with an average loss of 480 tons of topsoil per acre.

Small farmers contributed to the problem of wind erosion in the 1930s. They cultivated more of their land than did larger farmers, and were less likely to use costly wind erosion control techniques and equipment. Hansen and Libecap (2004b) argue that homesteads were too small to internalize many of the externalities associated with either the control of or failure to control wind erosion. Dust from eroding fields smothered downwind farms, and on very small farms, most of those effects were external. Conversely, small farmers could free ride on the erosion control activities of their larger neighbors. Indeed, all farms on the Great Plains in the 1930s were too small to effectively address regional erosion problems, and the large number of parties involved increased the costs of collective action.

The small farm problem was noted by government agencies investigating environmental damage and rural poverty on the Great Plains. The US Great Plains Committee (1936, pp. 3, 40–46, 75), appointed by President Roosevelt to investigate agricultural distress in the region concluded that 'although we now know that in most parts of the Great Plains a farm of this size [homestead] is far too small to support a family. They were required to put this land under plow, regardless of whether or not it was suited to cultivation'. Cooper et al. of the Bureau of Agricultural Economics (1938, pp. 146–8) claimed that farms 'are so small that the establishment of a system of farming that will conserve soil and produce a desirable family income is practically impossible'. Roland Renne of the Montana Experiment Station (1935, pp. 426–9) noted: 'Dealing with thousands of different owners slows up the adoption of a planned land use program . . .'.[30]

The control of wind erosion involved covering the exposed soil, slowing the surface speed of the wind and increasing the cloddishness of soil to make the particles more difficult to move. Pasture grasses, cover crops and stubble mulching to retain wheat stalks after harvest provided soil protection. Obstructions, such as trees, tall, drought-resistant crops like sorghum, or most importantly, strip crops with alternating bands of wheat and fallow (with stubble), placed perpendicular to the wind, reduced surface wind velocity and carrying capacity. Repeated obstructions were required to prevent surface wind speeds from regenerating. Investing in wind erosion control was costly. The major costs were the opportunity costs of leaving strips of cropland fallow. The benefits included saved topsoil and reduced crop, livestock and building damage from blowing sand.

As Hansen and Libecap argue, all farmers bore the costs of erosion control investments, such as strip fallow, but farmers with larger holdings internalized more of the downwind benefits. As a result, larger farmers would have been more likely to divert cropland to fallow. The presence of many small farms in a region, however, should reduce fallow incentives on larger farms. Drifting sand from unprotected fields on small farms would smother the crops and fallow strips on downwind larger farms, reducing the returns from erosion control investments. Hansen and Libecap examine the relationship between farm size and fallow share of cropland using census data for 285 counties in the Great Plains most vulnerable to erosion, where the share of crop acres was at least 40 percent of total farmland. This sample avoids including ranching counties of mostly pasture land where neither crops nor fallow were major options. The analysis covers each census period from 1930 to 1964, as well as a panel regression pooled across the entire period. The regression includes farm size, farm size squared and the standard deviation of farm size to capture the inhibiting effect on erosion control investments from many small farms in a county, surrounding a few larger ones.

The analysis reveals that farm size had a positive and statistically significant effect on fallow share in all periods. Fallow shares increased at a decreasing rate, and the standard deviation of farm size in a county exerted a negative effect on fallow. Using the coefficients for 1935, the fallow share was estimated to be 14 percent for a farm of 512 acres and 24 percent if the farm was 758 acres. Fallow shares rose to a maximum of 36 percent at a farm size of 1526 acres. The peak fallow share and farm size were close to what was considered optimal by agricultural economists in the 1930s.

Figure 2.6 illustrates the range of wind erosion across the Great Plains in 1934, based on soil erosion surveys conducted by the Soil Conservation Service. Since small farmers cultivated more of their land and left less in strip fallow than did larger farmers, one would expect that the intensity of wind erosion would vary across the Great Plains according to cultivation share, holding other natural factors constant. Hansen and Libecap regress an index of wind erosion severity across the counties against the deviation in rainfall from normal (1930–35), percentage sand in county soil (sandy soils were more likely to erode), average hourly wind speed in each county and percentage of total county farmland in cultivation. As predicted, counties with higher cultivation shares of total farmland faced more severe wind erosion. Moreover, the larger the cultivation share, the greater the predicted erosion. Accordingly, if farms on the Great Plains had been much larger, erosion control could have taken place within the boundaries of larger units, reducing external effects and coordination problems. Under those conditions, the costs of the Dust Bowl would have been reduced. Soil Conservation Service officials recognized this problem and pushed for the adoption of Soil Conservation Districts with regulatory authority to force and subsidize erosion control investments. The districts were adopted after 1937.

CONCLUSION: PATH DEPENDENCE AND GREAT PLAINS SETTLEMENT

Today, the North American Great Plains is an enigma. The region is not only relatively empty of population, but is emptying further. Out-migration continues. At the same time, the plains are dotted with abandoned farm buildings and town sites that suggest a past with a much greater promise and population – indeed, similar to patterns observed in the Midwest. Nowhere else in North America are the skeletal remains of past life so apparent. If the region is so risky for agriculture, why were so many small farms and associated small farming communities founded there?

This chapter addresses that issue in terms of path dependence. United States land policy, molded by climatic conditions in the East and political

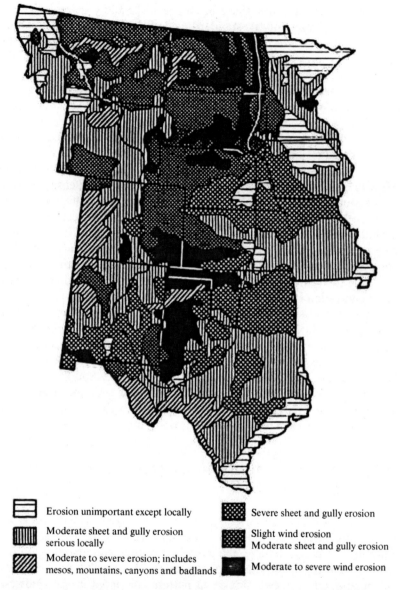

	Erosion unimportant except locally		Severe sheet and gully erosion
	Moderate sheet and gully erosion serious locally		Slight wind erosion Moderate sheet and gully erosion
	Moderate to severe erosion; includes mesos, mountains, canyons and badlands		Moderate to severe wind erosion

Note: Irregular line bounds the Great Plains Region as delimited by the Great Plains Committee.

Source: Kifer and Stewart (1938, p. 9).

Figure 2.6   Great Plains soil erosion, 1934

objectives favoring small farmers, brought a distribution of farms and population that *ex post* was inappropriate for a semi-arid region. Political goals of achieving dense settlement and a lack of understanding of the region's climate and its implications for agricultural success blocked land policy change toward larger allocations. During periods of high precipitation, small farm sizes and labor-intensive farming practices similar to those used in the eastern USA and northern Europe were successful. During droughts, however, those farms and techniques were found dangerously inadequate. Especially when the brutal droughts of the 1920s and 1930s appeared these farms failed, and the rural population began to migrate to more hospitable areas. This clustering of farm failures or 'homestead busts' was unprecedented in US experience both across time and across regions. Further, cultivation practices on these marginal farms contributed directly to wind erosion associated with the Dust Bowl and hindered collective action to control it.

In the 1930s government relief programs mitigated human suffering, but at the same time, slowed the necessary adjustment process of farm abandonment and consolidation. Even so, at that time, the greatest rural outmigration in the USA occurred on the Great Plains. Accordingly, there were clear costs from a mistaken land policy. It resulted in in-migration patterns and fixed investments in farms, communities and infrastructure that could not be maintained. Especially during drought, these investments had to be discarded and the population had to move away. The opportunity costs of the investments and the farm population in more favorable alternatives represent part of the costs of path dependence. The other costs were environmental – the lost soil from excessive wind erosion brought about by small farm cultivation practices.

These outcomes, however, generally were not anticipated during the period of settlement, 1880–1925. John Wesley Powell foresaw some of them, but there was little supportive scientific evidence to corroborate his concerns and there was stiff opposition from prospective Great Plains' settlers and politicians. Once in place, federal land policy could not easily or rapidly be adjusted to more effectively meet the demands of the region. As a result, the policies were not changed and migrants moved to the Great Plains to create new farms and to plow the land. As farms began to fail, state and federal government agencies attempted to mitigate the effects of farm failure and to limit depopulation. However, these were not successful.

In the end, important inefficiency losses cannot be linked to this institutional path dependence. Given the absence of information about the region during the settlement period, as well as intense political and constituent support for maintaining existing land policy, it is unlikely that things could have developed differently. The droughts of the 1920s and

1930s provided new information and initiated the adjustment toward farm sizes and population levels more appropriate for the Great Plains.

NOTES

1. 'Has North Dakota Farming a Future', Frank W. Reinoehl, M.L. Wilson Files, Merrill G. Burlingame Special Collections, 2001, Box 1, Montana State University Bozeman. Reinoehl blamed the Homestead Act for creating the problem (p. 5).
2. The data cover 363 counties in the Great Plains. For definition of the region, see Hansen and Libecap (2004b). County population data are from Forstall (1996).
3. These counties are in the western part of North Dakota and are semi-arid. They are picked randomly to illustrate the population decline in the region. They do not show the most extreme population declines.
4. This discussion draws from Puffert, www.eh.net/encyclopedia/?article=puffert.path. dependence
5. For analysis of some American frontier experiences, see Herscovici (1998) and Ferrie (1994).
6. For discussion of US land policies and the origins and administration of the Homestead Acts, see Gates (1968, pp. 387–461), Hibbard (1965) and Robbins (1942). In contrast, Mexico, Argentina, Brazil and other Latin American countries distributed much frontier land in very large blocks.
7. Quoted in Hibbard (1965, p. 143). An example of the congressional debate over the need to reserve federal land for small farmers ('free homes for homeless people') is in *Congressional Globe*, 37 Congress, 2nd Session, Wednesday, 7 May 1862 (p. 1915).
8. Gates (1968, p. 801).
9. Powell's report, 'Report on the Lands of the Arid Region', 45th Congress, 2nd Session, House Executive Document 73, was transmitted to the Commissioner of the General Land Office on 1 April 1878.
10. *Annual Reports of the Commissioner of the General Land Office* for the Fiscal Years, 1880–1925. The calculations are for state totals.
11. Recommended sizes varied, with somewhat smaller farms suggested for the southern plains and larger ones in the north. There were no important economies of scale beyond around 1500 acres. See Renne (1935, p. 427), Cochrane (1938) and Halcrow (1938).
12. For discussion of the reaction to Powell's report, see Stegner (1954, pp. 219–42). See Peffer (1951, pp. 8–62, 135–68) regarding the political controversy over homestead farm size, the claims of ranchers, and efforts to adjust the federal land laws.
13. As described by Libecap and Hansen (2002) until settlement of the Great Plains in the early twentieth century, there was no experience in the USA with semi-arid farming. Weather data were limited and interpretation even more primitive.
14. Warrick (1975, pp. 11–27; 1980) points out that although there is no general agreement on how normal circulation patterns are disrupted to cause droughts, the arid Southwest and Great Plains are most susceptible in North America.
15. Worster (2001, pp. 358–63) claims that congressional inaction came from a lack of desire of politicians to consider the scientific evidence on the region. More likely, the science was too inconclusive to support politically controversial changes in federal land distribution.
16. The theory argued that rainfall was endogenous to human activity. A classic discussion of rain follows the plow and the alleged transformation of the Great Plains is in Smith (1947, pp. 169–93).
17. Libecap and Hansen (2002) outline the claims of dryfarming experts and show how they contributed to the information problem facing migrants on the Great Plains.
18. Both notions were reflections of the Progressive Era and its belief in the evolutionary march of progress made possible through the practical adoption of science to advance human welfare.

19. *Congressional Record*, 45th Congress, 3rd Session, 1879, pp. 1202–3.
20. The data are drawn from county directories compiled by R.L. Polk & Company, of Montana, Helena, Montana. The directories include lists of farms by farmer name, location (rural post office), size, and assessed value. Part of the 1919 Agricultural Census Manuscript (about one-third) exists for Carbon County, Montana, US National Archives.
21. Webb and Brown (1938, p. 15).
22. National Resources Planning Board (1940, p. 1). This report focused on the northern plains.
23. Natural Resources Planning Board (1940, p. 3).
24. 'Activities of Federal and State Agencies in Solving Agricultural Problems of the Southwest', address by Roy I. Kimmel, Coordinator Southern Great Plains, 10 February 1939, Manhattan Kansas, History Collection, Special Collections, National Agricultural Library. General discussions of New Deal agricultural policies are provided in Saloutos (1982). An overview of New Deal relief in the Great Plains is provided by Link (1937).
25. Webb and Brown (1938, p. 87) provide lists of the different residency requirements and other eligibility rules for receiving relief.
26. Calculated from rural population figures from the Great Plains Dataset, ICPSR. The plains county portions are representative only – each state's total out-migration/rural population in Great Plains counties.
27. See also, Taylor (1942, p. 842), Hathaway (1960) and Maddox (1960).
28. The data in the figure do not account for natural increase. An adjusted out-migration figure for each county is used in the statistical analysis below.
29. See Hansen and Libecap (2004a) for discussion of the definitions used in constructing the data presented in Figure 2.5.
30. For further analysis of the relative disadvantage of small farms during this period see Starch (1935), Renne (1938; 1939), Montana Agricultural Experiment Station (1939), and Clawson et al. (1940).

REFERENCES

Arthur, W.B. (1989) 'Competing technologies, increasing returns, and lock-in by historical events', *Economic Journal*, **99**, 116–31.

Asch, B. and A.R. Mangus (1937), *Farmers on Relief and Rehabilitation*, Works Progress Administration Research Monograph VIII, Washington, DC: Government Printing Office.

Burke, E. and R. Pinckney (1914), 'A report on the Montana climate', *Montana Agricultural Experiment Station Bulletin No. 99*, Bozeman, MT, March.

Clawson, M., M.H. Saunderson and N.W. Johnson (1940), 'Farm adjustments in Montana: study of Area IV: its past, present, and future', *Montana Agricultural Experiment Station Bulletin No. 377*, Bozeman, MT, January.

Cochrane, W.W. (1938), 'Successful Montana Farms', MS Thesis, Montana State College, Bozeman.

Cooper, M.R., W.J. Roth, J.G. Maddox, R. Schickele and H.A. Turner (1938), 'The causes: defects in farming systems and farm tenancy', in *Soils and Men: Yearbook of Agriculture, 1938*, Washington, DC: Government Printing Office.

David, P.A. (1985) 'Clio and the economics of QWERTY', *American Economic Review* (Papers and Proceedings), **75**, 332–7.

Ferrie, J.P. (1994), 'The wealth accumulation of antebellum European immigrants to the U.S., 1840–60', *Journal of Economic History*, **54** (1), 1–33.

Forstall, R. (1996), *Population of States and Counties of the United States:*

1790–1990 from the Twenty-one Decennial Censuses, Washington, DC: US Department of Commerce, Bureau of the Census.

Gates, P.W. (1968), *History of Public Land Law Development*, Washington, DC: Public Land Law Review Commission.

Gillette, J.M. (1941), 'Some population shifts in the United States, 1930–1940', *American Sociological Review*, **6** (5), 619–28.

Halcrow, H. (1938), 'The problem of the unsuccessful dry farm in the Northern Great Plains', MS Thesis, Montana State College, Bozeman.

Hansen, Z. and G.D. Libecap (2004a), 'The allocation of property rights to land: US land policy and farm failure in the northern Great Plains', *Explorations in Economic History*, **41**, 103–29.

Hansen, Z. and G.D. Libecap (2004b), 'Small farms, externalities, and the Dust Bowl of the 1930s', *Journal of Political Economy*, **112** (3), 665–94.

Hathaway, D.E. (1960), 'Migration from agriculture: the historical record and its meaning', *American Economic Review*, **50** (2), 379–91.

Herscovici, S. (1998), 'Migration and economic mobility: wealth accumulation and occupational change among antebellum migrants and persisters', *Journal of Economic History*, **58** (4), 927–56.

Hibbard, B.H. (1965), *History of Public Land Policies*, New York: Macmillan.

Johnson, V. (1946), *Heaven's Tableland: The Dust Bowl Story*, New York: Farrar Straus.

Katz, M.L. and C. Shapiro (1985), 'Network externalities, competition, and compatibility', *American Economic Review*, **75**, 424–40.

Kifer, R.S. and H.L. Stewart (1938), *Farming Hazards in the Drought Area*, Works Progress Administration Research Monograph XVI, Washington, DC: Government Printing Office.

Lebergott, S. (1970), 'Migration within the U.S., 1800–1960: some new estimates', *The Journal of Economic History*, **30** (4), 839–47.

Liebowitz, S.J. and S.E. Margolis (1995), 'Path dependence, lock-in and history', *Journal of Law, Economics, and Organization*, **11**, 205–26.

Liebowitz, S.J. and S.E. Margolis (1998), 'Path dependence', in P. Newman (ed.), *The New Palgrave Dictionary of Economics and the Law*, vol. 3, London: Macmillan, pp. 17–22.

Libecap, G.D. and Z.K. Hansen (2002), 'Rain follows the plow and dryfarming doctrine: the climate information problem and homestead failure in the upper Great Plains, 1890–1925', *The Journal of Economic History*, **62** (1), 86–120.

Link, I. (1937), *Relief and Rehabilitation in the Drought Area*, Works Progress Administration Research Bulletin, Washington, DC: Government Printing Office.

Maddox, J.G. (1960), 'Private and social costs of the movement of people out of agriculture', *American Economic Review*, **50** (2), 392–402.

Montana Agricultural Experiment Station (1939), 'Farm adjustments in Montana: study of Area VII: its past, present and future', *Montana Agricultural Experiment Station Bulletin No. 367*, Bozeman, MT, January.

National Resources Planning Board (1940), *The Northern Great Plains*, Washington, DC: Government Printing Office.

Peffer, E.L. (1951), *The Closing of the Public Domain: Disposal and Reservation Policies*, Stanford, CA: Stanford University Press.

Powell, J.W. (1878), *Report on the Lands of the Arid Region of the United States*, 45 Congress, 2nd Session, Executive Document, No. 73, Washington, DC: Government Printing Office.

Puffert, D.J. (2000), 'The standardization of track gauge on North American railways, 1830–1890', *Journal of Economic History*, **60**, 933–60.

Puffert, D.J. (2002), 'Path dependence in spatial networks: the standardization of railway track gauge', *Explorations in Economic History*, **39**, 282–314.

Renne, R.R. (1935), 'Significance of the ownership pattern to land use planning', *Journal of Farm Economics*, **47** (3), 423–32.

Renne, R.R. (1938), 'Montana farm bankruptcies', *Montana Agricultural Experiment Station Bulletin No. 360*, Bozeman, MT, June.

Renne, R.R. (1939), 'Montana farm foreclosures', *Montana Agricultural Experiment Station Bulletin No. 368*, Bozeman, MT, February.

Robbins, R.M. (1942), *Our Landed Heritage: The Public Domain, 1776–1936*, Princeton, NJ: Princeton University Press.

Saloutos, T. (1982), *The American Farmer and The New Deal*, Ames, IA: Iowa State University Press.

Smith, H.N. (1947), 'Rain follows the plow: the notion of increased rainfall for the Great Plains, 1844–1880', *Huntington Library Quarterly*, **10**, 169–93.

Starch, E.A. (1935), 'Economic changes in Montana's wheat area', *Montana Agricultural Experiment Station Bulletin No. 295*, Bozeman, MT, January.

Stegner, W. (1954), *Beyond the Hundredth Meridian: John Wesley Powell and the Second Opening of the West*, Boston, MA: Houghton Mifflin.

Steinbeck, J. (1976), *The Grapes of Wrath*, New York: Penguin Books. First published in 1939.

Taeuber, C. and C.C. Taylor (1937), *The People of the Drought States*, Works Progress Administration Research Bulletin, Washington, DC: Government Printing Office.

Taylor, C.C. (1942), 'Rural life', *American Journal of Sociology*, **47** (6), 841–53.

Thornthwaite, C.W. (1936), 'The Great Plains', in C. Goodrich, B.W. Allin, C.W. Thornthwaite et al. (eds), *Migration and Economic Opportunity: Report of the Study of Population Distribution*, Philadelphia, PA: University of Pennsylvania Press, pp. 202–50.

US Department of Agriculture (1938), *Yearbook of Agriculture*, 'Soils and Men', Washington, DC: Government Printing Office.

US Great Plains Committee (1936), *The Future of the Great Plains*, Washington, DC: Government Printing Office.

US Weather Bureau (n.d.), 'Summary of the climatological data for the U.S., by sections', sections for Montana, Washington, DC: US Weather Bureau.

Vamplew, W. (ed.) (1987), *Australians: Historical Statistics*, Broadway, NSW: Fairfax, Syme and Weldon Associates.

Warrick, R.A. (1975), *Drought Hazard in the United States: A Research Assessment*, Boulder, CO: Institute of Behavioral Science.

Warrick, R.A. (1980), 'Drought in the Great Plains: a case study of research on climate and society in the USA', in J. Ausubel and A.K. Biswas (eds), *Climatic Constraints and Human Activities*, New York: Pergamon Press, pp. 93–123.

Webb, J.N. and M. Brown (1938), *Migrant Families*, Works Progress Administration Research Monograph XVIII, Washington, DC: Government Printing Office.

Worster, D. (1979), *Dust Bowl: The Southern Plains in the 1930s*, New York: Oxford University Press.

Worster, D. (2001), *A River Running West: The Life of John Wesley Powell*, New York: Oxford University Press.

3. Revisiting railway history: the case of institutional change and path dependence

Lena Andersson-Skog

INTRODUCTION

Railway history shows us that railway construction and railway policy is usually fairly stable during time, because of more or less irreversible physical, economical and institutional factors which constrain possible future policy outcomes. The magnitude of the investment required to construct an integrated national or even international, transport system, contribute to this development. Here, the assumption of path dependence, that pre-existing institutional structures or former decisions influence later or contemporary policy outcomes, are close in explaining the outcome of institutions and performance. A least common denominator in a definition of a path-dependence approach would be that early developments have profound and disproportionate effects on later developments (Arthur, 1994; David, 1985, p. 332; North, 1990, p. 94; Pierson, 2004, p. 44ff). Many decisions become almost irreversible, because high transformation costs and vested interests rule out other, and in some cases more efficient, institutions or policies. All policy outcomes are thus not equally plausible. Some have claimed that the notion that past experience and behavior influences present or future outcomes is 'as old as the writing of history' (Mowery and Rosenberg, 1998, p. 170). Put as broadly as this, path dependence can only serve as a philosophical truism: history matters. From this point of view, the concept of path dependence has a somewhat deterministic ring to it, and the risk of ruling out the possibilities for historical contingencies and institutional change is obvious.

The basic argument developed here, is that some of the significant fields to focus on in exploring path-dependent processes would be the technology-based industries operating in the intersection of international market forces and the demands of a strict political regulation. From this perspective, I would suggest that network industries in general, and perhaps the railway sector in particular, stand out. The railway sector has long since provided a battlefield where market forces and regulatory efforts from the state have clashed repeatedly, resulting in alternately negotiations and open conflicts in the making of institutions over almost the past two centuries. As a technical system, railways are characterized by both heavy investment costs and high costs for maintenance and technical renewal, thus emphasizing the importance of duration in long-term planning and strategic decision-making. At the same time, the structural shifts on the transport market during the twentieth century, most generally from rail to road, have radically changed the economic conditions for the railways. Adjustment to the new situation has generally not been swift, either in terms of changing organization, regulation or performance.

The railway sector is also an industry where distinct development paths and regulatory styles have developed in different nations, regardless of the common technological base. Even so, regardless of ownership and regulatory styles, in most countries railways, to a certain extent, are financed or subsidized by resource allocation in the political system. The railway sector (and infrastructure or network industries in general) thus makes an interesting case to explore in the pursuit of identifying different path-dependent processes and outcomes from several perspectives with different dynamics: technology, market and organization and regulation and policy feedback.

Given the comprehensive literature in the field of railway studies, it is only possible to touch upon a handful of examples from the USA and Europe to discuss path-dependence processes in the railway sector (for overviews of the state of the art in railway history, see Armstrong, 1998; Gourvish, 1993; Mom, 2003). In the chapter, I first discuss railways as technological systems and the use of path dependence, and then continue to studies of railway regulation, policy process and institutional change. In practice, some of the results of the vast array of neo-institutional studies and the more recent approaches in the history of technology that are concerned with path dependency issues and infrastructure are explored and summarized.

PATH DEPENDENCE AND RAILWAYS

The concept of path dependence has been imported in economic history, and other social sciences, from the history of technology and studies of technological innovation. The paradigmatic work is the one where Paul A. David uses the case of the QWERTY keyboard to illustrate a path-dependent development of a technological system (David, 1985; see also

Arthur, 1994). Liebowitz and Margolis have repeatedly criticized this concept, both from a standpoint regarding the weak empirical evidence in the case of QWERTY, as well as from its theoretical implications from a neoclassical perspective (Liebowitz and Margolis, 1990; 1995; 1996).

Nevertheless, there are parallel approaches, concerned with similar contingency issues. Nathan Rosenberg has long argued that technology and innovation has been put in a 'black box' in economic and economic historical studies. Rosenberg is focusing on the social learning process to explain the ongoing technological research. Technical progress should be understood as the attempt to extend and further explore certain trajectories of improvement made possible by the existing stock of technological knowledge at any given time. As a consequence, the actual technological choices available at any time are limited (Rosenberg, 1994, p. 16f). In this perspective, there is implicitly a strong trend towards technical convergence. One technology may support many others, and innovation spreads by this mutually reinforcing process.

While Rosenberg studies innovation and technological development, other scholars with a social-constructivist perspective have used path dependence in a wider societal context. The socio-technical systems approach includes not only the physical artifacts in the system, but also the people and organization that design, build and operate the artifacts, as well as the legal and economic framework of the system. Three major and interrelated approaches emerged during the 1980s and 1990s: the actor-network theory (ANT), the social construction of technology (SCOT) and the large technical system approach (LTS). From both a social-constructivist and an actor-network perspective, technical systems are regarded as the collective outcome of intertwined social, political, economic and cognitive processes and structures. Whereas social-constructivists focus on 'closure', for example, a kind of equilibrium that occurs when major user groups have accepted the properties of a new technology, the actor-network approach emphasizes the importance of actors: entrepreneurs, engineers, politicians, and so on, in controlling the technical artifact, the market and users' and competitors' options (see, for instance, Bijker, 1995; Callon, 1986). Whereas path dependence in both approaches is considered more of an empirical result than a problem to explore, the concept of momentum in the large technological systems approach has clear resemblance with the neo-institutional concept of path dependence.

Momentum is a central component in the LTS approach, developed by historian of technology Thomas P. Hughes (1983). Momentum is the last (of four) stages in the life cycle of a certain technological system and is reached when the system has matured. Now, change is counteracted by the embedded inertia of the system due to interrelated and interwoven economic, technical, social and regulatory resources mobilized and invested during the earlier stages (sunk costs or vested interests immediately come to mind). Change is promoted by reverse salients, or bottleneck situations. Reverse salients destabilize the system in various respects, for instance, economically by high costs for components, or politically, if decisions are not made in time. To solve the salient, the system builders/actors will have to succeed in turning the situation into what Hughes calls a critical problem; to redefine the situation and find an operative solution to it.

The technical properties of a system also influence the degree of coordination necessary for the operation and the possibility to change a technological system. Here, Charles Perrow (1984) made a distinction between tightly coupled and loosely coupled systems. The former category is made up by grid-based systems possessing a system-specific grid of rails, pipelines or wires. Traditionally these systems have called for a high degree of coordination, and a monopoly organization is common, whereas loosely coupled systems are characterized by the opposite features, for example roads and road traffic, in shipping and civil aviation. For researchers in the LTS tradition, this had created a widespread attention on tightly coupled systems, since the interrelatedness of technical and organizational aspects are more critical for further system development. An interpretation of the LTS approach, is that path-dependent processes are playing an important part in the success of the development of a technology.

Kenneth Lipartito suggests a similar concept altogether in his study of technological failure in the case of the picture phone in the USA in the 1960s: historical contingency. Lipartito argues that the failure did not stem from some functional flaw in the product or from a traditional notion of consumer demand (market failure), but rather from a contingent sequence of actions from technology producers, consumers and politicians that reflected the influence of expectations, assumptions, uncertainty, politics and self-reinforcing decisions that shaped the process (Lipartito, 2003, p. 75ff). The reception of a new technology involves open-ended choices that could go either way, but a contingent outcome is not wholly inexplicable, since each case is a part of a technological setting related to markets, technological knowledge, organizational styles and institutional restrictions.

From this short and sketchy overview, it would be possible to suggest that path-dependent processes probably are more frequent in technological systems that are tightly coupled, such as electrical networks and railways. Then again, as history has taught us, the same technology is constantly getting shaped and reshaped by the environment – socially, economically and politically – where it works (Levy and Spiller, 1996). Hence, another important conclusion would be that the economic, organizational and political context is of great importance for the outcome. This is an invitation to historians and social scientists with an inclination for history to study institutional outcomes as the result of dynamic social, economic or political processes.

How, then, do we study railway construction and railway policy governed by path dependence? One of the most widespread approaches in economic history today is perhaps the notions on path dependence brought forward by Douglass North. North emphasizes that in applying path dependence within the analytic framework of institutional change, both increasing returns and imperfect markets must exist. The mechanism of increasing returns is the micro fundament of a path-dependence process, and explains why early small events determine later developments. If a particular institution, policy or equilibrium does not provide increasing returns for one or more interest groups, regions, political parties or industries, then it is not a result of a path-dependence process (North, 1990). Here, access to the decision-making system and bargaining power of different interest are vital in shaping the outcome in a given situation (North, 1996). Even so, there are indications from various fields, that policy measures tend to give unforeseen outcomes due to the way they are implemented (Dixit, 1996; Krueger, 1996).

Path dependence does not rule out institutional change, but often provides a noteworthy obstacle. Shifts from increasing to decreasing returns, may lead to the emergence of new development paths, through learning, political, technical or social innovations combined with the actual institutional conditions. Here, 'timing, sequence and critical junctures' are of particular interest, as Paul Pierson puts it (Pierson, 2000, pp. 264–5; 2004, pp. 44–8, 54f). Pierson argues that public policies lock decision-makers into particular policy trajectories, partly due to the nature of pre-established policies, and partly because public policies shape decision-makers' information, experiences and interpretations (Pierson, 1994, pp. 17–26, 31–50). Put in a very simple way, the basic argument is that when an event occurs, it may have a different effect on the future development depending on when in the sequence of actions it occurred. As an example, an epidemic disease will have more severe effects on a population and an economy if its occurrence is preceded by a famine or an environmental disaster. Kathleen Thelen has pointed out that there are examples of cumulative effects of ongoing but often subtle changes in institutional arrangements that persist over long stretches of time. Institutional change may lead to what Thelen describes as institutional layering: the result of interplay between lock-in and institutional innovations, where combinations of new and old institutional elements coexist. This is more common in institutions that have strong biases against change (Thelen, 2003, pp. 210, 226–8).

In this respect, economic historical understanding of institutional change meets the new political institutionalism in regarding institutional change as a result of social and political processes, motivated by economic, ideological or other forces. The importance of self-reinforcing processes, increasing returns, the creation of lock-in situations and network externalities, together with timing and sequence of events, are common concepts of interest to further explore path dependence in policy-making both in neo-institutional economics and the new political institutionalism. In recognizing that the role of history and the importance of institutions may lead to an enduring suboptimal institutional setting, the concept of path dependence challenges the neoclassical paradigm with its emphases of increasing returns, learning effects and network externalities. The emphasis on the relations between exogenous events, timing and sequence, resembles the arguments about formative moments, windows of opportunity and veto points (Immergut, 1991). Human agency thus is of great importance in path-shaping or path-creating processes, even though the outcome may be unforeseen even by the actors themselves (Garud and Karnoe, 2001; Torfing, 1999). Other social scientists have criticized the lock-in argument in path-dependent processes. Recently, also the down-playing of ideational arguments as cognitive weapons in the path-shaping processes has been questioned (see, for instance, Blyth, 2001).

In furthering the understanding of the complexity and limitations of the concept, more empirical studies are indispensable. In economic history research, a multitude of case studies indicate that the interplay between technology, market conditions and institutions tends to create institutional solutions that are stable over time (even sometimes suboptimal). Whether or not the institutional outcomes actually are the result of market or policy failures is not evident at any given time. This indicates that we cannot consider path dependence as a homogeneous concept, but that it has to be examined as a multilayered process, with strong contextual links. The degree of reversibility, adaptation and change depends on what kind of technology or activity we discuss, its institutional settings, interest groups and market situation. In all those aspects, partial processes may be at play, with different time-lines and internal dynamics, thus creating strengthening or eroding forces at work simultaneously.

RAILWAYS, TECHNOLOGY AND GROWTH

In economic history research, railways are traditionally regarded as an essential catalyst for industrialization and economic growth and take-off. The railway system was generally completed in Europe some decades before the turn of the twentieth century. In the USA, this was achieved even earlier. In Europe, Sweden and Finland differ in this regard, since railway-building peaked in the 1920s–1930s, when railway-building ahead of demand was used to promote economic growth. In Finland there was even a law regulating the number of kilometers that had to be built every year (Andersson-Skog, 2000).

Investments in railways have generally been considered a conscious choice of action that marked the future economic development for a long time. Fogel's well-known work on American railroads is one of few exceptions. His claim was that almost the same outcome, measured in gross domestic product (GDP), would have been the case, had a similar investment been made in canals and small-scale transportation. In a path-dependent view, Fogel's contrafactual suggestion may serve as an alternative path not taken (Fogel, 1964; 1979; see also Fishlow, 1965). The concept of path dependence, however, is rarely used explicitly in railway studies, even if researchers frequently touch upon path-dependent issues. An early example of something considered as path-dependent effects, is Thorstein Veblen's explanation in 1915 as to why German economic growth overtook the UK's, even though the latter had an earlier start. According to Veblen, it was actually the early start that damaged the UK later (Veblen, 1915, pp. 130ff). One example Veblen put forward, was the early investments in railways, ports and other transport facilities, such as rolling stock, that left the UK with obsolete capital investments when Germany, and most other industrialized countries, adopted more modern technology, with larger capacity per unit, for instance, in wagons. The interrelated railway and port systems constituted a complex technical system, with inherited technical as well as economic obstacles favoring small, incremental changes at a time when the English transport system would have had to be changed as a whole at once, at a cost that would not be compensated by increased revenues. A similar argument is delivered by Derek H. Aldcroft concerning the difficulties of shifting from steam to electricity on the British railways in the 1930s. The interrelatedness between the coal industry and the railway companies made this transformation a slow and lengthy process (Aldcroft, 1968).

Peter Scott has argued that the reluctance in Britain to go from small coal wagons to larger ones, also had to do with the way the railway regulation provided the private owners an effective veto over rationalization. The railway companies could block any attempts from the state to enforce technological change. Scott's conclusion is that there was nothing inevitable about the British system; it has to be regarded as the product of institutional, technical and political constraints that locked the railways into a highly inefficient system. Sunk costs, together with the need to compensate the owners, made wholesale rationalization financially troublesome, while system interrelatedness blocked incremental changes (Scott, 2001, pp. 367–8, 380ff).

In the railway sector, a standardized gauge is the least common denominator necessary to create a large-scale well-integrated network. During the expansion period of the national railway systems, a convergence towards one standardized technological system was a prerequisite for an ongoing expansion of the market. Still, in Europe today, we have two gauges, at least three electrical power systems varying in, for example, voltage, alternating or direct current, frequency, and train control and signaling systems and other security measurements. This is an indication that the unification of the European railway system is a costly, slow and still uncompleted process. This cannot primarily be considered as a lack of early foresight in the mid-nineteenth century into the importance of long-distance, large-scale network integration from the late nineteenth century. In many cases gauge selection and gauge conversion was partly an outcome of institutional structures and the political map at the time, and partly due to transport demand on the market.

One aspect, still partly neglected, is how the spatial dimensions of a railway system co-evolved with market expansion and institutional arrangements over time and affected path-dependency processes. The spatial implications on organizational structure and management were one of the reasons Alfred Chandler named the American railroad companies the 'first big business'(Chandler, 1965). That spatial dimensionality is a critical distinguishing factor for the selection of gauge and thus for the path-dependent construction of the railway network is argued by Douglas J. Puffert. His argument arises from the localized nature of interactions among railway lines, as each seeks compatibility with the immediate neighbours (Puffert, 2000, p. 944ff). As a consequence, new railway lines in a variant gauge region adopt the gauges of these regions rather than the majority gauge of the system as a whole. The extent to which there is diversity of gauge in various regions has been proven to depend on the extent of early diversity, the level of demand for traffic across breaks of gauges and organizational innovation (Puffert, 2002, p. 308ff). To reduce the costs of gauge variation, gateway techniques, such as exchangeable wheel sets, have been used. While these techniques have sometimes substituted for gauge conversions, they have also hastened the process of standardization.

However, the use of different power sources on different lines both created coexisting and sometimes competing modes of traction as well as a need for security regulation and supervision. Competition on the tracks was another organizational arrangement that underlined the need for supervising 'third party' and trained technical expertise (Fremdling, 1999). Thus, the scale of operation itself and the geographical extension may during some periods be an incentive for actors to move from one path to another, or not.

In the 1930s Harold Innis pointed out the complex relations between transport systems, markets and economic political power. In the case of Canada, he claimed that the dependencies between production of staple commodities, such as fish, fur and wheat, and the international markets with the demand for different modes of transport, tended to both change over time and establish strong economic political interests and policy-making (Innis, 1930). To Innis, the tightly coupled transport systems, such as railways and canals, tended to create more rigid lock-in situations and limited options of actions for policy-makers than did the more loosely coupled transatlantic shipping. As a consequence, a tendency to create overhead capacity in existing transport systems was strengthened with the amount of capital invested and a limited number of strong economic interest groups depending on the trade flows (Innis, 1923; 1930).

To Innis, the spatial dimension of the railways was closely related to the geopolitical power relations and the increasing economic integration with the US economy from the mid-nineteenth century rather than a mere technological dependence. The pressure on revenues, interest rates and the building of excess capacity in branch lines and so on mirrored the market relations between the export-oriented Canadian economy and the consumption markets in the USA. According to Innis, the demands of transport improvement were reflected directly and indirectly in fiscal policy: land use, labor and capital were interwoven in Canadian railway policy (Innis, 1923). From this point of view it is obvious that the physical railway infrastructure reproduced the settlement and industry structure that maintained the railway polity's power relations and resource allocation. A growing mismatch between market opportunities and institutions may result in crises or an institutional breakdown. Established structures do not necessarily vanish in case of institutional changes. Here, informal institutions, such as ideology, a certain perception of the working of society and so on, may survive and develop further through new environments and institutions.

RAILWAY POLICY, INSTITUTIONS AND PATH DEPENDENCE

Increasing returns of scale and network effects, can, broadly speaking, provide two policy options: regulation or public ownership. The first has been frequent in the USA, and the latter in a number of European countries despite convergent or diverging markets and technological developments (Domberger and Piggot, 1994). In a study of the regulation of the British network industries in general from the 1820s onwards, James Foreman-Peck and Robert Millward set out to evaluate the efficiency of different institutional solutions in comparison with examples from other countries in Europe and the USA (Foreman-Peck and Millward, 1994). In the British case, a common pattern appeared. The first institutional setting was dominated by private ownership without political regulations or with a limited enforcement of restrictions. At first this promoted the growth of private networks, but later the demands on the state to intervene in order to for example regulate prices grew. Also, the second phase was dominated by private owners, but now restricted by a strong political regulation. During this stage, initiatives from the private owners to reorganize and modernize the industries were common. The final period saw a shift from private to public ownership. Nationalization led to the establishment of new state agencies to run business, or to institutional changes that strengthened the power of old state agencies. With certain variations, this pattern was valid for most other countries as well, even if the American pattern tended to halt in the second phase.

However, Foreman-Peck and Millward could not find any definitive evidence that private ownership was more efficient than state ownership. Their conclusion was that if 'reasonable' institutions are at hand, they may foster economic growth and efficiency, regardless if the owner is private or public. Foreman-Peck and Millward argued that the path-dependent processes at play, with strong vested interests in the private sector and weak regulation during most of the nineteenth century, contributed to the slow modernization of the British railways. Terry Gourvish reached the same conclusion in his discussion of the institutional changes in the British railway sector after 1845. But Gourvish also showed that the attempts made by the state to enforce institutional change often failed, due to bad timing in regard to economic and competitive strength of the private companies (Gourvish, 1999). As long as the railway companies could maneuver on the transport market, for example substituting rail traffic with lorries and busses, they refused to give in to the proposals from the government.

The importance of the relations between the timing of the political ambitions to change institutions not only to discussion in parliament, but also to the competition and trends on the transport market, is illustrated in the case of Swedish railway nationalization (Andersson-Skog, 1996; see also, Ottosson, 1997). The first political initiative came in 1918, but was turned down both by parliament and the private railways. During the

1920s, railway transportation went through a rapid structural shift, where the bulk transport of short-distance freights of agricultural products for a large number of companies were priced out of the market by lorries. In this situation, the government now forced the state railways to merge with the unprofitable local and smaller regional companies, but without making a general decision of total nationalization. That decision was instead taken in 1939. The profitable large private railways, surprisingly enough together with the state railways, formed a strong opposition against the ideas of nationalization. The state railways gave in to the government after promises to write off the cost of the purchase. Still, the last companies were not obtained by the state until 1952. The most profitable companies were the last to surrender, and tried to make a last profit during the Second World War and the years shortly thereafter (Andersson-Skog, 1993, p. 130ff). A study of regional railway interests in Sweden underlines the argument for timing actions to the sequence of events both on the market and on the political arena (Andersson, 2004).

Even if the examples above show that institutional change can be the result of path-changing actions from actors, most railway studies focus on the path-dependence developments under one institutional regime. The most commonly explored period covers the decades from the initial railway investments in the first part of the nineteenth century up to the First World War; the path-shaping period. Frank Dobbin sets out to explore the origins of national industrial policy strategies by charting the evolution of railway policy in the USA, France and Britain between 1825 and 1900. Departing from the empirical notion that national policy trajectories seem to exist over time, Dobbin emphasizes the political culture and its institutionalization in different nations as one important explanation of path dependence (Dobbin, 1994). The way the railways, as the first major policy issues in most industrializing countries in the nineteenth century, were regulated, tended to serve as a cognitive blueprint, setting a mental path for the solution of other regulatory decisions to take. As explanation, Dobbin stresses that the solutions in respective nations were decided in accordance with the political structure. He identifies three different national political cultures that helped shape the political structures. In the USA the federal structure created a dual structure with a local and a federal regulation. The legislation in Britain was aimed at protecting individual entrepreneurs from state intervention, whereas the traditionally strong central government in France also took a firm grip on railway planning and regulation (Dobbin, 1994, p. 26f).

Dobbin focuses on political culture, or informal institutions such as views on legitimacy, power, economic rationality and its impact on path-dependent policy-making. Colleen A. Dunlavy, on the other hand, examines how the formal institutional structure and the division of political power and the political decision-making affected the organization of the railway sector in the USA and Prussia/Germany up to the 1880s (Dunlavy, 1994). Dunlavy's result shows, paradoxically, that the many loci of power and judicial decision-making in the American institutional structure, made the state more active than in the case of Prussia/Germany due to the judicial responsibility to regulate conflicts. In Prussia/Germany the state had failed in its early attempts to regulate the private railway sector. Instead, private enterprises were free to organize the market without interference from the state. As a result, in Prussia/Germany, a strong railway association was formed in the 1840s, and maintained its power through almost all of the nineteenth century. In the USA, railroad associations were not established until the 1880s, when a more centralized railway regulation was imposed. The organizations of the professional railwaymen and engineers in each respective country were also structured in accordance with this.

In another study of railway regulation in the USA, from the 1840s to the late 1880s, Dunlavy explains why the organization is late compared with Germany. Dunlavy shows that the regulatory bodies in the states had difficulties in keeping up with the railways, 'the high-technology of their day'. When the railway lines began crossing state borders, the jurisdiction of the state no longer matched the scale of the enterprise. The right to regulate at all became a matter of bitter political dispute. The locus of power and the site of the conflict shifted from regional, to state and to national level in the American political structure numerous times before finally moving to the national level and the branches of government (Dunlavy, 2001, p. 48ff). Thus, the number of 'veto points' in the decision-making process contributed to a slow institutional change. In this case, the veto points were related to geographical constraints on jurisdiction. This exemplifies that the spatial dimension of regulation is worth exploring further than what has so far been the case.

Arne Kaijser, among others, has pointed out the significance of the institutional borderlines between local and national infrastructural systems in terms of jurisdiction. With examples from Sweden, he shows that there is a marked difference in which political level is primarily responsible for an infrastructural system, or an infrasystem. Local systems such as sewage, waste or gas works were the subject of local regulation, whereas national railway systems tended to be regulated by central government or its agencies (Kaijser, 1999, p. 227). There are several other examples that strengthen this notion. In the late nineteenth century, the telephone sector in Sweden was one of the most open markets in international perspective, and a vast system of privately owned local telephone networks emerged.

Interurban lines, however, were established as a state-owned system. As a result, a dual institutional system was established, with a great variation of regulatory arrangements, such as pricing, in respective subsystems. However, when the state purchased the remaining private networks, new regulations were formed, modeled as the institutions of the state railways, as the leading policy model (Andersson-Skog, 1999). In the British case, Foreman-Peck and Millward showed that the institutional arrangements and the policy implemented by the GPO became a role model for the way other network industries in Britain were regulated (Foreman-Peck and Millward, 1994). In conclusion, this indicates that informal institutions, such as ideas and beliefs may be vital in the shaping of path dependence, that is, as ideological tools used on the political arena (Blyth, 2001; Cox, 2001; Torfing, 1999).

CONCLUDING REMARKS

Examples from the history of the railway sector indicate that institutions in most cases are the result of path-dependent processes. Such processes reflect both technological system properties and the structure of the political system. The technological system develops around events such as gauge selection, network technical standardization and extension due to market conditions that take place in a certain institutional setting. The way the railway regulation evolves has not only to do with the situation on the transport market, but also on more general conceptions of what the state should do and the way this responsibility is divided among government bodies.

Here the degree of interrelatedness, either between railways and co-evolving transport systems or between railways and institutional arrangements, such as transport obligations and financial restrictions, seems to be of importance for continuity and change. Public ownership over a tightly coupled infrastructure system in a political structure with frequent veto points, would, from this point of view, be more characterized by inertia and path dependence than other institutional structures. However, path dependence is not a trench, which when once stepped down into is almost impossible to get out of, but rather a process, which when new opportunities are at hand – be these new technology, new markets or new ideas – is possible for key actors to either change or re-enforce. Here, political and historical institutionalism may be useful in providing insights of how change occurs among human actors. How, why and when informal institutions, cognitive conceptions such as ideas and norms, transform into blueprints and arguments used by economic organizations and political actors in shaping new or re-enforcing old trajectories, may increase our understanding of the nature of path dependence.

The critical assessments referred to above, underline that path dependence is both an attractive and a trying concept. It is appealing, because of the emphasis placed on history and the importance of sequences of events, which intuitively is a notion easy to grasp. But it is also bothersome, because history is known only in retrospect and the identification of critical events is *post hoc* and selective. Today, path dependence is a concept commonly used in the vast array of neo-institutional approaches in economics, history, sociology and political science. The multidisciplinary use naturally contributes to the confusion concerning the concept. Taken together, the future development of path dependence as a theoretical concept will depend on an interaction between the critical arguments from its opponents and the magnitude of different kinds of empirical processes, where we find examples of path-dependent developments.

REFERENCES

Aldcroft, D.H. (1968), *British Railways in Transition. The Economic Problems of Britain's Railways since 1914*, London: Macmillan.

Andersson, F. (2004), 'Mot framtiden på gamla spår? Regionala intressegrupper och beslutsprocesser kring kustjärnvägarna i Norrland under 1900-talet' ('Towards the future on old tracks? Regional interest groups and decision-making processes concerning coastal railways in Norrland during the 20th century'), diss., Umeå Studies in Economic History no 28, Umeå University, Umeå.

Andersson-Skog, L. (1993), 'Såsom allmänna inrättningar till gagnet, men affärsföretag till namnet'. SJ, järnvägspolitiken och den ekonomiska omvandlingen efter 1920' ('As public service by usage, but as business enterprise by name. The state railways, railway policy and economic transformation since 1920'), diss., Umeå studies in Economic History no 17. Umeå University, Umeå.

Andersson-Skog, L. (1996), 'From state railway housekeeping to railway economics. Swedish railway policy and economic transformation after 1920 in an institutional perspective', *Scandinavian Economic History Review*, 1, 23–42.

Andersson-Skog, L. (1999), 'Political economy and institutional diffusion. The case of Swedish railways and telecommunications up to 1950', in L. Andersson-Skog and O. Krantz (eds), *Institutions in the Transport and Communications Industries. State and Private Actors in the Making of Institutional Patterns, 1850–1990*, Canton, MA: Science History Publications, pp. 245–66.

Andersson-Skog, L. (2000), 'National patterns in the regulation of railways and telephony in the Nordic countries to 1950', *Scandinavian Economic History Review*, 2, 30–46.

Arthur, B.W. (1994), *Increasing Returns and Path Dependence in the Economy*, Ann Arbor, MI: University of Michigan Press.

Armstrong, J. (1998), 'Transport history, 1945–1995: the rise of a topic to maturity', *Journal of Transport History*, 19 (2), 103–21.

Bijker, W.E. (1995), *On Bicycles, Bakelites, and Bulbs: Towards a Theory of Socio-technical Change*, Cambridge, MA and London: MIT Press.

Blyth, M. (2001), 'The transformation of the Swedish model. Economic ideas, distributional conflict, and institutional change', *World Politics*, **54** (October), 1–26.

Callon, M. (1986), 'The sociology of an actor-network: the case of the electric vehicle', in M. Callon, J. Law and A. Rip (eds), *Mapping the Dynamics of Science and Technology*, Basingstoke: Macmillan, pp. 19–34.

Chandler, A.D. (comp and ed.) (1965), *The Railroads: The Nations First Big Business. Sources and Readings*, New York: Harcourt, Brace and World, Inc.

Cox, R.H. (2001), 'The social construction of an imperative. Why welfare reform happened in Denmark and the Netherlands but not in Germany', *World Politics*, **53** (April), 463–98.

David, P.A. (1985), 'Clio and the economics of QWERTY', *American Economic Review*, **75** (2), 332–7.

Dixit, A.K. (1996), *The Making of Economic Politics: A Transaction-Cost Perspective*, Cambridge, MA: MIT Press.

Dobbin, F. (1994), *Forging Industrial Policy. The United States, Britain, and France in the Railway Age*, Cambridge: Cambridge University Press.

Domberger, S. and J. Piggott (1994), 'Privatization policies and public enterprise: a survey', in M. Bishop, J. Kay and C. Mayer (eds), *Privatization and Economic Performance*, Oxford: Oxford University Press, pp. 32–61.

Dunlavy, C.A. (1994), *Politics and Industrialization: Early Railroads in the United States and Prussia*, Princeton, NJ: Princeton University Press.

Dunlavy, C.A. (2001), 'Bursting through state limits. Lessons from American railroad history', in L. Magnusson and J. Ottossson (eds), *The State, Regulation and the Economy. An Historical perspective*, Cheltenham, UK and Northampton, MA, USA: Edward Elgar, pp. 44–60.

Fishlow, A. (1965), *American Railroads and the Transformation of the Ante-Bellum Economy*, Cambridge, MA: Harvard University Press.

Fogel, R.W. (1964), *Railroads and American Economic Growth: Essays in Economic History*, Baltimore, MD: Johns Hopkins Press.

Fogel, R.W. (1979), 'Notes on the social saving controversy', *Journal of Economic History*, **1**, 1–54.

Foreman-Peck, J. and R. Millward, (1994), *Public and Private Ownership of British Industry, 1820–1990*, Oxford: Clarendon Press.

Fremdling, R. (1999), 'The Prussian and Dutch railway regulations in the nineteenth century', in L. Andersson-Skog and O. Krantz (eds), *Institutions in the Transport and Communications Industries: State and Private Actors in the Making of Institutional Patterns, 1850–1950*, Canton, MA: Science History Publications, pp. 61–92.

Garud, R. and P. Karnoe (eds) (2001), *Path Dependence and Creation*, Mahwah, NJ: Lawrence Erlbaum Associates.

Gourvish, T. (1993), 'What kind of railway history did we get? Forty years of research', *Journal of Transport History*, **14** (2), pp. 111–25.

Gourvish, T. (1999), 'The regulation of Britain's railways: past, present and future', in L. Andersson-Skog and O. Krantz (eds), *Institutions in the Transport and Communications Industries. State and Private Actors in the Making of Institutional Patterns, 1850–1990*, Canton, MA: Science History Publications, pp. 117–32.

Hughes, T.P. (1983), *Networks of Power: Electrification in Western Society 1880–1930*, Baltimore, MD: Johns Hopkins University Press.

Immergut, E.M. (1991), 'Institutions, veto points, and policy results: a comparative analysis of health care', *Journal of Public Policy*, **10** (4), 391–416.

Innis, H.A. (1923), *A History of the Canadian Pacific Railway*, London: P.S. King and Son.

Innis, H.A. (1930), *The Fur Trade in Canada: An Introduction to Canadian Economic History. With a Preface by R.M. MacIver*. New Haven, CT: Yale University Press.

Kaijser, A. (1999), 'The helping hand: in search of a Swedish institutional regime for infrastructural systems', in L. Andersson-Skog, and O. Krantz, (eds), *Institutions in the Transport and Communications Industries. State and Private Actors in the Making of Institutional Patterns, 1850–1990*, Canton, MA: Science History Publications, pp. 223–44.

Krueger, A.O. (1996), 'The political economy of controls: American sugar', in J.L. Alston, T. Eggertsson and D.C. North (eds), *Empirical Studies in Institutional Change*, Cambridge: Cambridge University Press, pp. 169–218.

Levy, B. and P.T. Spiller (eds) (1996), *Regulations, Institutions, and Commitment: Comparative Studies of Telecommunications*, Cambridge: Cambridge University Press.

Liebowitz, S.J. and S.E. Margolis (1990), 'The fable of the keys', *Journal of Law and Economics*, **33**, 1–25.

Liebowitz, S.J. and S.E. Margolis (1995), 'Path dependence, lock in, and history', *The Journal of Law, Economics and Organisation*, **11** (1), 205–26.

Liebowitz, S.J. and S.E. Margolis (1996), 'Typing errors', *Reason*, June, 28–35.

Lipartito, K. (2003), 'Picturephone and the information age. The social meaning of failure', *Technology and Culture*, **44** (January), 50–81.

Mom, G. (2003), 'What kind of transport history did we get? Half a century of JTH and the future of the field', *Journal of Transport History*, **24**, (2), 121–38.

Mowery, D.C. and N. Rosenberg (1998), *Paths of Innovation: Technological Change in the 20th Century America*, New York: Cambridge University Press.

North, D.C. (1990), *Institutions, Institutional Change and Economic Performance*, Cambridge, Cambridge University Press.

North, D.C. (1996), 'The new institutional economics and Third World development', in J. Hariss, (ed.), *The New Institutional Economics and Third World Development*, London: Routledge.

Ottosson, J. (1997), 'Path dependence and institutional evolution – the case of nationalisation of private railroads in interwar Sweden', in L. Magnusson and J. Ottosson (eds), *Evolutionary Economics and Path Dependence*, Cheltenham, UK and Northampton, MA, USA, Edward Elgar, pp. 186–96.

Perrow, C. (1984), *Normal Accidents: Living with High-Risk Technologies*, New York: Basic Books.

Pierson, P. (1994), *Dismantling the Welfare State?* New York: Cambridge University Press.

Pierson, P. (2000), 'Increasing returns, path dependence, and the study of politics', *American Political Science Review*, **94** (2), 251–67.

Pierson, P. (2004), *Politics in Time. History, Institutions and Social Analysis*, Princeton, NJ, and Oxford: Princeton University Press.

Puffert, D.J. (2000), 'The standardization of track gauge on North American railways, 1830–1890', *Journal of Economic History*, **60** (4), 933–60.

Puffert, D.J. (2002), 'Path dependence in spatial networks: the standardization of railway track gauge', *Explorations in Economic History*, **39**, 282–314.

Rosenberg, N. (1994), *Exploring the Black Box. Technology, Economics and History*, Cambridge: Cambridge University Press.

Scott, P. (2001), 'Path dependence and Britain's "coal wagon problem"', *Explorations in Economic History*, **38**, 366–85.

Thelen, K. (2003), 'How institutions evolve. Insights from comparative historical analysis', in J. Mahoney and D. Rueschemeyer (eds), *Comparative Historical Analysis in the Social Sciences*, Cambridge: Cambridge University Press, pp. 208–40.

Torfing, J. (1999), 'Towards a Schumpeterian workfare postnational regime: path-shaping and path-dependency in Danish welfare reform', *Economy and Society*, **28** (3), 369–404.

Veblen, T. (1915), *Imperial Germany and the Industrial Revolution*, London: Macmillan.

4. Path dependence in economic geography

Magnus Lagerholm and Anders Malmberg[1]

When an industry has thus chosen a locality for itself, it is likely to stay there long: so great are the advantages which people following the same skilled trade get from near neighbourhood to one another. The mysteries of the trade become no mysteries; but are as it were in the air, and children learn many of them unconsciously. (Marshall, 1890 [1916], p. 271)

[I]f there is one single area of economics in which path-dependence is unmistakable, it is in economic geography – the location of production in space. The long shadow cast by history over location is apparent at all scales, from the smallest to the largest. (Krugman, 1991c, p. 80)

INTRODUCTION

Economic geographers are interested in the spatial aspects of economic development. This interest can express itself in various ways. Some focus on macro analyses of the economic growth of spatial entities such as cities, regions or nations. Others are more interested in micro analyses of the development of firms or systems of related firms, such as industries, networks, production chains or clusters. In both cases, the two main concerns relate to difference in economic performance on the one hand, and difference in economic specialization on the other.

Thus, macro analyses in economic geography depart from questions like: why do some regions (cities, nations) prosper while others do not? Why is there regional specialization and how are such patterns reproduced? Differences in regional economic development exist not only in a global context but also within nations. Natural resources and demography have an impact here, but also institutional settings, knowledge structures and the general macroeconomic environment. The most influential models dealing with uneven regional development emphasize processes of cumulative causation and the fact that a region that, for one reason or another, has taken the lead in development will gradually tend to strengthen its position, at least partly at the expense of surrounding, less developed regions (Hirschmann, 1958; 1970; Myrdal, 1957; Ullman, 1958).

Micro analyses, on the other hand, focus on the location of the firm and ask questions like: how is the performance and competitiveness of a firm affected by the conditions that prevail in its immediate environment? Why do similar and related firms tend to agglomerate in certain places? The importance of spatial proximity between firms that interact in various ways (competition, collaboration, transactions) is a key factor here. The cost and skills of local labour, the cost and appropriateness of land and infrastructure, the barriers of entry and business culture, and so on, are other important factors for a good business location.

Even though space is the constituent aspect of economic geography, it should be obvious that most core questions of the discipline are also related to time. Different regions have various capabilities – resources, institutions, infrastructures, skills, norms and values – at their disposal and these capabilities make up the base of their development prospects. The capabilities of a region often date back in history as combinations of chance events, natural endowments and the effects of previous human activity. Some specific feature in the local environment may determine the locational choice of a firm, but the presence of the firm will also affect this environment.

The concept of path dependence is of explicit importance here. The origin of the concept lies in the analysis of technological trajectories. Nelson and Winter (1982) applied the concept in trying to understand how routines work in a firm and guide firm behaviour, innovation, competition and development of the economy.

Seeing path dependence as steps forward in a particular direction guided by past steps also embraces the idea of *increasing returns*. Arthur (1994) developed models for explaining why there are increasing returns and how they work. In a process of increasing returns each move down the path strengthens probability for additional steps along the same path. The process of increasing returns is self-reinforcing because of the benefits of sticking to the current path in comparison to the cost of shifting to an alternative path.

Arthur (1994) used the so-called Polya urn process to illustrate how elements of chance and sequencing play a crucial role for the outcome. Imagine a large urn containing at the start only two balls, one red and one blue. Pick one randomly and then return it to the urn accompanied by an additional ball of the same colour as the one picked. If you pick a red ball, then return two red balls. Repeat until the urn is filled and calculate the distribution. Make it over again, say a hundred times, and you will probably never end up on the same distribution. What does this show? It shows some of the key characteristics of path dependence. Pure chance determines which ball to be drawn first, the colour drawn will give positive feedback for that particular colour and the probability of picking the same colour in the next round is enhanced. Early picks can have a large impact on the outcome. This effect accumulates and makes a particular path more likely for the next draw. There is unpredictability within the process because we cannot predict the partly random outcomes beforehand; neither can we predict which of the possible final distributions it is going to be. There is also inflexibility since the more sequences being played, the harder it gets to change the path, and the more red balls in the urn, the higher probability that you pick one more of them. Another characteristic of increasing returns is that earlier events are not reduced with time. On the contrary, early events play a more important role than later events because of their impact on future choices. The last characteristic is that a lock-in on a specific colour is not necessarily the most efficient one; you may end up with a colour you do not like (see also Pierson, 2000).

Transferring these effects to the field of technological development implies that the winning technology is not inevitably the most efficient one but merely that the competing alternatives are long gone. According to Arthur, for a technological trajectory to accommodate to the characteristics of a path-dependent process, four core conditions have to be met. First, there has to be *large set-up* or *fixed costs*, which ensures that organizations have strong incentives to stay on the technological path. Secondly, there must be *learning effects* involved that make the technology more effective and workers gradually more experienced and productive. Third, *co-ordination effects* should occur when more people use the same technique. Finally, there should be *adaptive expectation* because individuals adapt to what they think others will choose, leading to a self-fulfilling disposition of expectations.

The path, in this context, is normally conceived of as a trajectory through time. As a matter of fact, however, the concept implies spatio-temporality. It is thus interesting to note that the metaphor in itself has spatial connotations: a path is not only a trajectory through time, but also a road, track or way, laid out in the landscape. Connecting space and time provides useful insights and important knowledge in analyses of regional economic development. Thus, economic geography has much to gain from incorporating concepts from evolutionary economics. Possibly, evolutionary economics has something to learn from economic geography as well. This is certainly what Paul Krugman has in mind in the quote at the start of the chapter.

Arthur (1994) too uses examples of industry location to illustrate the effects of increasing returns, positive feedbacks and the importance of history in economic development. The emphasis on the importance of spatial proximity is strongly related to two key concepts in economic geography, to be addressed below: agglomeration and clustering (Arthur, 1994, p. 49). His work is partly inspired by the type of spatial economics that adopts a process-oriented approach to agglomeration and clustering where successive rounds of new investments add layers to the sediments (physical, but also institutional, social, cultural and cognitive) of previous rounds (see also Massey, 1979; 1984).

Myrdal's (1957) models of regional disparity and the growth of regions build on such a framework. Once a region takes the lead as a cause of initial luck or chance, it tends to stay ahead of competitors because of its advantage over and gravitation on other surrounding regions. Within this view, no single output can be predicted or predetermined. The firms that locate first in a place create an attraction for new firms to move there, and these in turn make an even stronger attraction for more firms to move in. An entire industry may end up clustered in the initially chosen location. Historical accidents play a crucial role here (Arthur, 1994). The chosen location is not necessarily better than alternative locations but had some important features that triggered the first establishment.

Paul David (1985) and Douglass North (1990) have developed Arthur's work on increasing returns to explain economic development exploring the concept of path dependence. Specific patterns of timing and sequences matter for how a region will develop. Starting from similar conditions small events early in the development process can alter the outcome in several ways. Regarding path dependence as sequences of change in the economy, David sees temporally remote events such as chance, to be of importance for a region's (or a nation's) development. North makes the connection to the role of institutions. Once in place, the institutional set-up is hard to change and it has a remarkable impact on the capabilities for economic growth. The path dependence is highly integrated with the rigidity of institutional set-ups and this explains the divergence in economic performance. Several social sciences use the institutional approach to explain why things occur in one society and not in another. According to North all features leading to increasing returns on technology can be translated and used for explaining institutions' impact on economy, high or fixed start-up costs, learning effects, co-ordination effects and adaptive expectations. Also in economic geography, the impact of institutions on regional specialization and performance has become a growing concern (Amin and Thrift, 1994).

Thus, temporal and spatial variation in economic development is caused by specific institutional rules, routines and practices that govern economic action (Arthur, 1994; Hodgson, 1993; Lundvall, 1992; Nelson and Winter,

1982). Over time, particular choices, themselves framed by past decisions, open up new pathways of economic development, but preclude others (Arrow, 1962). Thus the downside of this tends to be expressed in terms of lock-in to a fated path where development is constrained within a progressively narrower range of possibilities that lead to decline. Lock-in can be seen as a product of over-specialization, associated with the progressive closure of knowledge systems and work practices in the face of wider technological shifts. By contrast, successful adjustment will involve a strategic upgrading and improvement of productive assets, which utilizes resources drawn from existing linkages and capabilities.

The aim of this chapter is to discuss how concepts such as path dependence and lock-in can be used to analyse regional economic development in general, and competitive advantage related to the spatial clustering of similar and related economic activity in particular. The creation and reproduction of localized capabilities, the positive and negative effects of specialization and the risk of deteriorating advantages in cases of lock-in are central in this context. In particular, we focus on the following two questions:

- Which mechanisms and processes generate spatial clustering of similar and related economic activity and how do these relate to path dependence?
- Why and when do localized capabilities, built over time, shift from being advantageous to become barriers against future success of a regional economy?

The chapter is structured as follows. In the next section the benefits of spatial clustering are introduced. Then, in the third section, we bring history into the picture by discussing which factors and processes contribute to the successful reproduction of the competitive advantage associated with such clustering and why, sometimes, the successful reproduction of competitive advantage deteriorates. In the fourth section, by way of conclusion, we argue that the concept of path dependence can indeed contribute to the understanding of the key questions in economic geography while at the same time highlighting a major predicament that this discipline finds itself in, arguably together with most other branches of economic analysis.

SPATIAL CLUSTERING: A KEY ISSUE IN ECONOMIC GEOGRAPHY

In the context of economic geography, the concept of agglomeration has to do with the spatial concentration of people and/or economic activity.

This phenomenon has attracted research interest over extended time periods. Throughout the twentieth century, a literature proliferated which, taken together, contributes to the formulation of a theory of why industry agglomeration emerges, and in what ways location in the proximity of similar or related firms contributes to the competitiveness of an individual firm. Among the classics in this field of research can be mentioned Marshall (1890 [1916]), Hoover (1937; 1948), Myrdal (1957), Hirschman (1958), Ullman (1958) and Pred (1966; 1977). More recent contributions have been signed by geographers like Scott (1983; 1988; 1998), Amin and Thrift (1992; 1994) and Storper (1997) with business strategists and economists like Porter (1990; 1994; 1998), Krugman (1991a; 1991b; 1991c) and Enright (1998).

Agglomeration Economies

The concept of agglomeration may have two different meanings in this context. One is related to the phenomenon that people and economic activity in general tend to concentrate in cities or industrial core regions. The advantages gained by such behaviour are often referred to as urbanization economies (cf. Dicken and Lloyd, 1990; Hoover, 1937). The other refers to the phenomenon that firms within the same or closely related industries tend to gather at certain places. Those mechanisms leading to such behaviour are correspondingly denoted localization economies. It is the latter aspect of agglomeration – that is, spatial clustering of similar and related economic activity – that makes up the main focus of this chapter.

There are several reasons to take the issue of spatial clustering seriously. One is that clustering phenomena do indeed lie at the core of what economic geography is all about. There is a lot to learn about the role of space and place in economic processes by trying to pinpoint the driving forces that make for spatial clustering of similar and related economic activity. Second, this task has obvious policy relevance today. Throughout and beyond the Organisation for Economic Co-operation and Development (OECD) world, cluster-based policies have in recent years increasingly been seen as the main option in the field of industrial and regional policy, and as an important element of these policies we find a doctrine saying that regions should specialize industrially and promote the dynamics of agglomeration in order to gain or sustain competitiveness and prosperity.

Traditional agglomeration theory has identified four types of localization economies that are held to explain spatial clustering. To start with, there are benefits to be gained from the possibility of clustered firms sharing the cost of certain collective resources among several firms. This applies in particular to the cost of infrastructures. When an agglomeration of similar or related firms is established, there is also a potential to adjust the local institutions, infrastructure, educational system and other types of collective goods to the needs of this particular industry. The first mechanism can thus be labelled *reduced costs for and gradual adjustment of shared infrastructures and other collective resources.*

The second mechanism is about *reduced transaction costs for co-located trading partners.* This mechanism is similar to the co-ordination effect identified by Arthur (1994) as one of the conditions for increasing returns to occur. Firms in agglomerations can reduce their transport and transaction costs as inter-firm transactions and shipments are simplified when the distance between firms is negligible. The customer firm which can place an order with a nearby supplier will gain an advantage in relation to a competitor which has to travel long distances to see its supplier or, alternatively, place the order by means of some communications system and then wait for the shipment to take place. Porter (1998, p. 80) describes this in the following way:

> the proximity of companies and institutions in one location – and the repeated exchanges among them – fosters better coordination and trust. Thus clusters mitigate the problems inherent in arm's-length relationships without imposing the inflexibilities of vertical integration or the management challenges of creating and maintaining formal linkages such as networks, alliances, and partnerships.

Third, the concentration of firms in similar or related industries creates *a market for specialized labour.* The establishment of a local pool of skilled labour has been proposed as a major element of the localization economies ever since Alfred Marshall more than a century ago wrote so elegantly about the advantages of being located in an industrial district (Marshall, 1890 [1916], p. 271):

> Again, in all but the earliest stages of economic development a localised industry gains a great advantage from the fact that it offers a constant market for skill. Employers are apt to resort to any place where they are likely to find a good choice of workers with the special skill which they require; while men seeking employment naturally go places where there are many employers who need such skill as theirs and where therefore it is likely to find a good market.

Theoretically, both employees and firms would benefit from the specialized market for labour skills that emerges in a spatial agglomeration of similar and related firms (Krugman, 1991a). This mechanism is subject to more and more attention as an important mechanism behind spatial clustering.

The fourth common agglomeration mechanism is about *localized learning and knowledge spillover in a local milieu*. These stimulate processes of interactive learning and diffuse knowledge from one company to the other in the local milieu. The idea that proximity between firms stimulates the development of firms is not new:

> a close relationship, almost a partnership, grows up among related firms in a given geographical area. The ability, for example, of members of the group to meet without inconvenience to discuss common problems and matters of mutual interest is a not inconsiderable advantage of close geographical association. (Estall and Buchanan, 1961, p. 109)

The assertion that spatial clustering triggers a process of learning and innovation within the local industrial milieu has attracted strong research interest in recent years. In a localized cluster, chances are greater that an individual firm gets in touch with actors that are early adopters of new technology or the innovator of it. The sociocultural environment of the firm becomes increasingly important in this context. Several different and sometimes overlapping models are in use to define local and regional innovative milieus. Lundvall uses the concept of national innovation system (Lundvall, 1992). Saxenian uses regional industrial system (Saxenian, 1994) to describe the growth in Silicon Valley, a system where the cultural and institutional context is part of the system and influences the industries' trajectory and development speed.

The local milieu can be defined as a territory that is characterized by consistency based on certain behavioural practices, norms and values as well as a common technical understanding. The 'innovative milieu' approach (Maillat, 1995) thus emphasizes the interaction that takes place between economic, sociocultural, political and institutional actors in a given place. Relations between firms, clients, research institutions, the education system and local authorities create a region which shares traditions and customs. This enhances the collective learning through intense interaction between a mixed set of actors. The milieu is a 'created space' that is both a result of and a precondition for learning – an active resource rather than a passive surface (Coffey and Bailly, 1996). The knowledge shared and exchanged within such milieus is in many cases of a tacit nature, only possible if the involved actors share the same background. Outsiders who do not have the common experience will fail to achieve tacit knowledge. Firms that are embedded in the right kind of milieu tend to learn faster and become more competitive. The agglomeration makes up a favourable milieu for knowledge creation and spillover effects, because of increasing returns and economies of agglomeration.

Clusters and Competitive Advantage

The modern upswing of research interest in the agglomeration/clustering phenomenon owes a lot to the influence of the American business strategist Michael Porter. Since the publication of his book, *The Competitive Advantage of Nations* (Porter, 1990), the cluster concept has become widely circulated in academic as well as in policy circles.

Porter's argument, in essence, is that if we want to understand how firms become innovative and competitive, we have to understand how firms link into systems of related industries (= industrial clusters) and how such clusters increase their dynamisms through spatial proximity:

> Today's economic map of the world is dominated by . . . critical masses – in one place – of unusual competitive success in particular fields. Clusters are a striking feature of virtually every national, regional, state, and even metropolitan economy, especially in more economically advanced nations. Silicon Valley and Hollywood may be the world's best-known clusters. Clusters are not unique, however; they are highly typical – and therein lies a paradox: the enduring competitive advantages in a global economy lie increasingly in local things – knowledge, relationships, motivation – that distant rivals cannot match. (Porter, 1998, p. 78).

The cluster approach as presented by Porter (1990) and subsequently developed by himself, his associates and others (Enright, 1998; Malmberg and Maskell, 2002; Malmberg et al., 1996; Porter, 1994; 1998; 2000), brings some genuine contributions to the analysis of the key issues of economic geography. First, it provides a way to describe the systemic nature of an economy, that is, how various types of industrial activity are related. In addition to the firms in the industry where we find the main producers of the primary goods in focus (be they heavy trucks, telecommunications equipment or popular music), the cluster comprises connected supplier firms and industries providing various types of specialized input, technology, machinery and associated services, as well as customer industries and more indirectly related industries.

This way of approaching the systemic character of economic activity has much in its favour. It opens up a scope for analysing interactions and interdependencies between firms and industries across a wide spectrum of economic activity. An additional advantage is that it contributes to the bridging of a number of more or less artificial and chaotic conceptual divides that characterize so much work in economic geography and related disciplines. These include, for example, manufacturing versus services, high tech versus low tech, large companies versus SMEs, public and private activities, and so on. A single cluster, defined as a functional industrial system, may embrace firms and actors and activities on both sides of each of these divides (see also Dicken and Malmberg, 2001).

Furthermore, Porter's model of the determinants of competitiveness in a cluster, known under the 'brand' of the diamond model, identifies a number of mechanisms proposed to foster industrial dynamism, innovations and long-term growth. Essentially, the model is built around four sets of intertwined forces related to factor conditions, demand conditions, related and supported industries, and firm structure, strategy and rivalry, respectively. Despite some more or less justified critique recently (see, for example, Martin and Sunley, 2003) it should be acknowledged that Porter's intervention has brought some genuinely new elements to the analysis of the spatial clustering phenomenon.

First, the treatment of factor conditions in Porter's account does offer some rather radical departures from the prevalent view, for example, in pre-1990 economic geography. One such departure is the emphasis of the role of specialized factors and factor upgrading, which redirects our focus from the classical notion of availability and cost for capital, labour and land towards the type of specialized factor conditions which are developed historically to fit the needs of a particular economic activity. These are important as factors of location since they are difficult to move and difficult to imitate in other regions (cf. Maskell et al., 1998). Another, perhaps more original, idea is that of selective factor disadvantages as a factor promoting dynamism and long-term growth. Arguably, no previous account had explicitly made the point that shortcomings in factor conditions (such as labour shortage and high wages, scarce natural resources, expensive electricity, and so on) can actually trigger technological and institutional innovations that will in the longer term contribute to the competitive success of the firms in a specific location.

Second, the treatment of the demand side as a primarily qualitative factor is original. Most previous models have emphasized access to a large market as an important location advantage. Porter's account, in contrast, alerts us to the fact that it is the sophistication of demand that matters – if we are interested in innovation and long-term competitiveness. According to this view, the locationally advantaged firm is the one that is in a position to receive and react to signals of sophisticated demand, rather than simply the one who is blessed with 'many customers' in the local market. This idea is also present in other recent approaches to the dynamics of industrial systems. In Eliasson's (2000) notion of the competence bloc, the 'competent customer' plays a key role.

Third, the importance of local rivalry is made much more explicit than in previously existing models of spatial agglomeration. That a firm may gain advantages from being located close to other firms in the same industry is, of course, a key insight in classical agglomeration theory. Rarely, though, has this advantage been attributed to the fact that spatial proximity between rivals will trigger dynamism and growth. The idea is that local rivalry adds intensity and an emotional dimension to the competition that most firms perceive in the global market. The firm down the road is often seen as the 'prime enemy', a bit like the rivalry between neighbouring football clubs. Firms in a local milieu tend to develop relations of rivalry, where benchmarking in relation to the neighbours is more direct, partly for reasons of local prestige, and partly, presumably, simply because direct comparison is simplified. One could speculate that there are at least two reasons for the latter. First, it is easier to monitor the performance of a neighbouring firm than a competitor far away. Second, if one firm displays superior performance, it is obvious to everyone that this cannot be blamed on different external conditions, since they are, in principle, identical for all firms in the local milieu (cf. Malmberg and Maskell, 2002).

On these points, at least, it should be acknowledged that the cluster approach, as developed by Porter and others, has contributed to genuine progress: the role of specialized production factors and selective factor disadvantages, sophisticated customer demand and local rivalry are novel and innovative proposals that have enriched our understanding of why conditions in a local milieu in general and agglomeration of similar and related firms in particular might promote superior firm performance.

BRINGING HISTORY INTO THE ANALYSIS OF SPATIAL CLUSTERING

Both the mechanisms behind localization economies identified in traditional agglomeration theory and the factors in focus on Porter's model for explaining cluster dynamics are largely ahistorical at the outset. They identify forces that give permanent advantages to firms located in a cluster of similar and related firms, once the structure is in place. Still it is obvious that a historical approach can contribute to our understanding of how clusters originate, develop and decline. In this section we look in more detail at these processes.

Phases in Cluster Development

The origin of clusters remains largely obscure. One reason for this is that agglomerations start out by chance in any location and can therefore not be predetermined (Arthur, 1994). A way to analyse the emergence of the agglomeration is thus simply to try to trace its roots backwards in history.

In most cases, we will then find some historical accidents, this or that entrepreneur did at some point in time start this or that type of economic activity, but it is not really possible to explain why this happened in one particular place and not in another (apart from the trivial fact that most new firms start at the place of residence of the founder). The role of such accidents is rather unexplored in economic geography, as in neighbouring disciplines presumably. So the event that actually triggers the clustering process remains in haze. What seems to be of particular importance is the emergence of a core or anchor firm for the cluster (Wolfe and Gertler, 2004).

But once an activity has started in a particular place, several mechanisms come into play, contributing to subsequent developments. The first is that a successful economic activity in one place is often followed by other similar or related activity. Whole clusters can develop out of the formation of one or two critical firms that feed the growth of numerous smaller ones. The spin-offs from these companies make the agglomeration dynamic and attract more firms to the cluster.

Another mechanism contributing to the development of agglomerations is related to the fact that firms, once they have been rooted in a place, rarely relocate. Large set-up or fixed costs and the learning effects are part of this (Arthur, 1994). Thus, Ross (1896) observed this more than a century ago and the observation has then been repeated and elaborated upon over time: 'The power of a locality to hold an industry . . . greatly exceeds its original power to attract. The new locality must not only excel the old, but it must excel it by margin enough to more than offset the resisting power of the matrix' (Ross, 1896, p. 265, quoted in Hamilton, 1967, p. 410). We may thus argue that the emergence of clusters of similar and related economic activity is related to three factors: they often originate in a rather random series of events leading to the start of a new firm at the place of preference by the entrepreneur; they develop through spin-offs and imitation within the local milieu; and they are sustained by various forms of inertia, meaning that firms rarely relocate once they have been reproduced in a place. Routines within firms are inherited to its spin-offs; the new firms carry some of their mother company's routines and implement them in a new company. The inertia spreads throughout the industrial system as there is a sharing of routines. Knowledge creation is strongly path dependent as today's practices, routines and types of knowledge are related to those of yesterday, just as those of tomorrow will be related to those of today (Nelson and Winter, 1982; Arthur, 1994).

This is, of course, not the end of the story. It is certainly possible to add to these three, another three or four elements that would contribute to portray not only the origin and rise of an agglomeration, but also its saturation, crisis and possible rejuvenation. Such an account would, in addition to pioneering, imitation and spin-offs, include concepts like the creation of networks between local firms; the creation of a local culture, supporting infrastructures and institutions adopted to the proliferation industry; and the establishment of the place as a brand of the industry and subsequent attraction on resources from the outside (people, capital, firms). Such a story would, ultimately also include a phase of consolidation – at some stage some firms tend to take on leading roles and often this means that they take over other firms in the agglomeration such that an initially small-firm based agglomeration often ends up being dominated by a limited number of larger firms. Also, history tells us that most spatial clusters, sooner or later, run into problems. Elements of petrifaction are often revealed at points in history when technological or other developments call for rapid restructuring. What was once a leading centre of dynamism within a given line of business may end up as a declining industrial region locked-in to its routines, technologies and institutions, facing great problems of renewal and finding itself being out-competed by firms located elsewhere. Then again, there are also examples of how industry agglomerations manage to reinvent themselves also in this phase, such that they can actually retrieve some of their former greatness.

Producing and Reproducing Competitive Advantage: Localized Capabilities, Institutional Endowments and Learning

Turning first to the virtuous circle by which clusters are able to successfully build and reproduce competitive advantage, we draw on the concept of localized capabilities (Maskell and Malmberg, 1999; Maskell et al., 1998). Locational advantage cannot be built on factors that are omnipresent. Factors that are ubiquitous do not make up an incentive for firms to agglomerate. In order for a factor to become a specific advantage, it has to be rare, valuable and difficult to imitate or move.

A specific combination of a region's infrastructure and built environment, its natural resources, the institutional endowments and the knowledge and skills available in the location, make up the unique localized capabilities of a region (Maskell and Malmberg, 1999; see also Malmberg and Maskell, 2006). The localized capabilities contribute not only to the competitiveness of the single firm, but also to the industrial strength of the entire region. These non-imitable capabilities are commodities formed in the past by the historical process.

There is much research in support of the idea that differences in economic performance and specialization across regions can be explained by the institutional endowments (Amin and Thrift, 1994; Dore, 1973;

Hirschman, 1970). The institutional (as well as the social and cultural) structure in a region is built up over a long period of time. The institutional endowments match the industrial system and support specific types of, for instance, knowledge-creation processes. As the needs of industries change, so does the function of the institutions in the region. Following the historical trajectory, each adaptation in the region is done to strengthen its local capabilities and make the industry more competitive.

The institutional endowment includes rules, routines, habits and traditions associated with the regional supply of capital, land and labour and the regional market for goods and services (Maskell and Malmberg, 1999). The region's institutional endowment represents the intricate contemporary interaction between elements of different ages – from the very old (religion, beliefs, values) to the recent/current (contemporary industry standards, current regulations, and so on). The contemporary institutional endowment is both the result of previous rounds of economic activity and the setting for subsequent rounds of localized knowledge creation. Localized capabilities construct the environment for creation of localized knowledge in a region, meaning that the knowledge created is not ubiquitous, but has the characteristics of tacit knowledge. The creation of tacit knowledge reinforces the institutional endowments and local competitiveness.

The regional institutional capacity can be created, reproduced and transformed through history, but at each point in time it has a directional effect on the efforts of the firms in the region by supporting and assisting some types of knowledge creation while hampering or preventing others. There is always an opportunity for choice where firms can trade-off present profits against the search for new knowledge and take the risk of trying a new path in the development process (Dosi, 1988). Thus, while the institutional endowments encourage and direct the progress of certain outcomes of the region's future, it will never be given beforehand what the outcome will be. Each set of localized capabilities attracts certain types of industries, to which it is especially suited. The resulting clustering of certain types of knowledge creation enhances the attractiveness of the region by adding economically attractive institutions. The process of regional economic development will, precisely because of this, tend to be highly path dependent (Krugman, 1991a; Malmberg, 1996).

Losing Regional Competitive Advantage: Lock-In and Deterioration of Localized Capabilities

In this section we argue that even though a region has several localized capabilities that promote the competitiveness of firms located there, these capabilities will tend not to last for ever. The localized capabilities can in some different ways deteriorate and place a region in a situation of decline (Maskell and Malmberg, 1999). Within economic geography, the concept of lock-in is used to describe the spiral of decline in a region that cannot change or adjust its path to new circumstances. This interpretation is somewhat different from the original one, where the emphasis is more towards a lock-in to a technology. The original issue was how a technology comes to dominate over other technologies, and not that much the effect of an over-specialization and decline of a region's advantage in localized capabilities. The institutional setting, the routines and practice formed by the path of earlier choices can keep the region competitive or, if it is rigid, lead the region to be out of date.

Thus, lock-in refers here to the case when successive adjustments of social, cultural, institutional and infrastructural structures in a region to the demand of the dominating cluster eventually leads to a situation where alternative developments paths are basically ruled out.

Even though each round of investment is an improvement of the past one, a strong lock-in can ultimately be a threat to the sustainability of the long-term competitiveness. It turns out that once successful adaptations of localized capabilities may become carriers of obsolete routines, hampering the rejuvenation of the cluster. The industry and region lose market shares and innovative capacity. The institutional settings are not capable of dealing with radical industrial restructuring. Martin (2003) suggests that it happens more often in introvert clusters with few extra-local linkages because of 'blind spots' that appear in the cluster when all the actors have adjusted their thinking towards each other and lose the perspectives of changes in demand, organization of production or new innovations, which makes the system more vulnerable. It is not necessarily that the actors do not realize that there is a problem, but rather that they do not know how to respond to it (Schoenberger, 2003).

Lock-in situations need not be problematic in a region, but they tend to become critical when, for some reason the successful reproduction of valuable localized capabilities is threatened. Capabilities can deteriorate for a number of reasons, thereby undermining the competitiveness of the firms located in the region. Following the argument in Maskell and Malmberg (1999), we briefly discuss three ways by which formerly strong localized capabilities can deteriorate: asset erosion (Dierickx and Cool, 1989), substitution (Porter, 1990) and ubiquitification (Maskell et al., 1998).

Asset erosion describes the process whereby previously important capabilities in a region are no longer reproduced in the same pace or to the same degree. The transmission mechanism can be broken for a variety of reasons. Young people are no longer interested in taking traditional jobs.

Attitudes and values can turn firms away from entrepreneurial activity. The interaction between customer and supplier firms in a local cluster can be broken by structural changes (concentration and mergers, buy-outs, closures, and so on) thus obstructing the knowledge creation that was based on the presence of knowledgeable, demanding and critical customers. Asset erosion can also refer to the exhaustion of natural resources, the congestion of the requisite infrastructure or the obstruction of the essential channels of communication in ways beyond repair.

Substitution represents the case where new technology or new customer preferences rapidly devalues former investments in, for instance, skills, education and infrastructure, thus undermining the region's capabilities. Regions in which the economic development was favoured by massive investments in channels were less fortunate when the technological development led to the construction of railroads, and so on.

Ubiquitification describes the process by which formerly localized capabilities are actively made practically worthless through a process of more or less instant global dissemination: a previously localized capability become a ubiquity. Reduction of transport costs makes large domestic markets and proximity to first-class suppliers less valuable. Many natural resources and built structures do not wear easily, but ubiquitification can sometimes make them lose most of their former value: when transport costs are sufficiently small, the actual location of a deposit of valuable minerals seldom in itself gives rise to a booming cluster of all the facilities needed to produce the production equipment or services demanded.

Asset erosion, substitution or ubiquitification can thus trigger a situation where lock-in suddenly becomes a lethal problem to the region. This phenomenon – that a region over time tends to develop institutions which hinder future success, as a result of decisions that were in themselves very advanced in their time – is sometimes referred to as penalties of taking the lead (Gerschenkron, 1962; Veblen, 1939). The fact that a region has previously been lagging behind, and not developed the structures of the last round of investment, and the ones before, might in certain cases become an advantage of backwardness. The absence of physical structures and social institutions adjusted to yesterday's level of technological and organizational development may become an advantage when trying to implement those of today or tomorrow.

CONCLUDING REMARKS

We have argued that several of the key research questions in economic geography have much to gain from integrating notions of path dependence into the analysis. If we want to explain why the economic performance and specialization of regions differ, or why there is so often spatial clustering of similar and related economic activity and why such settings seem to trigger innovation, learning and competitiveness, it seems obvious that forces of path dependence and increasing returns are in play.

The general character of innovation processes and knowledge creation has two implications for the argument put forward in the chapter (see also Maskell and Malmberg, 1999). The first is simply that history matters. In order to cope with the uncertain and incremental character of learning processes, firms develop various routines and procedures. Experienced success tends to make such routines durable, and this, in turn, will tend to establish path-dependent learning trajectories. The second implication is that proximity matters. The interactive character of learning processes will in itself introduce geographical space as a necessary dimension to take into account. Modern communications technology will admittedly allow more long-distance interaction than was previously possible. However, certain types of information and knowledge exchange continue to require regular and direct face-to-face contact. Put simply, the more tacit the knowledge involved, the more important is spatial proximity between the actors taking part in the exchange. The proximity argument is twofold. First, it is related to the time geography of individuals. Everything else being equal, interactive collaboration will be cheaper and smoother, the shorter the distance between the participants. The second dimension is related to proximity in a social and cultural sense. To communicate tacit knowledge will normally require a high degree of mutual trust and understanding, which in turn is related not only to language but also to shared values and 'culture'.

Two conclusions of the chapter may thus be summarized. First, the path-dependent and interactive character of knowledge creation is a key to the understanding of the contemporary emergence and reproduction of spatial agglomerations of related firms. Second, it is the region's distinct institutional endowment that embeds knowledge and allows for knowledge creation which – through interaction with the available physical and human resources – constitutes its capabilities and enhances or abates the competitiveness of the firms in the region. The path-dependent nature of such localized capabilities makes them difficult to imitate and they thereby establish the basis of sustainable competitive advantage.

So far, economic geography has been only partly successful in coping with these issues. We can recognize a regional success story when we face it, and we can fairly well capture the main processes behind this success, related as they are to the gradual growth and dynamism of a clustered structure of firms within the broader structure of a milieu that successfully develops and reproduces localized capabilities that underpin the success of the firms. We can also fairly well recognize a regional crisis, and pinpoint the structures and historical processes, that have put the region into a developmental dead end.

The problem, or predicament, as we see it, is twofold. First, it is somewhat discomforting that the very same type of factors – relating to institutions, infrastructures and skills – are used to explain both success and failure. Second, the discipline is, so far, rather empty-handed when it comes to identifying – let alone predicting – when we should expect successful specialization to turn into disastrous lock-in. Matthew's phrase 'For unto every one that hath shall be given' captures the prolonged and self-reinforcing success of clusters, while Bob Dylan's 'And the first one now will later be last for the times they are a-changin'', reminds us of the branching points at which leading clusters deteriorate and competing clusters take over. We urgently need to understand more of the conditions under which Bob will outperform Matthew in terms of predictive power on regional economic development.

NOTE

1. This chapter partly draws on previous work, notably Maskell and Malmberg (1999), Malmberg and Maskell (2002) and Malmberg (2003). The first few paragraphs of this chapter also appear, in slightly modified form, in Malmberg and Maskell (2009). We are grateful to Peter Maskell for permitting us to build upon some ideas that he was instrumental in first formulating, particularly in the third section of the chapter. We would also like to thank the editors, and the participants of the Visby seminar for encouraging and constructive comments on an earlier version of the chapter.

REFERENCES

Amin, A. and Thrift, N. (1992), 'Neo-Marshallian nodes in global networks', *International Journal of Urban and Regional Research*, **16**, 571–87.

Amin, A. and Thrift, N. (1994), *Globalization, Institutions, and Regional Development in Europe*, Oxford and New York: Oxford University Press.

Arrow, K.J. (1962), 'The economic implications of learning by doing', *Review of Economic Studies*, **29**, 155–73.

Arthur, W.B. (1994), *Increasing Returns and Path Dependence in the Economy*, Ann Arbor, MI: University of Michigan Press.

Coffey, W.S. and A. Bailly (1996), 'Flexible economy and services: new patterns of location of economic activity', in A. Bailly and W.F. Lever (eds), *The Spatial Impact of Economic Changes in Europe*, London: Avebury.

David, P. (1985), 'Clio and the economics of QWERTY', *American Economic Review*, **75**, 332–7.

Dicken, P. and P.E. Lloyd (1990), *Location in Space: Theoretical Perspectives in Economic Geography*, 3rd edn, New York: Harper and Row.

Dicken, P. and A. Malmberg (2001), 'Firms in territories: a relational perspective', *Economic Geography*, **77** (4), 345–63.

Dierickx, I. and K. Cool (1989), 'Asset stock accumulation and sustainability of competitive advantage', *Management Science*, **35** (12), 1504–13.

Dore, R. (1973), *British Factory–Japanese Factory*, London: Allen and Unwin.

Dosi, G. (1988), 'Institutions and markets in a dynamic world', *The Manchester School of Economics and Social Studies*, **61** (2), 119–46.

Eliasson, G. (2000), 'Industrial policy, competence blocks and the role of science in economic development', *Journal of Evolutionary Economics*, **10**, 217–41.

Enright, M.J. (1998), 'Regional clusters and firm strategy', in A.D. Chandler, P. Hagström and Ö. Sölvell (eds), *The Dynamic Firm. The Role of Technology, Strategy, Organization and Regions*, Oxford: Oxford University Press, pp. 315–42.

Estall, R.C. and R.O. Buchanan (1961), *Industrial Activity and Economic Geography*, London: Hutchinson.

Gerschenkron, A. (1962), *Economic Backwardness in Historical Perspective*, Cambridge, MA: Belknap Press.

Hamilton, F.E.I. (1967), 'Models of industrial location', in R.J. Chorley and P. Haggett (eds), *Models in Geography*, London: Methuen, pp. 361–424.

Hirschman, A.O. (1958), *The Strategy of Economic Development*, New Haven, CT: Yale University Press.

Hirschman, A.O. (1970), *Exit, Voice and Loyalty: Responses to Decline in Firms, Organizations and States*, Cambridge, MA: Harvard University Press.

Hodgson, G.M. (1993), *Economics and Evolution: Bringing Life Back into Economics*, Cambridge: Polity.

Hoover, E.M. (1937), *Location Theory and the Shoe and Leather Industries*, Harvard Economic Studies Series, vol. **55**, Cambridge, MA: Harvard University Press.

Hoover, E.M. (1948), *The Location of Economic Activity*, New York: McGraw-Hill.

Krugman, P. (1991a), *Geography and Trade*, Cambridge, MA: MIT Press.

Krugman, P. (1991b), 'Increasing returns and economic geography', *Journal of Political Economy*, **99**, 483–99.

Krugman, P. (1991c), 'History and industry location: the case of the Manufacturing Belt', *American Economic Review*, **81**, 80–83.

Lundvall, B.-Å. (ed.) (1992), *National Systems of Innovation: Towards a Theory of Innovation and Interactive Learning*, London: Pinter.

Maillat, D. (1995), 'Territorial dynamic, innovative milieus and regional policy', *Entrepreneurship and Regional Development*, **7**, 157–65.

Malmberg, A. (1996), 'Industrial geography, agglomerations and local milieu', *Progress in Human Geography*, **20** (3), 392–403.

Malmberg, A. (2003), 'Beyond the cluster. Local milieus and global connections', in J. Peck and H. Yeung (eds), *Remaking the Global Economy*, London: Sage, pp. 145–59.

Malmberg, A. and P. Maskell (2002), 'The elusive concept of localisation economies – towards a knowledge-based theory of spatial clustering', *Environment and Planning A*, **34** (3), 429–49.

Malmberg, A. and P. Maskell (2006), 'Localized learning revisited', *Growth and Change: A Journal of Urban and Regional Policy*, **37** (1), 1–18.

Malmberg, A. and P. Maskell (2009) 'An evolutionary approach to localized learning and spatial clustering', in R. Boschma and R. Martin (eds), *Handbook of Evolutionary Economic Geography*, Cheltenham, UK and Northampton, MA, USA: Edward Elgar, (in press).

Malmberg, A., Ö. Sölvell and I. Zander (1996), 'Spatial clustering, local accumulation of knowledge and firm competitiveness', *Geografiska Annaler*, **78B**, 85–97.

Marshall, A. (1890 [1916]), *Principles of Economics. An Introductory Volume*, 7th edn, London: Macmillan.

Martin, R. (2003), 'Institutional approaches in economic geography', in E. Sheppard and Barnes T.J. (eds), *A Companion to Economic Geography*, Oxford: Blackwell, pp. 77–94.

Martin, R. and P. Sunley (2003), 'Deconstructing clusters: chaotic concept or policy panacea?', *Journal of Economic Geography*, **3** (1), 5–35.

Maskell, P. and A. Malmberg (1999), 'Localised learning and industrial competitiveness', *Cambridge Journal of Economics*, **23** (2), 167–85.

Maskell, P., H. Eskelinen, I. Hannibalsson, A. Malmberg and E. Vatne (1998), *Competitiveness, Localised Learning and Regional Development. Specialisation and Prosperity in Small Open Economies*, London: Routledge.

Massey, D. (1979), 'In what sense a regional problem?', *Regional Studies*, **13**, 233–43.

Massey, D. (1984), *Spatial Division of Labour: Social Structures and the Geography of Production*, London: Macmillan.

Myrdal, G. (1957), *Economic Theory and the Underdeveloped Regions*, London: Ducksworth.

Nelson, R.R. and Winter, S.G. (1982), *An Evolutionary Theory of Economic Change*, Cambridge, MA: Belknap Press.

North, D.C. (1990), *Institutions, Institutional Change and Economic Performance*, Cambridge: Cambridge University Press.

Pierson, P. (2000), 'Increasing returns, path dependence and the study of politics', *American Political Science Review*, **94** (2), 251–67.

Porter, M.E. (1990), *The Competitive Advantage of Nations*, Basingstoke: Macmillan.

Porter, M.E. (1994), 'The role of location in competition', *Journal of the Economics of Business*, **1**, 35–9.

Porter, M.E. (1998), 'Clusters and the new economics of competition', *Harvard Business Review*, (November/December), 77–90.

Porter, M.E. (2000), 'Locations, clusters and company strategy', in G. Clark, M. Feldman and M. Gertler (eds), *The Oxford Handbook of Economic Geography*, Oxford: Oxford University Press.

Pred, A. (1966), *The Spatial Dynamics of U.S. Urban-Industrial Growth, 1800–1914. Interpretive and Theoretical Essays*, Cambridge, MA and London: Harvard University Press.

Pred, A. (1977), *City-Systems in Advanced Economies*, London: Hutchinson.

Ross, E.A. (1896), 'The location of industries', *Quarterly Journal of Economics*, **10**, 247–68.

Saxenian, A. (1994), *Regional Advantage. Culture and Competition in Silicon Valley and Route 128*, Cambridge, MA: Harvard University Press.

Schoenberger, E. (2003), 'Creating the corporate world: strategy and culture, time and space', in E. Sheppard and T.J. Barnes (eds), *A Companion to Economic Geography*, Oxford: Blackwell, pp. 377–91.

Scott, A.J. (1983), 'Industrial organisation and the logic of intra-metropolitan location – 1. Theoretical considerations', *Economic Geography*, **59**, 233–50.

Scott, A.J. (1988), *New Industrial Spaces: Flexible Production Organisation and Regional Development in North America and Western Europe*, London: Pion.

Scott, A.J. (1998), *Regions and the World Economy: The Coming Shape of Global Production, Competition, and Political Order*, Oxford: Oxford University Press.

Storper, M. (1997), *The Regional World*, New York: Guilford.

Ullman, E.L. (1958), 'Regional development and the geography of concentration', *Papers and Proceedings of the Regional Science Association*, **4**, 179–98.

Veblen, T. (1939), *The Imperial Germany and the Industrial Revolution*, London, Macmillan.

Wolfe D.A. and M.S. Gertler (2004), 'Path dependency and discontinuities in cluster formation', paper prepared for a Workshop on the Genesis of Clusters, Waxholm, Sweden, 4–5 July.

5. The deceptive juncture: the temptation of attractive explanations and the reality of political life

PerOla Öberg and Kajsa Hallberg Adu

To assert that 'history matters' is insufficient: social scientists want to know why, where, and how. (Pierson, 2000a, p. 72)

OUTLINE

The following chapter discusses path-dependence theory in relation to analysis of political processes, suggesting that path-dependence explanations are only sometimes helpful, but often overlook critical features of political life. We argue that a path-dependence approach has to take into account rational actors in a broader way, and in so doing would make a great difference. Furthermore, we discuss the nature of chance – whether it is continuous or non-continuous, exogenous or endogenous, common or rare – and propose that this part of the theory should be more elaborated. Accordingly, this has consequences for how we view one of the cornerstones of path dependence: in our view, there are good reasons to be more careful about singling out critical junctures.

We illustrate our position with three empirical cases often used in path-dependence discussions. These three cases are examples of central components of the Swedish model. Before concluding, we discuss what methods are suitable for understanding stability and change. However, before doing that, we briefly review some of the recent path-dependence studies and take a closer look at the ideas that have transitioned from economics.

POLITICS, HISTORY AND DIFFERENT PATHS

From the birth of the discipline, scholars of politics have gone back in time to be able to, with history, explain more current events. For instance Marx, Hegel, Weber, Durkheim and, later, Almond and Verba, Huntington and

Skocpol have had a historical approach to research, thus giving explanatory power to timing and historical narration is not in any way new to the field of political science. However over the past decade, economic historians and the concept of path dependence have significantly influenced political historical ventures as well as the study of development of political institutions. Sociological and demographic changes have resurfaced as explanations to political events, and the discussion of how institutions are created and sustained is yet again central. The approach, sometimes summarized as 'history matters', has been criticized for being deterministic and too general.

Stinchcombe's historical explanation model from 1968 suggests there are two types of explanations in social sciences: what causes the starting up of a tradition and what later reinforces it. Mahoney (2000) incorporates these two different social science causes in a more focused approach to path dependence than those who claim it entails 'history matters'. He suggests that a path-dependent process has a start, often called critical juncture (also called formative or unsettled moment or policy window), which is followed by a trajectory with deterministic features (Collier and Collier, 1991; Katznelson, 2003; Mahoney, 2000, pp. 511–12; for a discussion on the importance of actors in formative moments see, for example, Rothstein, 1992, p. 26n.; for a useful presentation of path-dependence concepts and their origins see Greener, 2005, pp. 63–5). The sequence of events following a contingent start or critical juncture is characterized by what the economists call 'increasing returns' or self-reinforcing processes (Arthur, 1989; Pierson, 2000c). Early developments, according to the path-dependency school can have important effects on cases that make generalizations difficult since the outcomes will vary with the settings or early developments (Hall, 2003, p. 385). Mechanisms will be structural, but outcomes will be self-reinforcing and dependent on early contingent developments (Katznelson, 2003, p. 291). Hence, the analogy of a path suggests that turning around and going back becomes more difficult with each step (Katznelson, 2003, p. 290; Thelen, 1999, p. 392).

The overall awareness of these insights has generated a spurred interest in issues of stability and change in political institutions. Under the label of 'new institutionalism', the longstanding focus on institutions in political science has been fused with the economic perspective including rational choice and game theory. The very influential political scientist Robert Putnam, in his important publication *Making Democracy Work*, built his argument around the two maxims of 'institutions shape politics' and 'institutions are shaped by history'. Putnam states: 'individuals may "choose" their institutions, but they do not choose them under circumstances of their own making, and their choices in turn influence the rules within which their successors chose' (1993, pp. 7–8). This quote summarizes well how more than a few political scientists have thought about the theoretic concept or ideal type of path dependence. Historical institutionalism is now the main approach for analysing institutions as well as one of the core political science approaches (Peters et al., 2005, p. 1276). However, the literature also shows that the path-dependence discourse has inherited some problems from its historical institutionalism roots.

First, and most important, the approach is too deterministic. When change happens it cannot be explained within path-dependence thought. The historical institutionalists' determinism can be derived from the great importance given to institutions as well as the marginal mention of political conflict (Hall and Taylor, 1998, p. 962; Peters et al., 2005, p. 1277). Second, it is methodically challenged with a constant bias in singling out cases enlightened with 'retrospective rationality' (Kay, 2005, p. 561; Mahoney, 2000, p. 527; Peters et al., 2005, p. 1277; Thelen, 2003, pp. 221–2). Only in hindsight it is possible to identify a path, hence the possible cases chosen always support the idea of a path.

However, it is not at all strange that political scientists have turned to path-dependence type of explanations in order to understand political processes. Obviously, certain politically constructed systems have qualities that seem highly stable over time. The belief is that systems are at some point contingently chosen and their impact could not be foreseen. The much applauded 'Dr. Seuss'-critique[1] towards the historical institutionalism school has influenced followers of path dependence to try to map distinct arrangements with intrinsic logics that hold for groups of cases (Goldstone, 1998, p. 832; Pierson, 2000b). Indeed, political structures like types of governing (for example, Peters and Pierre, 1998; Peters et al., 2005), political-economical systems (for example, Hall and Soskice, 2003) and welfare regimes (for example, Esping-Andersen, 1990) divide groups of nations that apparently stay on different paths over a long period of time.[2] These are important observations that have attracted particular interest from political scientists interested in continuity and change, since they call for explanations. Let us briefly sum up these observations.

Types of governing, or bureaucratic systems, seem to be distinctly separate between groups of nations, but remarkably stable within the groups. Peters (2000) describes four different administrative traditions or ideal types, linking them to path-dependent thought. The administrative traditions are described as follows:

1. Anglo-Saxon (minimal state).
2. Continental European: Germanic (organicist).
3. Continental European: French (Napoleonic).
4. Scandinavian (mixture of Anglo-Saxon and Germanic).

These distinct traditions have long historical roots and are important in order to understand differences in politics and policy. Peters himself develops a theory on how administrative reforms can be received within the different traditions. He argues that friendly traditions make success of a certain type of reform more probable. Peters groups reforms into six categories and argues which reforms are compatible with which administrative tradition. Hence, he convincingly shows that a decision that affects a country's type of governing is clearly embedded in separate administrative traditions (Peters, 2008).

Not only state structures, but also market economies can be characterized by adherence to separate groups. Students of the so-called varieties of capitalism (VoC) approach have convincingly argued for such grouping. The VoC approach, coordinated agreeably by Hall and Soskice in 2003, says there are two basic types of production models: co-ordinated market economies (CMEs) and liberal market economies (LMEs). The distinction between the two varieties of capitalism is upheld be the mechanism of institutional complementarities. Two institutions are complementary if the presence of one increases the returns from the other. The basic argument is that nations with a particular kind of institution in one sphere of the economy tend to develop complementary practices in other spheres too. Since institutional practices are not distributed randomly, there are, according to these researchers, clusters of countries that empirically converge along important dimensions. Hence, examples of CMEs are Germany, Netherlands and Sweden. Typical LMEs are the USA and the UK. The two economy types can be distinguished from one another by 'the extent to which firms rely on market mechanisms to coordinate their endeavors as opposed to forms of strategic interaction supported by non market institutions' (Hall and Soskice, 2003, p. 33). The outcomes vary between the production systems and hence the policy direction as well as the state capacity for various challenges.[3] For example, the approach predicts varying company strategies and variations in, for example, skill formation between the different market economies, which have a decisive influence on how welfare state arrangements will be designed.

Hence, the interconnection between economy and politics is evident, especially in studies of the development of welfare states. Esping-Andersen (1990) for example, opposes the division of state and market, advocating 'markets are often politically created and form an integral part of the over all welfare regime', thus he discusses 'regimes' rather than 'states' (1990, p. 4). Esping-Andersen has himself contributed with the most well-known argument that welfare states can be described using designated group-labels. He sketches three worlds of welfare capitalism, the conservative, the liberal and the social-democratic, exemplified with Germany, the USA and Sweden, and their different implications on de-commodification of labor, social stratification and employment. Departing from social rights, Esping-Andersen convincingly shows that social policy (and other institutions) created in the past has affected the labor market and the citizens' relation to the market and to other citizens and hence distinct 'worlds' or welfare trajectories. Even though Esping-Andersen himself is rather careful of forecasting, Kathleen Thelen suggests that regimes will react very differently to exogenous shocks, like changing family values (Thelen, 1999, pp. 397–8).

To conclude so far, independently of whether studies of governing structures, political-economic systems or welfare regimes explicitly adhere to path-dependence theory or not (for example, Esping-Andersen does not), there are clearly distinct paths with self-reinforcing features that call for explanations. Path-dependence theory can clearly be of help here, but some caution must be attended when we integrate a theory originally developed by (historical) economists with political science. We elaborate on this in the following section.

A REMINDER OF POLITICAL ACTORS

The economic mechanisms of self-reinforcement or positive feedback consist of high set-up costs, learning and coordination effects and adaptive expectations. High set-up costs concern any complicated system, learning effects are results of experience and could concern adjustment because of pricing mechanisms. Coordination effects arise from cooperating with others leading to higher efficiency (Pierson, 2005, p. 26). These mechanisms in turn produce stronger reasons for sticking with the system due to the high costs of changing, and the path is well under way. In economics, self-reinforcing processes are also an explanation as to why sometimes less efficient options are persistent.[4]

The core of the path-dependence argument is indisputably shared between economic historians and scholars of politics, namely, that institutions (standards, norms, rules, and so on) are seen as enduring entities that cannot be changed quickly (see, for example, Kay, 2005, p. 555; Mahoney, 2000, p. 512; North, 1991, p. 97). The economists' way of thinking in aspects of settings with particular institutional rules producing certain 'strategies and outcomes' have also been valuable contributions (Skocpol, 1995, p. 106). Even if most social scientists agree that it has been fruitful to apply the concept to political science, some scholars stress there are differences between the market and the political arena that need to be considered (Kay, 2005, p. 569; Pierson, 2005, p. 30; Thelen, 1999, p. 400;

2003, p. 234; 2004, p. 31). A few of those arguments are presented in brief below.

Important concerns in the literature on differences between economic markets and political arenas are predominantly occupied with politics being 'messier' or more complex compared to the market, and therefore the theory does not easily translate between the two spheres; more specifically, how the different settings influence the way mechanisms operate and the behavior of the actors.

The complexity of politics possibly affects self-reinforcing mechanisms such as learning and competition, making them less effective (Bennet and Elman, 2006, p. 256; Mahoney, 2000, pp. 508–9; Pierson, 2005, p. 129). Bennet, Elman and Mahoney conceptualize the complexity on politics as complementary mechanisms. Apart from positive feedback proposed by economists, they also introduce negative feedback, reactive sequences as well as cyclical processes (Bennet and Elman, 2006, pp. 256–9; Mahoney, 2000, pp. 509, 530–31). Mahoney focuses on the reactive sequences and explains that they do not just reinforce an earlier decision like positive feedback; instead the reactive sequence sets 'in motion a chain of tightly linked reactions and counteractions' that can even reverse early events (2000, pp. 526–7). These additions shed light on the imperfect relationship between actions and outcomes in politics, and hence the vagueness of political efficiency. Similarly, Kay suggests there are 'policy specific' path-dependent mechanisms that do not apply to the market. He claims they are policy distinctive since they are based on 'definite, conscious choices'. Also they are not self-reinforcing. The non-increasing returns include: positive or constraining effects by policies adopted on groups, transformations on government capacity due to implementation of policy, and the introduction of formal and informal contracts with citizens which are expensive to break up (Key, 2005, p. 563). Again, the claim is that the concept of path dependence exhibits unique mechanisms when changing the economic setting for a political one. However, Key takes a different approach by stressing that policy preferences are not contingent, but 'conscious choices'.

While some political scientists claim economic mechanisms are not as effective in politics, others quite surprisingly advocate the opposite. The consequence being that path dependence might be both more prevalent and prevailing in politics. Political scientist Paul Pierson suggests the economic positive feedback mechanisms might even be stronger in politics where the compulsory – rather than the voluntary – nature of events is in effect due to the legally binding laws that are the center of the political sphere (Pierson, 2005, p. 31ff). Pierson summarizes his argument in four points: first, in politics there is collective activity – political arenas are not as fluid and flexible as economic markets; therefore a lock-in is embedded (ibid., p. 33). Second, Pierson stresses the role of formal institutions, which in politics narrow the choices by law, not just by practice (ibid., p. 34). Third, political authority and power asymmetries or even power cleavages may be enforced over time since self-reinforcing mechanisms tend to strengthen certain actors and paradoxically, suggests Pierson, make power asymmetries less visible since open conflict is minimized in very polarized situations – or not needed if power distribution is highly unequal (ibid., p. 36). Finally, ambiguity on processes and outcomes – when in the market, firms seek to maximize profits and workers and consumers are reasonably well informed on wages and prices, however, in politics, the relationship between choices and outcomes is less clear. Therefore, argues Pierson, reliance is high on 'mental maps' which are self-reinforcing (ibid., p. 37). Pierson borrows from sociology in his fourth argument for strong self-reinforcing processes in politics, and thereby uses the same base as the scholars above (complexity of politics) to arrive at a different conclusion!

Additionally, there are many arguments that actors behave differently in politics, compared with the market. Actors' preferences are not acted out in the same way in the market compared with in politics. Political actors form alliances more often than not, and cannot always act out their preference. This is why the 'losers' of one game (or election) do not perish like 'losers' do in the market – in other words, processes in the periphery have greater impact in politics than in economics (Thelen, 2004, p. 296). Political actors often both negotiate and struggle for outcomes.

In the historical institutional context political actors' room to maneuver has been deferred in time (to critical junctures) and in organizational space (in already existing institutions). The unsuccessful view on actors and political struggle is summarized by historical institutionalist Skocpol: 'I am primarily interested in studying political processes and outcomes, and I see as brought about, usually without intentional foresight and control, by actors whose goals and capacities and conflicts with one another are grounded in institutions' (1995, p. 105). If historical institutionalists display little interest for actors, new institutionalists acknowledge strategic political actors but downplay their ability and preference for conscious choice leading to change. For instance Thelen proposes that time horizons are short for political actors (mainly due to elections) and therefore they are likely to support the trodden trail. Also, switching costs to a different path would be due short term, and payoffs would likely come later and are therefore less probable, argues Thelen. Consequentially, there is a bias towards the status quo, since politicians tend to bind themselves and secure the policies they have created (Thelen, 1999).

However, we claim, as others have done before us (for example,

Campell, 1997; Magnusson and Ottosson, 1997, p. 5; Ottosson, 1997), that downplaying actors' room to maneuver might be a mistake and hence, we explore a rather common and more compelling approach based on bounded rationality. For this reason, we find it fruitful to integrate a rational choice perspective into studies of historical political processes. Jon Elster accurately describes our position in a 'deceptively simple sentence': 'When faced with several courses of action, people usually do what they believe to have the best overall outcome' (Elster, 1989, p. 22). Despite its brevity, the formulation is loaded with complexity (Elster, 1985, pp. 5–8, 29). Rational actors are often misinformed and make wrong decisions, they are only 'doing the best that is humanly possible, in the multiply constrained situation that constitutes the human condition' (Goodin, 1999, p. 68). Hence, rational choice is 'not an infallible mechanism, since the rational person can choose only what he *believes* to be the best means' (Elster, 1989, p. 25; original emphasis). Our understanding of rationality is in line with the work of scholars who have been willing to relax some assumptions of the theory (Thelen and Steinmo, 1992, p. 31). This wide conception of rationality is more fruitful theoretically since it allows for other than only egoistic preferences and does not assume that subjects are fully informed (cf. Opp, 1999, p. 175).

While researchers with a non-rational perspective try to convince us that rationality is an exception and non-rationality the rule (March and Olsen, 1989, p. 25), we think it is the other way around. It is probably true that 'most of us, most of the time, follow societally defined rules' (Thelen and Steinmo, 1992, p. 8); that is in everyday life. But we argue that there are good reasons to believe that centrally positioned politicians normally act very rationally when it comes to important decisions. They make very elaborate calculations before acting. Often, quite a few persons are working full-time for a long period of time to find out alternatives and calculate different outcomes. Reality does in some cases resemble the ideal type of 'political man' more than was ever imagined. Furthermore, it is true that ordinary people often 'justify action by logic of consequentiality' (March and Olsen, 1989, p. 162), but there is also ample evidence to suggest that elite political actors are much more rational than they are willing to admit (Johansson, 2000; Svensson, 1994). Although it is 'appropriate' to be rational, no politician wants to be described as being strategic to the point of being cynical. Hence, we have to be just as critical to sources that say that they have *not* been acting rationally, as we usually are when they say that they have.

Moreover, students of politics have to take into account that our research objects, the political actors, are versatile, adaptable and autonomous. This might, in the extreme case, be when our research objects in fact read or listen to presentations of research about themselves and learn from it. An interesting example is a presentation that political scientist Bo Rothstein held in front of the board of the Swedish employers' confederation on his findings about the very stabile corporatism in Sweden, which in fact – in itself – contributed to the important changes in the trajectory of corporatism a few years later (Rothstein, 1992, p. 350 'epilog'; Rothstein and Bergström, 1999, p. 34; cf. Johansson, 2000, p. 178 n. 496).

Taking all this into account, what might look like pure institutional stability with actors following standard operating procedures within a path may, rather, be the result of successful rational (strategic) action from either insiders or even outsiders, winners as well as initial losers. What might look like a critical juncture that suddenly occurs, may very well be the result of a long-range rational struggle to *create* such a critical juncture. Hence, a process of change may resemble a temporarily open window of opportunity, although the strategic actors themselves through a rational process may have opened it up.

QUESTIONING THE CRITICAL JUNCTURE

When studying institutional change the time horizon of causes and outcomes can be long or short. The causal processes of interest often vary greatly in the time they take to develop. Pierson (2003) argues that social science focuses too much on quick/quick cases, where both the cause and the outcome of a process arrive over a very short period of time. The prevalence of quick/quick case studies is a function of what is the easiest type of study to perform, claims Pierson. It is difficult and costly to aggregate processes and watch them unfold over time. In a case where a country is democratizing, for instance, it is easier to focus on the last 'threshold' of the process, maybe the situation around the founding election, than to overlook the whole development. However, Pierson argues, most political events are probably not quick/quick cases that evolve and reach an outcome very fast. More likely, these processes are often quick/slow, slow/quick and slow/slow in cause and effect. Also, both the periodization of cause and of outcome must be considered when setting a time frame for the study. Figure 5.1 visualizes Pierson's argument.

When a social science phenomenon is studied over a longer period of time it can be shown that threshold effects, cumulative effects or cumulative causes are the background to the event described, argues Pierson. The main reason why time should be a key factor in social science analysis is that causation might be mistaken when focusing the study at a very short period of time. In line with this argument, Peters et al. suggest that the

		Time horizon of outcome	
		Short	Long
Time horizon of cause	Short	I	II
	Long	III	IV

Source: Pierson (2003, p. 179).

Figure 5.1 The time horizons of different causal accounts

path-dependence idea is often supported on false premises since actual instability is overlooked when the changeable politics is separated from the more, over time, stable policy and hence an explanatory factor is ruled out (2005, p. 1277). Also, triggering effects might be given too much attention as a consequence.

Pierson's cumulative, threshold and causal chain models resemble the slow/fast aspect of change, however, they also provide another dimension; they explain the closeness between events (cause and outcome/outcomes) or the clustering of events. The cumulative model suggests change occurs continuously, because the cause of change is replacement (Pierson, 2003, p. 189ff). Threshold change is signified by major, sudden shifts. This is explained in the threshold model by that cumulative effects are small until they reach a critical level. Revolutions are the typical example, where tensions build up over time until they reach a critical level and the revolution is a fact (ibid., p. 186). Causal chains are 'a sequence of key developments over extended periods of time'. This is a model that tries to explain complex correlations over often long stretches of time, involving multiple causes as well as multiple consequences (ibid., p. 187f).[5] Thus, Pierson supports the theoretical advantages of describing change in 'critical junctures' and gives examples of when these junctures take place long before an outcome arguing that the causal effect is still there after a temporal separation (ibid., p. 197f).

Another viewpoint is that political change is fast and cultural change is slow. Both politics and culture create institutions, furthermore; institutions could be viewed as interaction of cultural and political institutions (Roland, 2004, p. 128). The influence of anthropology, cognitive psychology and sociology has suggested that institutional preferences are created in the defining of boundaries of diverse cultural groups. Katznelson proposes these approaches 'can help clarify when and how agency operates not quite on its own making, and how the pursuit of preferences underpins continuity without closing off prospects for new moments of large-scale change' (2003, p. 294). However, again it is unclear when change should be expected and exactly how agency 'operates not quite on its own making'. The big and slow moving changes – to use Pierson's description – can obviously be combined with the recognition of critical junctures or change points, but the theoretical advantages of creating such a clear distinction between slow, cultural change and sudden, political change has not yet convinced.

Building on this dilemma, the general theory of today is focused more on change than stability. 'Despite the importance assigned by many scholars to the role of institutions in structuring the political life, the issue of how these institutions are themselves shaped and reconfigured over time has not received the attention it is due', Kathleen Thelen points out in her article on how institutions *evolve* (Thelen, 2003, p. 208; also 2004, pp. 292–6). Thelen supports the idea that political institutions are enforced over time, but according to her it is not because of self-reinforcing mechanisms but, rather, because once an institution is in place there is an overall bias for the status quo in politics. The reason, according to Thelen, is the political actors operate with a different strategy from the economic actors. Thelen focuses her argument on strategic political actors, but claims that – which has been earlier criticized – political actors are short-sighted and want to minimize transaction costs and hence prefer the status quo (Peters et al., 2005, p. 1285; Thelen, 1999). However, even if Thelen's view on stability differs from ours, she has successfully reopened the debate on path-dependence theorizing and its strict separation of issues of institutional innovation and institutional reproduction (Thelen, 1999; 2004, pp. 23–31). Accounts have often been based on a punctuated equilibrium model, emphasizing that change comes about in situations of momentary openness created by some exogenous shock. Only in these moments are agency and choice important. Such moments of change are followed by long periods of institutional stability when strategy and choice is less important than processes of adoption of institutional incentives and constraints. According to many researchers, employing path-dependence ideas, periods of institutional reproduction persist until another exogenous shock opens up for change (Thelen, 2003, p. 212). However, Thelen argues that institutions experience conversion, rather than 'breakdowns'. The latter, she claims, is empirically very unusual (ibid., p. 220f). The current institutionalism acknowledges institutions as stable entities, however, suggesting that they at the same time are subject to constant change (Thelen, 2003, pp. 218–20; 2004, p. 31). In that sense, historical institutionalism has fully merged with the path-dependence perspective, and most historical institutionalists today use the concept (although in various ways).

Here advancing further than Pierson, Thelen advocates strongly the continuous change approach and therefore is critical towards the path-dependence school and its 'choice points' or critical junctures (cf. Magnusson and Ottosson, 1997, p. 4 and the discussion on adaptation and learning). Thelen proposes that choice points add very little explanatory power and that the broad definition of path dependency can be used only to *ex post* explain that a trajectory was followed. By introducing a more specific agenda, Thelen poses questions such as 'what aspects of institutions are renegotiable?' and 'under what conditions?' The key is to distinguish between what constitutes stability and what creates change (Thelen, 2003, pp. 221–2).[6]

Hence, we agree with Thelen that analysis of institutional innovation and reproduction 'could be brought to a more sustained dialogue' (Thelen, 2003, p. 209). She supports her critique with examples of exogenous shocks that one would expect to induce change but have had very little effect, and institutional arrangements that have persisted over a long period of time but have gone through ongoing subtle changes (Thelen, 2003, p. 210).

From the perspective of a punctuated equilibrium model, there often seems to be too much continuity through breakpoints in history, but also too much change beneath the surface of apparently stable formal institutional arrangements (Thelen, 2003, p. 211).

As we too have suggested in the first section of this chapter, Thelen argues that critical junctures and development pathways capture something important about institutional development over long stretches of time. However, she also claims, that 'at the highly aggregated level at which they are often invoked, these concepts also sometimes obscure some of the most interesting questions of all, regarding surprising institutional continuities through apparent break-points, as well as "subterranean" but highly significant changes in periods of apparent institutional stability' (Thelen, 2003, p. 233). By obscuring the interesting mechanisms of change with the simple label of a critical juncture, political scientists unfortunately move away from robust explanations. As alarming is that the idea of choice periods hide 'significant changes' during its antithesis, periods that are labeled stable.

Thelen's conclusion is that it may not be so useful to think of institutional development in terms of a sharp dichotomy between periods of institutional innovation and change (2003, p. 233). This is a flaw imported from studies of economics: 'Models of path dependence appropriated from economies tend to focus on single process in isolation, bringing history in only at bookends – at the critical juncture moment and then again at the end of a reproduction sequence' (2003, p. 234). We agree that this is a very important argument. Hence, if we want to understand institutional evolution, we have to accept that it is not that easy to distinguish stability from change. We cannot presuppose that it is possible to find a clearly defined breaking point, which 'explains' the subsequent development. Unfortunately, this means that we defuse one of the analytically strongest parts of a path-dependence explanation, the critical junctures. However, this does not exclude the insight that once a path is taken 'once-viable alternatives become increasingly remote' (Thelen, 2003, p. 219). But we would like to express a fair warning; critical junctures are attractive explanations, but because of that also deceptive when we want to understand the reality of political life.

In conclusion, we argue that path-dependency explanations may be very useful in political science. However, the path-dependency perspective has to be developed in order to capture the essence of politics, which is a continuous struggle between contending interests. We have to bring actors back in. Political life consists of organized and less organized actors that make decisions, often based on a continuous analysis of the current situation, and with a long- or short-term aim to secure or strengthen their position. Any perspectives that ignore this, at least as a possibility, run the risk of missing the essential part of social science explanation. Furthermore, in line with Thelen's (2003) argument, since politics is a continuous struggle between contending interests, it is difficult to discern stability from change. Change as a consequence of constant renegotiation, is sometimes a prerequisite for stability.

We illustrate our points concerning some problems with the approach using empirical studies of Swedish political history related to what sometimes is called the Swedish model. We will not engage ourselves in the rather futile discussion about what that model really is (Cox, 2004, p. 215). Rather, we focus on a central theme in path-dependency studies: the persistence and change of welfare systems. Diverse historical processes are supposed to have created ideal-typical welfare regimes (Esping-Andersen, 1990), which are more or less intact because of stabile power resources (Korpi, 1989; 2006), cross-class alliances (Luebbert, 1991; Swenson, 2004) or other self-reinforcing patterns of 'locking-in' processes (Pierson, 1996). The work on welfare systems has presented many insights into and explanations of developments of such states and emphasizes the interrelatedness of state and market; in Thelen's words placing 'political and economic development in a historical context and in terms of processes unfolding over time and in relation to one another' (1999, p. 390). Distinct trajectories of regimes, capitalisms or production models inclusive of firm behavior and administrative traditions have been discovered. By using writings on the Swedish welfare system or the Swedish model we can illustrate our arguments. We focus on three rather distinctive traits of

Swedish politics in the 1900s: its comprehensive welfare state, the extensive integration of interest groups into public policy and the very coordinated wage-bargaining system.

REVISITING PATHS OF THE SWEDISH MODEL

The Social Democratic Party and the Welfare State

The Swedish welfare state is often taken as an example of a very persistent system. Historians have pointed out that some prerequisites for the welfare state were established in the eighteenth and very early nineteenth centuries (Mörner, 1989). However, it is more reasonable to argue that the underlying principles of the welfare state – universalism and uniform social benefits based on financing through taxes – was established in relation to the pension reform in 1913. The reform was mostly backed up by liberals but, after an internal strife, also by the Social Democrats (Svensson, 1994, p. 194). These principles were further established in the 1920s and 1930s, when a number of social reforms – considered very important by contemporary politicians in charge (Möller, 1946; Svensson, 1994) although less so by some scholars today (Swenson, 2004, p. 1) – were implemented. During the heydays of Social Democracy in the 1940s through the 1960s, the most ambitious welfare projects were launched, and the ideological foundation of the 'Swedish model' became what it – if only on a rhetorical level (Cox, 2004) – still is. Consequently, researchers agree that the Swedish welfare state (like many other welfare states) has appeared astonishingly persistent over the years, at least until the 1990s. However, the development after the 1990s is contested, partly depending on different definitions of the model (Bergh, 2004; Cox, 2004). Some scholars argue that important changes have indeed taken place (Blomqvist, 2004; Clayton and Pontusson, 1998). While others, although admitting that changes have occurred, still state that the model's 'defining characteristics' have remained astonishingly persistent over the years (Bergh, 2004; Lindbom, 2001; Rothstein, 2002), and that the Swedish Social Democratic model still 'continues to set a standard for public generosity in the OECD' (Brooks and Manza, 2006, p. 916). In any case, during most of the 1900s, the Swedish welfare state seems to be a prime example of path dependence.

There are, of course, many causes for this stability, but we argue it would be a mistake to describe the development of a welfare state as a self-propelled organism, that developed itself without nursing from those who cared for it. The Swedish political scientist Torsten Svensson convincingly shows this in his detailed study on Social Democratic Party strategy during the mid-1900s (Svensson, 1994). Svensson's aim is to explain the Social Democratic dominance in Sweden that was prolonged for an essential part of the 1900s in spite of a crumbling core electorate – blue-collar workers. While others have described the dominance as more or less occurring by pure chance, he shows that it can be explained by a carefully designed strategy by the leading Social Democrats at the time. At centre stage was the design of the welfare state. Svensson shows how the inner circle of the party very early on, almost by scientific means, ana-lysed the situation. Around 1920, it was clear to important persons in the party that the electoral base was diminishing, and they were considering alternative choices, especially possible alliance partners. As a consequence of this process, it was decided that the long-term goals were not going to be accomplished together with farmers, and that parts of the middle-class, that is, salaried employees, were a better choice (Svensson, 1994, p. 310).

Based on secret internal material, Torsten Svensson shows how the party leaders, after having assessed the situation, defined the long-term goal and chosen the means that the party leaders considered best adapted to this purpose, launched a number of projects in order to implement the strategic decisions taken.

An effort to widen the electoral base is a strategy full of risks, which the party leaders were aware of. While the situation with a marginalized com-munist party is sometimes considered a structural prerequisite for Social Democratic dominance in Sweden, it was in fact a consequence of the party's strategic action. The efforts

> were manifested in a systematic mobilization of Social Democrats at the union elections, the creation of Social Democratic cells within the unions, hiring (in the party and in the LO [Landsorganisationen i Sverige – the Swedish Trade Union Confederation]) of secretaries dedicated to battle with the Communists, massive propaganda and, from the second world war, a systematic registration of Communist union members. With this work the Social Democratic Party managed to influence its own possibilities of choice. (Svensson, 1994, pp. 309, 64–75)

However, securing the left flank was not enough, of course. It was impor-tant also to fight the Conservatives and the liberals for the votes of the salaried employees. In order to analyse choices and means, a special inter-nal party committee was appointed. An organization with direct access to the party chairman (Tage Erlander) was established in order to keep the leadership informed of white-collar views and reaction to different proposals. This information was also used in an astute strategy to present information adjusted to the respective groups addressed (Svensson, 1994, pp. 103–9).

This new wage-earners strategy (in contrast to a workers strategy) was also very important for welfare politics. The most obvious example is how propositions that led to the important decision on the Supplementary Pension Reform (1959) were designed in line with the long-term strategy. After tough internal fighting (partly with the blue-collar union), but also after a lot of elaborate calculations on different outcomes, this and other important welfare reforms were deliberately shaped to establish the cross-class alliance with salaried employees:

> But the new policies were adjusted to the interest of wage-earners and consumers. The policy against unemployment was in the interest of both workers and salaried employees. Instead of flat-rate formulas for pensions and comparable benefits, the principle of earnings-related benefits was introduced. The old understanding of equality was replaced by new visions, emphasizing social security. (Svensson, 1994, p. 310)

Furthermore, Svensson shows that the strategic action also mattered. As a consequence of carefully prepared propositions, salaried employees became as positive towards Social Democratic reforms as workers, which lay the foundation for electoral success (Svensson, 1994, chs 5–7).

As Blomkvist and others have argued, this kind of politically strategic action from the Social Democrats was essential to the stability of the Swedish welfare state in the years to come. Only by elaborating the universal system could broad public support for it be maintained: 'The overwhelmingly public character that the welfare sector assumed in Sweden after the 1950s cannot . . . be attributed solely to historical circumstance. It is also the result of conscious political choices by reformist Social Democratic party . . .' (Blomqvist, 2004, p. 143). Hence, the Swedish welfare state has appeared strikingly stable over a long period of time, indicating path dependency. But the reason for the persistence of the system is not that it could not be changed for some technical reason, or that it was never questioned in a Social Democratic hegemonic environment of consensus. Even the balance of power was not clear enough to guarantee continuance. Instead, a very important part of the explanation for the stability was that some politicians acted remarkably astutely to keep, but also to develop, the system. If they were on a path, they had to fight vigorously and cleverly to stay on it.

The Employers' Confederation and Corporatist Governance

A comprehensive formal involvement of interest groups into public policy-making is another characteristic trait of the Swedish model. Formal representation in the workings of government agencies, for example, membership in agency executive boards, has been one of the most important incorporations of interest groups into public policy-making (Lewin, 1994, p. 70). This kind of 'administrative corporatism' has been a significant part of the Swedish model since the early 1900s (Öberg, 2002; Rothstein, 1992). The first government proposal to establish a corporative institution was put forward in a Conservative bill for workers' occupational accident insurance in 1902. Other important decisions were the approval of Parliament for government grants to the corporatist local labor exchange system in 1906, and the decision to admit leading persons from the Employers' Confederation and the Confederation of Trade Unions to participate in major decisions in the board of the newly established National Board for Social Affairs in 1912 (Rothstein, 1991, pp. 157–66). The Swedish social scientist Bo Rothstein has argued, from a path-dependency inspired approach, that a decision in 1932 when the dominating farmers' organization was given privileges that put the organization in a position to control the dairy products market was a 'formative moment' (Rothstein, 1992, ch. 6). However, taking his other publications into account, there seems to have been a continuous chain of formative movements. Besides the early decisions described above, which Rothstein has denominated 'the roots of corporatism' (Rothstein, 1988), the important restructuring of the labor market administration in the years following the Second World War seems just as important (Rothstein, 1996).

Over the decades to come, corporatism was institutionalized in the Swedish state (Rothstein, 1991, p. 163). Especially from the mid-1930s and until the 1970s, organizations were constantly drawn into public affairs (Hermansson, 1993; Lewin, 1994). Following an animated discussion in the 1970s, administrative corporatism decreased, but was still alive and kicking in the late 1980s (Hermansson et al., 1999, p. 37). However, in 1991, the Confederation of Employers decided to unilaterally withdraw its representatives from government agency boards. This functioned as the basis for a parliamentary decision in 1992, when all interest group representation in government agency boards – at least formally – came to an end (Johansson, 2005). Hence, administrative corporatism, also, seems to be a prime example of path dependency, with a typical critical juncture that changed the path in the 1990s.

How should we understand the apparent critical juncture in the 1990s? It has been argued that the organized employers reacted to 'a course of events beyond its control' (Rothstein and Bergström, 1999, p. 46). The political scientist Joakim Johansson, on the other hand, uses unofficial material in order to investigate whether the Swedish Employers' Confederation (SAF) decided to withdraw its representatives in government agencies, as part of a long-term plan with the objective to change 'fundamental rules defining the conditions for the participation of labour market parties in labour market policy processes, and to strengthen the influence of SAF in relation to that of the trade union organisations' (Johansson, 2005, p. 80). Johansson credibly exposes that the employers' decision was taken after an almost 20 year-long deliberation, a process that makes what is sometimes called a straw man of rational man to come alive (Johansson, 2000; 2005).

By the late 1970s, key persons in the employers' confederation were dissatisfied with the balance of power between employers and trade unions. The unions were in a position to set the agenda, so it was important to tip the balance back to the advantage of employers. Administrative corporatism was identified as the main problem, since the working-class movement was benefiting from it more than the employers (Johansson, 2000, pp. 82–9). The alliances between union representatives, agency officials and the Social Democratic government, were seen as having the 'agenda-setting privilege'. Of course, the SAF wanted to break this privilege but such an effort was seriously impeded by the SAF's very presence on the boards. Centrally positioned actors in the SAF argued that a more offensive SAF strategy was needed but it was: 'Difficult to reconcile with traditional participation in government agencies, in which all important issues are managed according to the agenda and needs of the government agencies' (Redbrandt, cited by Johansson, 2005, p. 89).

The decision to restructure this important part of the Swedish model would not have been much of a rational plan, if the actors had not considered the consequences and other actor's potential countermoves. In order to really tip the balance of power, the SAF needed to use its resources in other, more efficient, ways. This was also clearly spelled out in internal strategy plans. The SAF should focus more on lobbying and public opinion-making, which was perceived to offer the organization the greatest influence on policy-making: 'Informal contacts between SAF and the government agencies are to be increased. Initiatives are to be taken by SAF. This holds for the managerial level as well as for the relationship between SAF experts and the government agencies' (Redbrandt, cited in Johansson, 2005, p. 89).

However, an open strategy for acquisition of power would of course alert all other parties concerned, which a rational actor is aware of. First, it was important to 'Keep a low profile'. Reluctance to reveal the plan in public was characteristic especially for the most active employees in the secretariat of the SAF. They even wrote a memorandum with the intriguing headline: 'Emergency plan in case of leakages' (*Beredskapsplan för läckor*). It was stated in the memorandum that the organization should be ready to handle a potential situation where they had to inform the public about the SAF's intentions:

> *Our image outwards* had better be to talk about a considerable change in the SAF's working methods, 'a modern SAF'. However, we ought not to let ourselves be provoked to polemicize against malicious contributions or discuss SAMPOL [an internal committee where strategies concerning administrative corporatism were discussed] in *terms of power*. (Cited in Johansson, 2000, p. 183, our translation; Johansson's emphases).

The effects of a unilateral withdrawal, which was also dependent on choices made by others, were of course important. Early in the process, careful steps were taken and could be 'adjusted in relation to choices made by other interest organizations' (Johansson, 2000, p. 111). Eventually, after considerable internal deliberation, persons with top positions in the SAF were convinced that a unilateral withdrawal would be troublesome as far as the legitimacy of other parties was concerned, including the legitimacy of representation for the trade unions. In a conference in 1989, an influential person stated: 'If SAF decided to leave the National Labour Market Board (AMS) today, the construction of AMS would collapse like a house of cards. It is built on party representation . . . [T]he whole construction would go to rack and ruin' (Jan-Erik Larsson, cited in Johansson, 2005, p. 93).

Based on a solid base of evidence, Joakim Johansson concludes that there 'existed a long-term and well-planned power-political design, a relatively sophisticated strategy, behind the withdrawal of SAF' (Johansson, 2005, p. 96). Although the SAF may not have accomplished all of their aims (yet), they certainly managed to create and use what at first looks like an 'ideal-type' critical juncture. But notice, that it, of course, was important for the organization to make it look like one. Part of the strategy was to give the impression of an exogenous shock that not only made it possible, but even necessary, to change the system: in internal strategy memorandums they encouraged personnel in the organization to stimulate the debate from the 'West European perspective', that is, give the impression that an irresistible process of change was going on outside Sweden that the country had to adjust to (Johansson, 2000, p. 184).

Hence, it is possible to find critical junctures in the development of Swedish corporatism. As a matter of fact, we can find several if that is what we are looking for. But too many junctures makes each of them less critical. Furthermore, from this case we must learn that what might be considered a juncture may be intentionally created by rational actors. Consequently, actors were not at all dependent on the path, and did not have to wait for an external shock to change fundamental rules. Moreover, although the decision to de-corporatize government agencies was important, it did not have the immediate effects that some expected. A lot of interest groups were still represented in government agencies 15 years later, although sometimes informally. Even today, the SAF's successor, Swedish Enterprise, is represented in a few agencies (Hallberg, 2006; Hermansson et al., 1999, ch. 2; Svensson and Öberg, 2003). Hence, once again, it is difficult to discern stability from change.

Unions, Employers, and the Wage-Bargaining System

Aside from Social Democratic dominance in combination with the generous welfare state, and the comprehensive administrative corporatism, the centralized wage-bargaining system has drawn the attention of international scholars to Swedish politics. This is yet another example of what might be described as a path-dependent institution that has quite recently changed through a critical juncture.

The first central agreement between the LO and the SAF was concluded in 1952. However, this was not a sudden window of opportunity, but something that better may be described as a key event in a long process. The process began in the 1930s (Alexopoulos and Cohen, 2003, p. 332), or at least in 1947/48 when the SAF started internal discussions about the strategy of the organization. Affiliated organizations were reluctant to accept centralization, but key persons agreed that centralization would make it possible to continue to 'maintain the interest of employers in a period of enterprise expansion and strong state' (De Geer, 1986, p. 87). Although the trade union was also in favour of centralized bargaining, it was the employers that took the most active part. The Employers' Confederation had strong economic motives: centralized bargaining avoided competition among the employers themselves, which cushioned inflationary effects of competitive sectoral pay increases (De Geer, 1986; Törnqvist, 1999; cf. Alexopoulos and Cohen, 2003, p. 336 who argue that the SAF also was hoping to relieve labor shortages).

Although the central agreement in 1956 was the first in an unbroken series which lasted more than 30 years (Törnqvist, 1999, p. 74), there was a lot of questioning and renegotiation during the whole period (for example, De Geer, 1986, pp. 87–93).

In 1990, the Swedish employers' confederation made it clear that the organization would no longer take part in centralized collective bargaining, a decision that 'could be viewed as the death of the Swedish model of industrial relations' (Törnqvist, 1999, p. 71). This event may be perceived as a typical case of a critical juncture. It was a major change at a specific moment of time, and influential scholars have argued that it was due to an exogenous pressure. The employers' change of policy is typically explained by the need for new production strategies, especially evident for employers in engineering industries: a more flexible and diversified production required more wage flexibility, and centralized bargaining was perceived as an impediment to achieve that (Pontusson and Swenson, 1996; other exogenous explanations are discussed in Alexopoulos and Cohen, 2003, pp. 335, 354–6).

Although path dependence with a critical juncture is a plausible explanation here, we argue, in relation to this case, that there are firm reasons to question it. First, 'the juncture' was the end of a long process with continuous renegotiations. Second, the exogenous push explanation is at best incomplete, therefore, it is questionable whether this should be considered a juncture at all.

As we have already emphasized, the period that on the surface looks stable, was in fact a period of ongoing internal struggle within both the employers' confederation and the trade union movement. A complete central agreement was reached in 1956 and the first signals to change were registered in the late 1960s (Traxler et al., 2001, p. 156).

When it comes to explaining the decision by the employers in 1990, we should remind ourselves of Thelen's persuasive argument that it is a mistake to assume that an institution's origin, maintenance and dissolution all have the same explanation. We have to take research beyond such 'constant/cause explanations' (Thelen, 2003, p. 214). Hence, it is *not* credible to argue, as economists in essence usually do, that 'any explanation of centralised bargaining in Sweden must also be able to explain its demise' (Alexopoulos and Cohen, 2003, p. 354).

Furthermore, explanation put forward especially by Jonas Pontusson and Peter Swenson is important, however – as in the case of dismantling of administrative corporatism – it is also important to notice that this is the argument that the SAF itself gave for decentralization (Törnqvist, 1999, p. 71). Hence, it relates to the 'West European perspective' put forward in the decision to leave agency boards, and was intended to make it seem the only possible choice of action. However, historian Christer Törnqvist, who has studied the process in detail, argues that ideological motives, linked to a shifting balance of power, were just as important. The reason was that many employers – erroneously – thought that their managerial rights settled in earlier agreements were threatened (Törnqvist, 1999, p. 78). Changes in some labor market laws spurred the SAF 'to develop a strategy for future victories . . . [and] therefore started an ideological offensive without precedent' (Törnqvist, 1999, p. 80). Törnqvist argues convincingly for the 'primacy of the politico-ideological rational':

> we can conclude that decentralization threatens to weaken LO's position . . . It is in this light that we must understand SAF's active propaganda role: to a great extent, its deep involvement in political campaigns from the mid 1970s paved

the way for changes in industrial relations. SAF abandoned the centralized system only when it no longer appeared politically advantageous. (Törnqvist, 1999, p. 82)

We also question how critical this juncture really was. It is true that this was an important event in Swedish industrial relations, but is it the major change that some have argued? Is it really the end of the Swedish model of industrial relations?

When the SAF announced its decision to withdraw from centralized negotiations, the Social Democratic government immediately appointed an expert group that carried through a successful stabilization drive that took the form of a pattern agreement 1991–93. In 1993, they managed to set the terms for an agreement that were followed by all parties in the following sectoral negotiations (Elvander, 2002, p. 199). They were less successful in 1995, however. The government tried to make the peak organizations come to an agreement on mediation, but they were reluctant. Instead, a 'new Swedish regime for collective bargaining and conflict resolution' was settled after the introduction of the industrial agreement in 1997 and its equivalence in the public sector in 2000 (Elvander, 2002). It is true that wage coordination had indeed been in 'rapid and subsequent decline in Sweden, from the break down of centralization in 1982 to the establishment of the Industrial Agreement in 1997' (Lindgren, 2006, p. 53). However, the agreements marked a situation where wage-bargaining was decentralized, but not to the extent some employers had hoped for. The important negotiations were still held on a national level, but within different sectors of the economy. Nils Elvander has argued that the parties of the Industrial Agreement have 'to a large extent created a functional equivalent to the centralization through SAF and LO' (Elvander, 2002, p. 214).

In most literature on wage-bargaining, Sweden stands out as the prime example of change from centralized to decentralized negotiations. However, a less noted trend back towards more coordinated negotiations started early in the 2000s. The LO's representative assembly decided on recommendations to the unions with joint demands in October 2000; a norm of what is 'fair wage increases [*rätt löneökning*] in the total economy, would shrink the space for short-sighted demands that are good for one group, but harmful to everyone' (LO's Representantskap, 2000). In October 2002, the Trade Union Confederation launched an intensive internal campaign – Coordination for solidarity (*Samordning för solidaritet*). Four staff from the central secretariat were responsible for initiating internal deliberation about guiding principles for coordinated negotiations. The aim was to have all the affiliated unions within the confederation agree on joint wage demands in coordinated negotiations with employers in the round of wage negotiations in 2004 (LO, 2003a). In a brochure from the project, LO stated: 'Currently, the understanding of the need to coordinate and collaborate grows stronger among both unions and employers. The 1990s are over. *Things have turned around*' (LO, 2003b, p. 4, our translation; original emphasis). The reason given was that cooperation within sectors was not enough, there was a risk of increasing competition between different sectors on the labor market and 'fairness [*rättvisa*] have to include the whole labour market in order to reach stability' (LO, 2003b, pp. 4–5). In specific *Guidelines for coordinated negotiations*, the LO decided how the work should be organized. The most important part was that the board of the confederation draws up recommendations for what joint demands should be insisted upon in the round of negotiations. The LO's representative assembly (*Representantskapet*) should thereafter confirm the guidelines (LO, 2003c).

The project worked out well. In the autumn of 2003 it was clear that all affiliated unions within the confederation were united. They agreed on wage demands levels and also on a low-wage profile on the demands (see *Svenska Dagbladet*, 2003-10-21; 2003-10-15). Analysts of the negotiations concluded that not only were the unions united, but coordination within Swedish Enterprise was also firmer than before, '"upgraded collaboration" [uppgraderad samverkan] is the employer term for the unity this year' (*Svenska Dagbladet*, 2003-11-19). When negotiations started, the centralized part was obvious: 'A bit simplified, this year's beginning of negotiations may therefore be described as centrally coordinated negotiations headed by Swedish Enterprise and LO, even though none of them take part in the negotiations' (*Svenska Dagbladet*, 2004-01-27).

The round of negotiations in 2004 had some mixed ingredients. Parties in the industrial sector came to an agreement on time (after tough negotiations), but especially some low-wage unions were involved in conflicts. However, one of the most involved journalists concluded that the outcome in these conflicts, especially concerning work environment issues, did bear the traits of peak organizations rather than sectors: 'The collaboration, a concept that is associated with the past SAF-LO negotiations, has experienced a renaissance this year. This is true on both sides of the negotiation table. Earlier, the collaboration was primarily a union concept. This year, the employers have been cleverer [duktigare] than in a long time' (*Svenska Dagbladet*, 2004-06-12).

The LO followed the same procedures as in preparations for negotiations in 2004 during the next large round of negotiations in 2007. Its representative assembly approved of the boards' suggestions for 'joint demands before Agreement 2007'. The internal agreement was built on a recommendation from decision-making boards within the peak organization, where the affiliated unions confirmed in writing that they were committed to the joint demands and to support each other. This time, the leaders of the LO decided there were 'reasons for a more detailed coordination that takes its point of departure in more distinct rules and specified joint demands' (LO, 2006). Hence the LO's board should decide that a first agreement reached by a union could have 'a strong standard setting effect (normerande verkan) on the rest of the labor market' (LO, 2006). After fierce internal discussion, the LO's board reached an internal compromise (LO-tidningen, 2006-10-13) whereby all the unions in the confederation jointly agreed to give low-wage earners, and especially women, top priority.

Hence, in spite of the insistence among international scholars that Sweden has undergone a remarkable change since centralization formally broke down in 1990 (Swenson and Pontusson, 2000; Traxler et al., 2001, p. 156), peak organizations still hold key positions (Svensson and Öberg, 2005). The model may accurately be described as renegotiated as well as changed. Furthermore, the development illustrates Jelle Visser's (2005, p. 303) statement that a distinction between 'old' and 'new' is insufficient to capture changes in industrial relations institutions in Europe in the last decades.

To sum up this part, while it is possible to discern path dependence and critical junctures in wage-bargaining institutions in Sweden, we recommend certain cautions before a final conclusion is reached. Once again it is clear that what may at first look like a distinct juncture marked off from periods of stability, may in fact be embedded in continuous renegotiations. What looks like a change driven by exogenous forces may have been driven by central actors' strategical action, perhaps also making use of these forces in their public argumentation. Moreover, what from one perspective may look like a critical juncture may not be as critical after all. Stability and critical junctures may be constructions that mislead us from a solid explanation of the historical events.

CONCLUDING REMARKS

There are definitely patterns of specific politics that are remarkably stable over time, at least from a bird's-eye view. Moreover, these patterns differ between groups of nations. For instance, although there are differences between welfare policies in the Scandinavian countries, from a comparative politics perspective, there are also striking similarities persistent over time. These countries seem to be on a different path compared with groups of other countries, for example, countries in southern Europe. Apparently, path dependence is an apt metaphor, often very much to the point and with an astonishing pervasive force, which makes it useful when addressing audiences outside the community of social scientists.

However, we must avoid being carried away by the attractiveness of a beautiful metaphor. At least, when the metaphor is turned into a theory of stability and change and applied in political science, some cautions are necessary. A theory appropriate to explain macroeconomic developments over a very long period – say industrialization of the western world – may be less useful in explaining micro political processes, for example, analysing the development of the pension system in Sweden.

In this chapter, we have argued that there is a need for a reminder of the behaviour of political actors in order to improve theories on evolution of institutions. Although we admit that it is improbable that people in their everyday lives calculate all possible outcomes on a multitude of possible choices, we do not find it likely, either, that discontented politicians politely wait for a policy window to open some decades in the future. As illustrated in this chapter, winners calculate how they can prolong their successes, and initial losers make plans with the intention to turn things around. This is one of several reasons why we think that research from a path-dependence perspective tends to make the distinction between stability and change too clear-cut. In agreement with Kathleen Thelen, we propose that stability and change cannot be studied as separate processes. While change is often a prerequisite for maintenance, institutions that seem stable are often in a state of continuous renegotiations below a calm surface.

Consequently, our position is that researchers of institutional evolution have to look deeper, that is, dare to dive below that surface. Researchers that *presume* that there has been a critical juncture somewhere along the path will most likely find one. But, it is mistaken to trace a path back only until a break point is found, stopping there, overjoyed of the discovery of a presumed critical juncture, instead of continuing the investigation. In case the backwards process-tracing continues, there is a chance – or a risk – that the event comes out less critical, and not even a juncture. Critical junctures are attractive, almost beautiful explanations, but also deceptively so for researchers who honestly want to understand evolution of institutions. Likewise, case selection should refrain from using the term 'path dependence' to describe obvious lock-ins.

Hence, we argue that social scientists shall not give up on micro studies based on methodological individualism. We have briefly illustrated such studies in our empirical examples, and showed that the Swedish model has constantly been renegotiated on initiatives of winners as well as initial losers, but at the same time has maintained some of its characteristic traits. A practical way forward is to continue to make use of theory-driven process-tracing, where historians' ability for astute narrative is combined with social scientists' interest in theory (cf. George and Bennet, 2005; Hall, 2003). In addition, research based on micro process-tracing has to be put into perspective by cross-country comparisons. Only then can we distinguish different trajectories. The questions should focus on *what* part of an institution is renegotiable, *when* and *how* (Pierson, 2000a; Thelen, 2004). By doing so, we may get more solid evidence to tell if we are on a path at all or merely wandering around but with a vague and reappraised idea of direction; whether we came from a distinct juncture or a vague, winding road of various verdicts; and whether we really are dependent on a path or just for the moment satisfied with the direction taken.

NOTES

1. The critique is directed towards 'purely narrative explanations of particular sequences of events' such as the children's book-like principle 'it just "happened to happen" and was not very likely to happen again'.
2. Events that have benefited from the path-dependence approach also concern causes and consequences of social movements and revolutions (for example, Collier and Collier, 1991), diversity in regimes (for example, Luebbert, 1991) as well as democratic transitions (for example, Bratton and van de Walle, 1997; Przeworski et al., 2000). For an extensive review see Mahoney (2003).
3. Although other political scientists, for example, Blyth (2003), rather sharply contradict this grouping of political economies, claiming that Germany is not really a typical, stable CME. Neither can the economic success of the USA be linked to it adhering to LME strategies. Rather, Germany is going through extensive institutional transformations and the success measured as high rate of employment in the USA can be linked to the fact that a large proportion of the workforce is jailed! Blyth implies that the VoC approach holds a normative bias for the LME model, something which Hall and Soskice refute as 'a striking and neo-Darwinian conclusion' (Hall and Soskice, 2003, p. 243).
4. However, whether path dependence in politics also leads to lock-in of inefficiencies has not been discussed. Is that because it is harder to measure?
5. Elster does not agree that a cause and outcome often can be temporally separated, since that jeopardizes the strength of the causality. He advocates 'local' causes as close as possible in time to the outcome. Pierson counter argues by claiming this viewpoint unluckily rejects all social explanation factors (Elster, 1983, in Pierson, 2003, p. 200).
6. Thelen talks about three types of change in institutions: layering, functional change and diffusion.

REFERENCES

Alexopoulos, M. and J. Cohen (2003), 'Centralized wage bargaining and structural change in Sweden', *European Review of Economic History*, 7, 331–66.

Arthur, B.W. (1989), 'Competing technologies, increasing returns, and lock-in by historical events', *Economic Journal*, **99** (394), 116–31.
Bennet, A. and C. Elman, (2006), 'Complex causal relations and case study methods: the example of path dependence', *Political Analysis*, **14** (3), 250–67.
Bergh, A. (2004), 'The universal welfare state: theory and the case of Sweden', *Political Studies*, **52** (4), 745–66.
Blomqvist, P. (2004), 'The choice revolution: privatization of Swedish welfare services in the 1990s', *Social Policy & Administration*, **38** (2), 139–55.
Blyth, M. (2003), 'Same as it never was: temporality and typology in the varieties of capitalism', *Comparative European Politics*, **1** (2), 215–25.
Bratton, M and N. van de Walle (1997), *Democratic Experiments in Africa: Regime Transitions in Comparative Perspective*, Cambridge: Cambridge University Press.
Brooks, C. and J. Manza (2006), 'Why do welfare states persist?', *Journal of Politics*, **68** (4), 816–27.
Campbell, J. L. (1997) 'Mechanisms of evolutionary change in economic governance: interaction, interpretation and bricolage', in L. Magnusson and J. Ottosson (eds), *Evolutionary Economics and Path Dependence*, Cheltenham, UK and Northampton, MA, USA: Edwards Elgar, pp. 10–32.
Clayton, R. and J. Pontusson, (1998), 'Welfare state retrenchment revisited: entitlement cuts, public sector restructuring, and egalitarian trends in advanced capitalist countries', *World Politics*, **51** (1), 67–98.
Collier, R.B. and D. Collier (1991), *Shaping the Political Arena: Critical Junctures, the Labor Movement, and Regime Dynamics in Latin America*, Princeton, NJ: Princeton University Press.
Cox, R. (2004), 'The path-depencency of an idea: why Scandinavian welfare states remain distinct', *Social Policy & Administration*, **38** (2), 204–19.
De Geer, H. (1986), *SAF i Förhandlingar*, Stockholm: Svenska arbetsgivareföreningen.
Elster, J. (1983), *Explaining Technical Change*, Cambridge, Cambridge University Press.
Elster, J. (1985), *Making Sense of Marx. Studies in Marxism and Social Theory*, Cambridge: Cambridge University Press.
Elster, J. (1989), *Nuts and Bolts for the Social Sciences*, Cambridge: Cambridge University Press.
Elvander, N. (2002), 'The new Swedish regime for collective barganing and conflict resolution: a comparative perspective', *European Journal of Industrial Relations*, **8** (2), 197–216.
Esping-Andersen, G. (1990), *The Three Worlds of Welfare State Capitalism*, Princeton, NJ: Princeton University Press.
George, A.L. and A. Bennet (2005), *Case Studies and Theory Development in Social Sciences*, Cambridge, MA: MIT Press.
Goodin, R.E. (1999), 'Rationality redux: reflexions on Herbert A. Simon's vision of politics' in J.E. Alt, M. Levi and E. Ostrom (eds), *Competition and Cooperation. Conversations with Nobelists about Economics and Political Science*, New York: Russel Sage Foundation.
Goldstone, J.A. (1998), 'Initial conditions, general laws, path dependence, and explanation in historical sociology', *American Journal of Sociology*, **4** (3), 829–45.

Greener, I. (2005), 'The potential of path dependence in political studies', *Politics*, **25** (1), 62–72.

Hall, P.A. (2003), 'Aligning ontology and methodology in comparative politics', in J. Mahoney and D. Rueschmeyer (eds), *Comparative Historical Analysis in the Social Sciences*, Cambridge: Cambridge University Press.

Hall, P.A. and D. Soskice (2003), 'Varieties of capitalism and institutional change: a response to three critics', *Comparative European Politics*, **1** (2), 241–50.

Hall, P.A. and R.C. Taylor (1998), 'The potential of historical institutionalism: a response to Hay and Wincott', *Political Studies*, **46** (5), 958–62.

Hallberg, K. (2006). 'Is corporatism in Scandinavia on decline or not? Reviewing recent findings and assessing possibilities for a cross-national study', Master's thesis, Uppsala University.

Hermansson, J. (1993), *Politik som intressekamp (Politics as Struggle Between Interests)*, Stockholm: Norstedts.

Hermansson, J., A. Lund, T. Svensson and PO Öberg (1999), *Avkorporativisering och lobbyism*, SOU 1999:121.

Johansson, J. (2000), *SAF och den svenska modellen. En studie av uppbrottet från förvaltningskorporatismen 1982–91*, Skrifter utgivna av Statsvetenskapliga föreningen 142, Uppsala: Acta Upsaliensis Universitatis.

Johansson, J. (2005), 'Undermining corporatism', in P. Öberg and T. Svensson (eds), *Power and Institutions in Industrial Relation Regimes. Political Science Perspectives on the Transition of the Swedish Model*, Work Life in Transition 2005:12, Stockholm: National Institute for Working Life, pp. 77–106.

Katznelson, I. (2003), 'Periodization and preferences: reflections of purposive action in comparative historical social science?' in J. Mahoney and D. Rueschmeyer (eds), *Comparative Historical Analysis in the Social Sciences*, Cambridge: Cambridge University Press, pp. 270–301.

Kay, A. (2005), 'A critique of the use of path dependency in policy studies', *Public Administration*, **83** (3), 553–71.

Korpi, W. (1989), 'Power, politics, and state autonomy in the development of social citizenship: social rights during sickness in eighteen OECD countries since 1930', *American Sociological Review*, **54** (3), 309–28.

Korpi, W. (2006), 'Power resources and employer-centered approaches in explanations of welfare states and varieties of capitalism. Protagonists, consenters, and antagonists', *World Politics*, **58** (January), 167–206.

Lewin, L. (1994), 'The rise and decline of corporatism: the case of Sweden', *European Journal of Political Research*, **26** (1), 59–79.

Lindbom, A. (2001), 'Dismantling the social democratic welfare model? Has the Swedish welfare state lost its defining characteristics', *Scandinavian Political Studies*, **24** (3), 171–93.

Lindgren, K.-O. (2006), *Roads from Unemployment. Institutional Complementarities in Product and Labour Markets*, Uppsala: Department of Government, Uppsala Universitet.

LO (2003a), *Kallelse till Förtroendevalda och medlemmar i LOs förbund*, Sams – samordning för solidaritet inför avtalsrörelsen 2004, Stockholm: Landsorganisationen i Sverige.

LO (2003b), *Dagordning*. Sams – samordning för solidaritet inför avtalsrörelsen 2004, Stockholm: Landsorganisationen i Sverige.

LO (2003c), *Riktlinjer för samordnade förhandlingar*, Sams – samordning för solidaritet inför avtalsrörelsen 2004, Stockholm: Landsorganisationen i Sverige.

LO (2006), *Gemensamma krav inför avtal 2007*, www.lo.se (accessed 26 October 2006).

LO-tidningen 2006-10-13, 'Kompromiss bäddar för samordning' (Tommy Öberg.)

LO's Representantskap (2000), *Rekommendationer till förbunden med gemensamma krav inför Avtal 2001*, 27 October, Stockholm: Mimeo Landsorganisationen i Sverige.

Luebbert, G.M. (1991), *Liberalism, Fascism, or Social Democracy: Social Classes and the Political Origins of Regimes in Interwar Europe*, New York: Oxford University Press.

Magnusson, L. and J. Ottoson (1997), 'Introduction', in L. Magnusson and J. Ottosson, (eds), *Evolutionary Economics and Path Dependence*, Cheltenham, UK and Northampton, MA, USA: Edwards Elgar, pp. 1–9.

Mahoney, J. (2000), 'Path dependence in historical sociology', *Theory and Society*, **29** (4), 507–48.

Mahoney, J. (2003), 'Knowledge accumulation in comparative historical research: the case of democracy and authoritarianism' in J. Mahoney and D. Rueschemeyer, *Comparative Historical Analysis in the Social Sciences*, Cambridge: Cambridge University Press, pp. 131–74.

March, J.G. and J.P. Olsen (1989), *Rediscovering Institutions. The Organizational Basis of Politics*, New York: Free Press.

Möller, G. (1946), 'De planerade sociala reformerna', *Tiden* (2), 70–85.

Mörner, M. (1989), '"The Swedish model": historical perspectives', *Scandinavian Journal of History*, **14** (3), 245–67.

North, D.C. (1991), 'Institutions', *Journal of Economic Perspectives*, **5** (1), 97–112.

Öberg, P.O. (2002), 'Does administrative corporatism promote trust and deliberation?', *Governance*, **15** (4), 455–75.

Opp, K.D. (1999), 'Contending conceptions of the theory of rational action', *Journal of Theoretical Politics*, **11** (2), 171–202.

Ottosson, J. (1997), 'Path dependence and institutional evolution – the case of the nationalisation of private railroads in interwar Sweden', in L. Magnusson and J. Ottosson (eds), *Evolutionary Economics and Path Dependence*, Cheltenham, UK and Northampton, MA, USA: Edwards Elgar, pp. 186–96.

Peters, B.G. (2000), *Four Main Administrative Traditions*, Washington, DC: World Bank, http://go.worldbank.org/8W85CKFC80 (accessed 14 October 2008).

Peters, B.G. (2008), 'The Napoleonic tradition', *International Journal of Public Sector Management*, **21** (2), 118–32.

Peters, B.G. and J. Pierre (1998), 'Governance without government? Rethinking public administration', *Journal of Public Administration Research and Theory*, **8** (2), 223–43.

Peters, B.G., J. Pierre and D.S. King (2005), 'The politics of path dependency: political conflict in historical institutionalism', *Journal of Politics*, **67** (4), 1275–300.

Pierson, P. (1996), 'The new politics of the welfare state', *World Politics*, **48** (2), 143–79.

Pierson, P. (2000a), 'Not just what, but when: timing and sequence in political processes', *Studies in American Political Development*, **14** (Spring), 72–92.

Pierson, P. (2000b), 'Dr. Seuss and Dr Stinchcombe: a Reply to the commentaries', *Studies in American Political Development*, **14** (Spring), 113–19.

Pierson, P. (2000c), 'Increasing returns, path depencence, and the study of politics', *American Political Science Review*, **94** (2), 251–8.

Pierson, P. (2003), 'Big, slow-moving, and . . . invisible: macro social processes in the study of comparative politics', in J. Mahoney and D. Rueschmeyer (eds), *Comparative Historical Analysis in the Social Sciences*, Cambridge: Cambridge University Press, pp. 177–207.

Pierson, P. (2005), *Politics in Time*, Princeton, NJ: Princeton University Press.

Pontusson, J. and P. Swenson. (1996), 'Labor markets, production strategies, and wage bargaining institutions: the employer offensive in comparative perspective', *Comparative Political Studies*, **29** (2), 223–50.

Przeworski, A., M. Alvarez, J.A. Cheibub and F. Limongi (2000), *Democracy and Development: Political Institutions and Well-Being in the World, 1950–1990*, Cambridge: Cambridge University Press.

Putnam, R. (1993), *Making Democracy Work: Civic Traditions in Modern Italy*, Princeton, NJ: Princeton University Press.

Roland, G. (2004), 'Understanding institutional change: fast-moving and slow-moving institutions', *Studies in Comparative Institutional Development*, **38** (4), 109–31

Rothstein, B. (1988), 'Sociala klasser och politiska institutioner. Den korporativa korporatismens rötter', *Arkiv för studier i arbetarrörelsens historia*, **40**, 27–46.

Rothstein, B. (1991), 'State structure and variations in corporatism: the Swedish case', *Scandinavian Political Studies*, **12** (2), 149–71.

Rothstein, B. (1992), *Den korporativa staten (The Corporatist State)*, Stockholm: Norstedts.

Rothstein, B. (1996), *The Social Democratic State. The Swedish Model and the Bureacratic Problem of Social Reforms*, Pittsburgh, PA: University of Pittsburgh Press.

Rothstein, B. (2002), 'The universal welfare state as a social dilemma', in B. Rothstein and S. Steinmo (eds), *Restructuring the Welfare State: Political Institutions and Policy Change*, New York: Palgrave Macmillan, pp. 206–22.

Rothstein, B. and J. Bergström (1999), *Korporatismens fall och den svenska modellens kris*, Stockholm: SNS.

Skocpol, T. (1995), 'Why I am an historical institutionalist', *Polity*, **28** (1), 103–06.

Svenska Dagbladet (2003-10-21), 'Låglönesatsning i fokus för LO-krav' (T. Öberg).

Svenska Dagbladet (2003-10-15), 'Uppslutningen är bred bakom låglönesatsningen' (A. Danielsson).

Svenska Dagbladet (2003-11-19), 'Ett spel om nästan 30 miljarder' (T. Öberg and A. Danielsson).

Svenska Dagbladet (2004-01-27), 'Upptakt med högt tonläge' (T. Öberg and A. Danielsson).

Svenska Dagbladet (2004-06-12), 'Lugn start men stökig final' (T. Öberg).

Svensson, T. (1994). *Socialdemokratins dominans. En studie av den svenska socialdemokratins partistrategi*, Skrifter utgivna av Statsvetenskapliga föreningen i Uppsala, nr 120, Uppsala: Upsala Universitatis Upsaliensis.

Svensson, T. and PO. Öberg (2003), *Korporatismen i det nya Millenniet. Tre uppsatser om intresseorganisatinernas deltagande i svensk politik*, Svensk Modell i Förändring – SMIF Forskningsrapport 2003:2, Stockholm: Arbetslivsinstitutet.

Svensson, T. and PO. Öberg (2005), 'How are coordinated market economies coordinated? Evidence from Sweden', *West European Politics*, **28** (5), 1075–100.

Swenson, P. (2004), 'Varieties of capitalist interest: power, institutions, and the regulatory welfare state in the United States and Sweden', *Studies in American Political Development*, **18** (Spring), 1–29.

Swenson, P. and J. Pontusson, (2000), 'The Swedish employer offensive against centralized wage bargaining' in T. Iversen, J. Pontusson and D. Soskice (eds), *Unions, Employers, and Central Banks. Macroeconomic Coordination and Institutional Change in Social Market Economies*, Cambridge: Cambridge University Press, pp. 77–106.

Thelen, K. (1999), 'Historical institutionalism in comparative politics', *Annual Review of Political Science*, **2**, 369–404.

Thelen, K. (2003), 'How institutions evolve', in J. Mahoney and D. Rueschemeyer (eds), *Comparative Historical Analysis in the Social Sciences*, Cambridge: Cambridge University Press, pp. 208–40.

Thelen, K. (2004), *How Instititons Evolve. The Political Economy of Skills in Germany, Britain, the United States, and Japan*, Cambridge: Cambridge University Press.

Thelen, K. and S. Steinmo (1992), 'Historical institutionalism in comparative politics', in S. Steinmo, K. Thelen and F. Longstreth (eds), *Structuring Politics. Historical Intitutionalism in Comparative Analysis*, Cambridge: Cambridge University Press, pp. 1–32

Törnqvist, C. (1999), 'The decentralization of industrial relations: the Swedish case in comparative perspective', *European Journal of Industrial Relations*, **5** (1), 71–87.

Traxler, F., S. Blashke and B. Kittel (2001), *National Labour Relations in Internationalized Markets. A Comparative Study of Institutions, Change and Performance*, Oxford: Oxford University Press.

Visser, J. (2005), 'Beneath the surface of stability: new and old modes of governance in European industrial relations', *European Journal of Industrial Relations*, **11** (3), 287–306.

6. The role of institutions and organizations in shaping radical scientific innovations

Rogers Hollingsworth[1]

INTRODUCTION

This chapter confronts several interrelated problems as to how the institutional environments of organizations influence their innovativeness. Using a path-dependent perspective, it addresses (1) how institutional environments influence organizational isomorphism within countries, and (2) how institutional environments influence both the founding of new kinds of organizations and the founding of radically new departments and divisions within existing organizations.

To confront these problems, I draw on some of the data from the study of 290 major discoveries (that is, radical innovations in basic biomedical science) which took place throughout the twentieth century in four countries (Britain, France, Germany and the USA). The data relate to approximately 250 research organizations which varied in the number of major discoveries made, some having no major discoveries. Because of limitations of space, most of this chapter will focus primarily on organizations in the USA, but from time to time soft comparisons will be made with the institutional environments and organizations in the other three countries. Even though the empirical research for this chapter pertains to radical innovations in the basic biomedical sciences, many of the chapter's generalizations also apply to radical innovations in other sectors and to countries other than the four considered in this research. Two major arguments of the chapter are that (1) the path-dependent nature of the institutional make-up of societies influences variability across societies in the rate of major discoveries, and (2) the path-dependent culture and structure of individual research organizations influence which organizations are likely to have many, few or no major discoveries.

PATH DEPENDENCY

The subject of path dependency is 'tricky business'. Hardly anyone is a strict determinist, assuming that actors are totally determined by choices made in the past, or by the institutional and/or organizational environment in which they are embedded. If we were strict determinists, we could make confident predictions about the social world. Scholars who use the term 'path dependency' usually vary in the meaning they attach to it. At one extreme is the view that path dependency simply refers to the causal relevance of preceding events in some type of temporal sequence. For example, a number of authors writing about path dependency suggest that what happens at an earlier point in time, and the sequence with which certain events occur in the history of a society, influence processes and events at subsequent points in the history of the society (Grew, 1978). In short, history matters: what actors do today is shaped by what they did yesterday (Garud and Karnøe, 2001; Pierson, 2000, p. 252). A different, and more narrow conceptualization of path dependency but with a bit more rigor is that offered by Margaret Levi (1997, p. 28). Once a country, organization or individual has 'started down a track, the costs of reversal are very high. There will be choice points, but the entrenchments of certain institutional arrangements obstruct an easy reversal of the initial choice'. As Paul Pierson (2000, p. 252) observes, 'the costs of exit – of switching to some previously plausible alternative – rise'. The farther along a path a society or an organization is in developing a set of practices, the more difficult it becomes to shift to alternative paths. As a result, extensive movement down particular paths, whether at the societal or organizations levels, tends to have 'lock in' effects (Arthur, 1994). This is the way in which path dependency is used here.

A critical issue in path dependency is in understanding how history matters. While there is considerable variation in the literature on this issue, most path-dependent analysts tend to take one or more of the following perspectives:

1. Small events often have major consequences.
2. Specific courses of action – once introduced – are very difficult to reverse.
3. There is a great deal of chance and contingency to the unfolding of history.
4. The timing and sequence of events are very importing in shaping longer-term social processes and outcomes.

In scientific organizations where considerable emphasis is given to priority in the discovery process, being early in developing a novel technique, adopting a new type of instrumentation or developing a new discipline may make a great deal of difference in shaping the status of an investigator or a laboratory, but adopting a process or instrument, or establishing a particular kind of disciplinary-based department at a much later date may be of little consequence in the competitive discovery process. As Tilly (1984, p. 14) observes, *when* things happen in a sequence affects *how* they happen and the consequences of their occurrence (for the importance of the sequences of events, see Grew, 1978; Pierson, 2000, p. 264).

When it comes to designing organizations, actors generally have no way of knowing a priori the consequences of their actions. Experienced and wise decision-makers are generally aware that they are gambling, that they may well be introducing components and processes which will later prove to have undesirable consequences. Unfortunately, many social scientists who study social change tend to be excessively optimistic, rational and functionalist in their approach to problems and tend to exaggerate their ability to gauge the consequences of their actions.

Most institutional and organizational change unfolds in processes which are somewhat blind and random. Societies that excel in being innovative in various sectors or spheres over extended periods of time do so because of their good fortune in having an institutional environment which offers them the capacity to perform well (see the discussions in Allen, 2004; Hall and Soskice, 2001; Hollingsworth and Boyer, 1997; Hollingsworth et al., 1994). At best, we can hope to discern retrospectively whether there are regularities in the way that history unfolds. Generally, we cannot predict what processes will definitely lead to particular outcomes, but hopefully, as a result of appropriate research strategies, we will be able to specify which ones are most likely not to lead to particular types of outcomes.

INSTITUTIONAL ENVIRONMENTS

The institutional environment of organizations provides resources for organizations that often play a major role in shaping their behavior. How resources are allocated to organizations is inextricably bound up with the relationship between organizations and their institutional environment (Aldrich, 1979; Baum, 1996; Pfeffer, 1981). For the purposes of this chapter, the analysis focuses on four aspects of institutional environments that externally constrain the behavior of research organizations. These are environmental or external (1) control over the appointment of scientific personnel, (2) control over whether or not a particular scientific discipline will exist within a research organization, (3) control over the level of funding for the organizations, and (4) control over the type of training needed for appointment in a research organization. In the following analysis, societal or institutional environments are coded in terms of whether they are weak or strong. In those societies in which external controls over organizations are highly institutionalized and strong, there is less variation in the structure and behavior of research organizations. In such instances, the connectedness between research organizations and their institutional or external environments is so strong that research organizations have low autonomy to pursue independent strategies and goals. Conversely, the weaker the institutional environment in which research organizations are embedded, the greater the variation in the structure, behavior and performance of research organizations. Moreover, where the institutional environments are more weakly developed, organizations generally have greater autonomy and flexibility to develop new knowledge and to be highly innovative. Hence, it is in those societies where the institutional environments are most developed and rigid, and where there is less organizational autonomy and flexibility, that fewer radical innovations in basic and applied science as well as in fundamentally new products and industrial sectors have emerged. In strong institutional environments, actors and organizations may not be so successful in making radical innovations, but quite successful in making incremental innovations and producing high-quality products (Hage and Hollingsworth, 2000).

The data on the institutional environments of these four countries suggest that there is a high degree of complementarity among the four concepts describing institutional environments: when one is weakly developed the others tend to be weakly developed, and vice versa. This perspective has led a number of analysts to emphasize the concept of institutional complementarity.[2]

Even though there are prototypes of strong and weak institutional environments, there can be exceptions to the way institutional environments affect organizations. For example, German universities are greatly constrained by being embedded in a strong institutional environment, but in the same society Max Planck Institutes have had much more organizational autonomy (Ash, 1997; Mayntz, 2001). In a weak institutional environment, which is the case with Britain, there are research establishments operated by governmental research councils or departments (the Agriculture and Food Research Council, Defense) which have had little choice about personnel, budget or research programs. Most governmental research units in Britain have long been concentrated in a relatively small number of large organizations, have operated in a very bureaucratic manner and have been heavily directly dependent on Whitehall (which determines personnel policies, research plans and financial resources). In contrast, British universities historically had much greater organizational autonomy and more independence to shape their personnel and research policies than was the case with most governmental research units (Ziman, 1987, ch. 2).

INSTITUTIONAL ENVIRONMENTS AND ORGANIZATIONAL ISOMORPHISM

In weak institutional environments, there is likely to be much more heterogeneity in types of research organizations and among organizations of the same type than in strong institutional environments. Hence, in the USA, with a relatively weak institutional environment, there have long been many more different types of universities than has been the case in Germany where universities have been embedded in a strong institutional environment and are much more similar to one another. Thus, in the USA, there have been small elite private universities such as Rockefeller University, the California Institute of Technology, Rice University and the Scripps Research Institute. There have been medium-sized private universities: Johns Hopkins University, the University of Chicago, Vanderbilt University and Princeton. And there have been large private universities such as Harvard, Stanford, Massachusetts Institute of Technology, New York University. In addition, there are the large public universities in California (Berkeley, University of California Los Angeles, University of California, San Diego) and in the Midwest (Michigan, Indiana, Wisconsin, Illinois, Minnesota). Each of these separate types of university is in a distinct type of population, somewhat differentiated from each of the other types because their dominant competencies are not easily learned or transmitted across organizational populations (McKelvey, 1982, p. 192; Aldrich et al., 1984, p. 69).

Of course, in both strong and weak institutional environments every organization is unique, meaning that there is always heterogeneity within each type of organization. But organizations of the same population and in the same institutional environment are likely to share many of the same attributes. Even if weak institutional environments lead to more heterogeneity among types of organizations in any particular population, there are forces at work within each society that lead over time to organizational isomorphism both across and within organizational types. There are several bodies of literature which empirically have provided support to the idea of organizational isomorphism even among different types of organizations in the same society. One is the varieties of capitalism literature (Crouch and Streeck, 1997; Hall and Soskice, 2001; Hollingsworth and Boyer, 1997; Hollingsworth et al., 1994; Streeck and Yamamura, 2001).

Another literature is that on the history of research organizations – particularly that involving universities in Britain, France, Germany and the USA. While within each of these four countries, organizational diversity persists within their university systems, there nevertheless have been pressures toward organizational isomorphism, though these pressures have been strongest in those countries (that is, Germany and France) in which universities have been embedded in strong institutional environments (Clark, 1993; 1995).

There is also empirical literature from the field of population ecology, though the theoretical basis for much of this literature is derived from evolutionary biology. For example, McKelvey (1982, ch. 7) argued that different populations of organizations within the same society have a set of competencies and routines which are societally specific, and as a result of these competencies, actors in both different and similar organizations engage in a great deal of common learning and socialization. Scientists, technicians and administrators, even if from different types of organizations but in the same society, acquire a great deal of common 'organizational know-how'. DiMaggio and Powell (1983) picked up on these ideas when they pointed out that organizations engage in 'mimetic processes'. More recently, Hodgson (2003) developed the argument that routines are organizational meta-habits which diffuse across populations of organizations within an institutional environment. As suggested above, a good bit of this insight was borrowed from evolutionary biologists (Mayr, 1963; 2001) who have demonstrated that interbreeding and gene flow stabilize biological species. Picking up on these ideas, Astley (1985), a population ecologist, did more than anyone else to establish clear linkages among the different literatures in biology, population ecology and organizational isomorphism. And where there are high degrees of organizational isomorphism, organizations are not likely to diverge widely in their historical processes. In short, they are likely to share many of the same path-dependent processes.

Thus far I have raised several interrelated historical processes: how institutional environments relate to organizational isomorphism, path dependency and innovativeness. The concept of path dependency keeps us mindful of the fact that the way things were organized yesterday – or last year, and so on – influences the way they are organized today. But institutional environments, organizations and individual actors are always changing. The stronger the institutional environment, the greater the degree of organizational isomorphism, and the higher the degree of common path-dependent processes. But there are also pressures toward organizational isomorphism even in weak institutional environments. Moreover, within most organizations – irrespective of their institutional environments – there are pressures for differentiated internal divisions and departments to become somewhat isomorphic and to share common path-dependent processes. In short, a common organizational culture tends to become pervasive in most organizations: individuals in different departments of the same organization become socialized into common ways of addressing problems. There are pressures both across and within organizations in the same society to emphasize homogeneous competencies. The pressures toward homogenization are especially strong when actors in highly saturated environments are competing for the same finite resources (Hawley, 1950).

CONSTRAINTS ON ISOMORPHISM

Isomorphism, no matter how powerful as a force, does not sweep unimpeded through history. There are counter-currents which place constraints on isomorphic tendencies. For example, Stinchcombe (1965) many years ago made the observation that organizations – even of the same type but founded at different points in time – are likely to be imprinted with many of the 'social technologies' and cultural attributes at the time of their creation. When Stinchcombe made his observation, social scientists had not yet explicitly developed the concept of path-dependency, but his emphasis on how the history of organizations is permanently influenced by the moment of their founding is of course clearly suggestive of a path-dependency perspective at the level of organizations. In short, Stinchcombe was implicitly making the profound point that organizations do not necessarily closely track changes in their environment. Instead, they are somewhat inert, preserving certain 'nonadaptive' qualities which often have deleterious effects on their capacity to be highly adaptive to their environments and to be innovative.

There is substantial literature which suggests that continuous innovativeness in modern societies requires diversity in organizational forms, heterogeneity in organizational structures and diversity in ideas (Garud and Karnøe, 2001; Nooteboom, 1999; Rizzello and Turvani, 2002). Thus, individual societies are constantly confronting contradictory pressures. They are subjected to processes which move organizational populations toward greater homogeneity and uniformity. But if a society is to be creative and innovative, it must have sustained variation and diversity in organizational forms and ideas. Thus, biologists and population ecologists alike have long realized that homeostatic forces within populations constrain evolutionary change and thus preserve nonadaptive forms (Astley, 1985, p. 229; Gould, 1980; Mayr, 2001).

However great the force of path dependency at the institutional and organizational level, new organizational forms do emerge from time to time (Romanelli, 1992). Indeed, the emergence of new organizational forms might be classified as a radical innovation.

What are the conditions under which new organizational forms emerge? Unfortunately, we lack the theoretical tools to specify when and where such innovations will occur. For theoretical insights into this problem, perhaps our best sources are the biologists who study the processes of speciation. We might think of the emergence of a new organizational form as a kind of organizational mutant. As Astley (1985, p. 232) reminded us, mutations occur all the time, among both biological and organizational species. However, most do not take hold since they are crowded out, are outnumbered in their population environments and 'rapidly dissipate through the normal intermixing process' (Mayr, 1963; 2001). Indeed, we know from numerous population ecology studies that new organizations have low survival rates (Hannan and Freeman, 1984; 1989). *Ipso facto,* they have little path dependency.

If considered to be like a mutation, the emergence of a new organizational form is more likely to survive if it occurs in lowly populated environments but with ample resources for the new type to develop and it is not crowded out by the more normal processes of intermingling with other organizations. In the short term, a new form may be immune to the pressures of organizational isomorphism. In other words, environments where there is an excess of resources relative to demand offer a new organizational form a greater opportunity to survive than is the case in more competitively saturated environments.

USING PATH DEPENDENCY TO UNDERSTAND THE MAKING OF MAJOR DISCOVERIES[3]

Historically and geographically, western, industrialized societies having weak institutional environments have had more different types of organizations and lower levels of organizational isomorphism primarily because they have had environments which were not so highly saturated relative to the demand for resources. The USA during most of the twentieth century was such a society, and for that reason it was possible for new organizational forms to emerge in its research sector – private research institutes, research-oriented medical centers, small universities oriented toward research, even federally owned and operated research centers. Private research institutes such as Rockefeller Institute for Medical Research (now Rockefeller University), the Salk Institute, the Carnegie Institution and the Scripps Research Institute came into existence. The creation of the Johns Hopkins University Medical School has been much described, representing, as it did, the inauguration of a medical school which would engage in serious basic science (Hollingsworth, 1986). The establishment, and growth, of the campus of the National Institutes of Health in Bethesda, Maryland, as a governmentally operated research institute, is another example. In short, the institutional and resource environment in the USA during the twentieth century facilitated the emergence of new, but diverse forms of research organizations.

Several key factors are important for understanding why the USA had an impressive record across much of the twentieth century in making major discoveries in biomedical research. With its weak institutional environment and its abundance of resources, the USA had the conditions which made it possible for new types of organization to emerge which could then quickly adapt to the latest scientific knowledge, and often to become the pace setter in new fields of science. This pattern of the emergence of new types of organizations that quickly incorporated the latest trends in science is consistent with Stinchcombe's argument (1965) about the founding and imprinting of organizations.

Critical to our work is our definition of a major discovery. A major breakthrough is a finding or process, often preceded by numerous 'small advances', which leads to a new way of thinking about a problem. This new way of thinking is highly useful in addressing problems by numerous scientists in diverse fields of science. This is very different from the rare paradigm shifts Thomas Kuhn analysed in *The Structure of Scientific Revolutions* (1962). Major breakthroughs about problems in biomedical science occur within the paradigms about which Kuhn wrote. Historically, a major breakthrough in biomedical science was a radical or new idea, the development of a new methodology or a new instrument or invention. It usually did not occur all at once, but involved a process of investigation taking place over a substantial period of time and required a great deal of tacit and/or local knowledge. My colleagues and I have chosen to depend on the scientific community to operationalize this definition, counting as major discoveries bodies of research having at least one of the ten criteria listed in Box 6.1.

Previous literature has not provided us with the theoretical tools to understand what the particular organizational environments are which facilitate major discoveries, on how types of organizations or the structures and cultures of individual organizations are associated with the making of major discoveries. It is these issues which are addressed below.

As a result of an in-depth cross-national and cross-temporal organizational study of 290 major discoveries in Britain, France, Germany and

BOX 6.1 INDICATORS OF MAJOR DISCOVERIES

1. Discoveries resulting in the Copley Medal, awarded since 1901 by the Royal Society of London, insofar as the award was for basic biomedical research.
2. Discoveries resulting in a Nobel Prize in Physiology or Medicine since the first award in 1901.
3. Discoveries resulting in a Nobel Prize in Chemistry since the first award in 1901, insofar as the research had high relevance to biomedical science.
4. Discoveries resulting in ten nominations in any three years prior to 1940 for a Nobel Prize in Physiology or Medicine.*
5. Discoveries resulting in ten nominations in any three years prior to 1940 for a Nobel Prize in Chemistry if the research had high relevance to biomedical science.*
6. Discoveries identified as prizeworthy for the Nobel Prize in Physiology or Medicine by the Karolinska Institute committee to study major discoveries and to propose Nobel Prize winners.*
7. Discoveries identified as prizeworthy for the Nobel Prize in Chemistry by the Royal Swedish Academy of Sciences committee to study major discoveries and to propose Nobel Prize winners.* These prizeworthy discoveries were included if the research had high relevance to biomedical science.
8. Discoveries resulting in the Arthur and Mary Lasker Prize for basic biomedical science.
9. Discoveries resulting in the Louisa Gross Horwitz Prize in basic biomedical science.
10. Discoveries in biomedical science resulting in the Crafoord Prize, awarded by the Royal Swedish Academy of Sciences, if the discovery had high relevance to biomedical science.

Note: * We have had access to the Nobel Archives for the Physiology or Medicine Prize at the Karolinska Institute and to the Archives at the Royal Swedish Academy of Sciences in Stockholm for the period from 1901 to 1940. Because the archives have been closed for the past 50 years for reasons of confidentiality, we have used other prizes (Lasker, Horwitz, Crafoord) to identify major discoveries in the past several decades.

the USA, my colleagues (Jerald Hage and Ellen Jane Hollingsworth) and I have learned that major discoveries tend to occur in organizational contexts which have the characteristics described in Box 6.2 and Figure 6.1. The organizational contexts associated with major discoveries may exist in different types of organizations.

BOX 6.2   ORGANIZATIONAL CONTEXTS
           FACILITATING THE MAKING OF MAJOR
           DISCOVERIES

1. **Moderately high scientific diversity**. This existed when the organizational context had (a) a variety of biological disciplines and medical specialties and sub-specialties, (b) numerous people in the biological sciences with research experience in different disciplines and/or paradigms. Scientific diversity exerted maximum beneficial effect when the organizational context had high depth (that is, individuals highly competent in different task areas – theoreticians, methodologists, scientists highly conversant with literature in various fields, scientists highly competent in the latest instrumentation in diverse fields).

2. **Communication and social integration among the scientific community**. This was the bringing together of scientists from different scientific fields through *frequent* and *intense* interaction in the following types of collective activities: (a) joint publication, (b) journal clubs and seminars, (c) team teaching, (d) meals and other informal activities.

3. **Organizational leadership with the capacity to understand the direction in which scientific research was moving and the ability to integrate scientific diversity**. These activities were both task oriented and socio-emotional in nature and applied to organizational leaders who had (a) strategic vision for integrating diverse areas and for providing focused research, (b) the ability to secure funding for these activities, (c) the capacity to recruit individuals who would confront not only important scientific problems but ones which could be solved and (d) the capability to provide rigorous criticism in a nurturing environment.

4. **Recruitment**. Organizational capacity to recruit individuals who internalized a moderate degree of scientific diversity.

---

5. **Organizational autonomy and organizational flexibility.**
   Organizational autonomy was the degree to which the organizational context where the research took place was relatively independent of its institutional environment, and organizational flexibility was the ability of the organizational context to shift rapidly from one area of science to another. To attain organizational autonomy and flexibility, it was necessary that the organizational context be loosely coupled to its institutional environment if the organizational context was an entire organization, but if the organizational context was a subpart of a larger organization, it could attain flexibility and autonomy only if it was loosely coupled both to the larger organization and the institutional environment in which it was embedded.

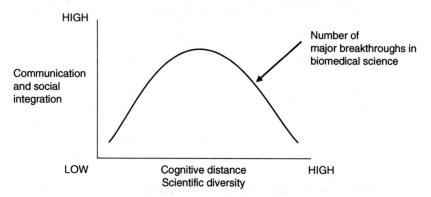

Figure 6.1   The relationships among scientific diversity, communication/ integration and making major discoveries

The few organizations where a sizeable number of major breakthroughs occurred again and again were relatively small, had both high autonomy and flexibility, and had the capacity to adapt rapidly to the fast pace of change taking place in the global environment of science. Such organizations tended to have moderately high levels of scientific diversity but internal structures which facilitated the communication and integration of ideas across diverse scientific fields. Moreover, these organizations tended to have scientific leaders with a keen scientific vision of the direction in which new fields in science were going and the capacity to develop a strategy for recruiting scientists capable of moving a research agenda in that direction. Internationally, most organizations having this kind of flexibility and autonomy in strategy have tended to be located in weak institutional environments.

To provide some sense of the path dependency of research organizations, I focus briefly on the distinctive culture of the Rockefeller Institute (after 1964 called Rockefeller University). Applying the criteria listed in Box 6.1, scientists made more major discoveries in basic biomedical science in this very small organization than in any other organization in the twentieth century – more than all the Kaiser Wilhelm and Max Planck Institutes combined. The variables listed in Box 6.2 and Figure 6.1 have special relevance to the Rockefeller. First, there has been its very small size throughout its history. Second, Rockefeller historically has not had academic departments and disciplines as we know them in the large American research universities. It has been structured around laboratories, and historically when the head of a laboratory retired, died or left, the laboratory was closed, and this provided the organization the opportunity to stand back and assess what to do next. This capability provided the organization an enormous amount of flexibility to adapt to the rapidly changing larger world of science (Hollingsworth, 2002).

Most research universities are structured around departments and academic disciplines, and for that reason they lack organizational flexibility and acquire a great deal of organizational inertia. The Rockefeller organization historically had a great deal of scientific diversity, but whereas most universities have differentiated diversity into departments and subspecialties, the Rockefeller organization had a path-dependent tendency to have a great deal of scientific integration, unlike Max Planck Institutes which have been structured very much around a single area of research or discipline. The mechanisms for integrating the diversity in organizations are present in different variations in organizations, but the emphasis here is on integration – on communication across different fields – and this can take place in a variety of ways in different organizations. During the first 60 years of the Rockefeller organization, much of the scientific integration took place in the lunchroom. The idea was to have a fairly good lunch and to have tables at which generally no more than eight people would be seated, and scientists could have a single conversation about a serious problem. This took place day after day with very eminent people on hand. Foreign scientists coming to America generally arrived in New York, and many of the most distinguished visited the Rockefeller organization. This added to a very exciting environment. And the lunchroom, lectures and afternoon tea did a great deal to promote and facilitate the integration of what I call scientific diversity.

At Rockefeller, there was for many years a certain style of leadership.

It had leaders who had a good sense of the direction in which science was moving, leaders who had an extraordinary ability to recruit people who internalized a scientific diversity and who could lead the organization in the direction in which science was moving. Finally, they had leaders who were willing to take risks. When the Institute was established, John D. Rockefeller, Sr informed the leaders within the Institute that even if they never discovered anything of great importance, that would not matter. He simply wanted the Institute to do the best it could – creating an invigorating and nurturing environment, doing its best to advance the understanding of nature.

One of the things worth observing about the path-dependent culture at the Rockefeller was the development of its young scientists, a subject often overlooked. Here was an organization that had more major breakthroughs in biomedical science than any other organization in the world in the twentieth century, but when we focus just on the Nobel prizes that were awarded to Rockefeller scientists, one of the things that catches the observer's attention is the large number of Nobel prizes that were awarded to people who went to this organization as very young scientists and made their careers there in its extraordinarily nurturing environment, where they did not have to apply for research grants and where people were encouraged to engage in high-risk research. In short, the Institute 'grew' many of their most creative scientists. Note the names of those who went there as very young scientists and eventually were awarded Nobel prizes for work which they did there. There were Peyton Rous, Albert Claude – one of the most important people in the development of cell biology – George Palade, Wendell Stanley, John Northrop, Gerald Edelman, William Stein, Stanford Moore, Bruce Merrifield, Gunther Blobel and Rod MacKinnon. The number of young people who went there and ultimately were awarded Nobel prizes is greater than the combined number of all Nobel prizes awarded to Harvard (or Cambridge) professors for work accomplished there in the biomedical sciences. At Rockefeller, there were also a number of other Nobel laureates, scientists who had done their work there and elsewhere (for example, Karl Landsteiner, Haldan K. Hartline). But what is especially impressive is the culture in which young people were able to mature and become some of the world's most creative scientists.

On the other hand, as suggested above, there is in most societies a great deal of organizational isomorphism, even in such weak institutional environments as the USA. And most large universities in the USA, as well as in the other three countries, have tended to have the characteristics described in Box 6.3. They have been differentiated into large numbers of scientific disciplines, have had relatively little communication across scientific

---

BOX 6.3 ORGANIZATIONAL CONTEXTS CONSTRAINING THE MAKING OF MAJOR DISCOVERIES

1. **Differentiation.** Organizations were highly differentiated internally when they had sharp boundaries among subunits such as (a) basic biomedical departments and other subunits, (b) the delegation of recruitment exclusively to departments or other subunit level and (c) the delegation of responsibility for extramural funding to the department or other subunit level.
2. **Hierarchical authority.** Organizations were coded as being very hierarchical when they experienced (a) centralized decision-making about research programs, (b) centralized decision-making about number of personnel, (c) centralized control over work conditions and (d) centralized budgetary control.
3. **Bureaucratic coordination.** Organizations which had high standardization of rules and procedures.
4. **Hyperdiversity.** This was the presence of diversity to such a deleterious degree that there could not be effective communication among actors in different fields of science or even in similar fields.

---

disciplines, and tended to have less autonomy and flexibility to adapt to the fast pace of scientific change than is the case with those organizations having the characteristics described in Box 6.2 and Figure 6.1.

Why do organizations having the capacity to integrate scientific diversity have an advantage in making major discoveries over those which have a low capacity to facilitate communication across diverse fields? In our study of 290 major discoveries, every single one reflected a great deal of scientific diversity. Very good science may occur in those organizational environments where there is little connection across disciplines and subspecialties and which are highly specialized within a very narrow field. But in such narrow and specialized environments, the science which is produced reflects insufficient diversity for the scientific community with its vast diversity to recognize the work as a major discovery.

Major breakthroughs do not occur only in organizational environments which are small and which are not internally differentiated into departments or divisions. There are exceptions to these findings. How is it that major discoveries might also occur in large organizations which are internally differentiated into separate departments? First, clusters of discoveries might be explained by the rare conditions under which a mutant type department/division emerges and performs extraordinarily well for a relatively short period of time. Second, breakthroughs can occur in the type of organizational context described in Box 6.3, but only if the laboratory is structured quite differently from most other laboratories in Box 6.3 type organizational contexts (see also Figures 6.2, 6.3 and 6.4). In other words, the lab is headed by a scientist operating in an organizational environment which generally would not be expected to have a major discovery.

EXCEPTIONS TO THE PROCESSES OF ORGANIZATIONAL ISOMORPHISM

As suggested above, there are in most societies – regardless of whether institutional environments are weak or strong – pressures for cultural homogeneity and organizational isomorphism across units within any single organization. However, at certain moments in time, there are exceptions to this generalization. In those organizations in which there is very little centralized control, where internal units have high levels of autonomy and good access to human, physical and financial resources, there is the potential that a fundamentally new discipline or scientific program could emerge in a sub-part and which could be incorporated into a departmental structure. This type of radical innovation I equate as being a type of organizational mutation. Of course, universities are constantly establishing new departments or appointing someone with a new scientific agenda within an existing department. But when a fundamentally new discipline or program – by world standards – emerges within a particular university, this is indeed a very radical innovation. And just as we lack the theoretical tools to predict where and when a new kind of organization will emerge, neither can we predict where and when within existing research organizations there will be the emergence of a radically new program, discipline or paradigm. However, the sociological conditions for the emergence of this kind of innovation within a single organization are somewhat similar to those under which new organizational forms will emerge. The following two conditions must exist: (1) the organization must be extremely decentralized (permitting the actors creating the radical innovation to have high autonomy), and (2) the actors within the organization must have access to sufficient diverse types of resources so that their scientific practices and administrative routines are not crowded out by those which might already have become institutionalized within the larger environment of the host organization. According to evolutionary logic, those in the new field must be able to escape the homogenizing pressures in the existing organizational environment and be able to intermix, interbreed and reproduce their own progeny. In short, such organizational mutations within a sub-part of a larger research organization will occur only under specific conditions.

These types of radical innovations are, of course, very rare events. The following are a few examples. One occurred when the University of Cambridge (UK) established its Department of Physiology in the late nineteenth century. Another occurred a few years later with the emergence of the Cambridge Department of Biochemistry. Later, also at Cambridge, a new research paradigm occurred in biology, but in the Cavendish Laboratory (a physics department) (de Chadarevian, 2002; Geison, 1978; Hollingsworth, 2009; Needham and Baldwin, 1949). In each of these departments, a number of major discoveries emerged in the basic biological sciences within a relatively short period of time. At Harvard in the period between the mid-1950s and the mid-1970s, a similar innovation occurred with the establishment of two new departments: the Department of Biochemistry and Molecular Biology, and the Department of Organismic and Evolutionary Biology, and again, each of these departments had a number of major discoveries.

Over time, however, departments have institutionalized routines, as do universities, and inertial processes set in, making it difficult for the new sub-part to continue being as innovative on the world stage of science. Hence, the level of innovativeness of the new department eventually declines. Over time, even organizations which at one time were highly decentralized with high autonomy for each separate unit are likely to institutionalize a set of routines which slowly establish interlocking, sequential and conditional behaviors among all of its various sub-parts and their members. Eventually, these routines establish collective capabilities and capacities which lead to the emergence of shared behavior throughout the organization (Hodgson, 2003, p. 376).

This kind of historical process occurred in the Departments of Physiology and Biochemistry at Cambridge, and in the Departments of Biochemistry and Molecular Biology and Organismic and Evolutionary Biology at Harvard. At the Cavendish Laboratory, there were such strong organizational pressures for the laboratory to return to its mission of physics research that the molecular biologists were strongly encouraged to exit the University of Cambridge. The biologists in the Cavendish (for example, Francis Crick, Fred Sanger, Max Perutz and John Kendrew) were doing some of the most novel biological science of the entire twentieth century. However, they worked outside the disciplinary frameworks of existing Cambridge biological departments, and the pressures of organizational isomorphism were so great that the group, with funding from the Medical Research Council, exited the university and moved to the suburbs of Cambridge where the Laboratory of Molecular Biology (LMB) was established. The LMB eventually became one of the world's leading research centers in basic biomedical science in the latter part of the twentieth century.

Initially each of the Cambridge and Harvard departments had an outstanding leader, and considerable scientific diversity, which was highly integrated – in short, the characteristics listed in Box 6.2 above. Each department had a distinctive culture or glue which held it together, even though each individual scientist tended to pursue a separate body of research – but research which was highly complementary to that of the research program in the entire department.

Eventually, the distinctive scientific excellence of these departments declined for reasons which were common to all. Over time, the scientific agenda of the new department tended to diffuse to other organizations throughout the world. Second, many of the members of the department either retired, died or left the organization. Third, scientific practices became routinized, but no new leader emerged with a radically new agenda, capable of transforming the department to being once again at the cutting edge of science. Fourth, the routines of the larger organization in which the department was embedded slowly began to penetrate the department, leading to isomorphic administrative routines and practices throughout the organization. For all of these reasons, it is difficult for a research department to remain at the cutting edge of research for more than two or three decades. It may be possible for a new department with a new agenda to emerge within another part of the same organization or in a sub-part of another large organization. However, these outstanding departments were very rare events – the equivalent of sub-organizational mutations – which unpredictably were able to 'take hold'. But over the longer term the distinctiveness of the 'new species' diminishes as it interacts with the rest of the organization.

PATH DEPENDENCY WITHIN AN ORGANIZATION

Because organizations are embedded in institutional environments which are path dependent over long periods of time, institutional environments place constraints on the behavior of organizations. However, organizations also have path-dependent processes. But several forces operate to alter the structure and culture of research organizations over time. First, because of the way the research organizations interact with each other over time, there are isomorphic pressures which narrow the range of variation in their behavior and culture. Second, the historical record demonstrates that over time, the institutional environments in which research organizations are embedded tend to change. Weak institutional environments – such as those in the USA and Britain – have become stronger as the central governments have become more involved in funding research. Hence, the trends toward stronger institutional environments have also tended to generate greater isomorphic pressures among organizations.

Thus far much of the discussion has focused primarily on the institutional environment of research organizations. But when we think of path-dependent processes, we also must be attentive to these processes within organizations. It is within the research organization where research and major discoveries occur. Figures 6.2, 6.3 and 6.4 suggest the path-dependent processes which occur among institutional environments, organizations and laboratories. The figures suggests that in the basic biomedical sciences, there are two general types of laboratories in research organizations. Those in which major discoveries may be made, for simplicity are called Type A, and their characteristics are (1) having a moderately high level of scientific diversity (that is, not highly specialized), (2) being well-connected to invisible colleges in multiple fields of science, (3) having access to instrumentation and funding for high risk research, and (4) having laboratory heads who internalize high cognitive complexity, have a good grasp of the direction in which science is moving and have a good sense of how different scientific fields might be integrated in order to move research in a chosen direction. As Figures 6.2, 6.3 and 6.4 suggest, laboratories can have all of these characteristics and yet have no major discoveries. In other words, a laboratory could be in an organization having characteristics associated with major discoveries and the laboratory could have the general structural and cultural characteristics associated with major discoveries, but have no major discovery. There is a certain amount of chance and luck in the making of major discoveries (Edelman, 1994, pp. 980–86; Jacob, 1995). But virtually every laboratory in our study of 290 major discoveries tended to have characteristics similar to those listed for Type A. Moreover, the organizational environments with characteristics similar to those listed in Box 6.2 were more likely to have a number of Type A laboratories.

Type B laboratories are at the opposite end of the continuum on virtually all the laboratory characteristics listed above. That is, the laboratories (1) have little scientific diversity, (2) are well-connected to invisible colleges in a single discipline, (3) have limited funding for high risk research, and (4) have laboratory heads with low levels of cognitive complexity, a tendency to avoid high-risk research and little concern with integrating

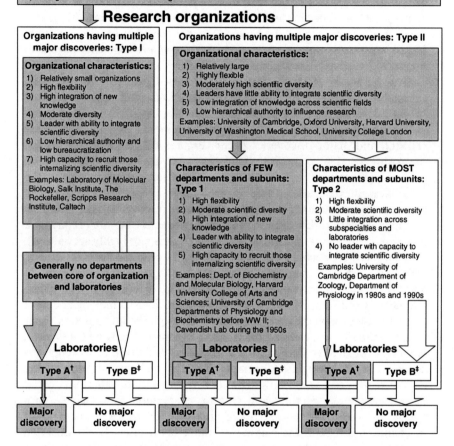

Weak institutional environment

Institutional characteristics: 1) Weak control over personnel; 2) Weak control over scientific disciplines; 3) Weak control over funding for scientific research; 4) Many different types of training systems; 5) Strong normative environment for high risk research

Research organizations

Organizations having multiple major discoveries: Type I

Organizational characteristics:

1) Relatively small organizations
2) High flexibility
3) High integration of new knowledge
4) Moderate diversity
5) Leader with ability to integrate scientific diversity
6) Low hierarchical authority and low bureaucratization
7) High capacity to recruit those internalizing scientific diversity

Examples: Laboratory of Molecular Biology, Salk Institute, The Rockefeller, Scripps Research Institute, Caltech

Generally no departments between core of organization and laboratories

Laboratories

| Type A† | Type B‡ |

| Major discovery | No major discovery |

Organizations having multiple major discoveries: Type II

Organizational characteristics:

1) Relatively large
2) Highly flexible
3) Moderately high scientific diversity
4) Leaders have little ability to integrate scientific diversity
5) Low integration of knowledge across scientific fields
6) Low hierarchical authority to influence research

Examples: University of Cambridge, Oxford University, Harvard University, University of Washington Medical School, University College London

Characteristics of FEW departments and subunits: Type 1

1) High flexibility
2) Moderate scientific diversity
3) High integration of new knowledge
4) Leader with ability to integrate scientific diversity
5) High capacity to recruit those internalizing scientific diversity

Examples: Dept. of Biochemistry and Molecular Biology, Harvard University College of Arts and Sciences; University of Cambridge Departments of Physiology and Biochemistry before WW II; Cavendish Lab during the 1950s

Laboratories

| Type A† | Type B‡ |

| Major discovery | No major discovery |

Characteristics of MOST departments and subunits: Type 2

1) High flexibility
2) Moderate scientific diversity
3) Little integration across subspecialties and laboratories
4) No leader with capacity to integrate scientific diversity

Examples: University of Cambridge Department of Zoology, Department of Physiology in 1980s and 1990s

Laboratories

| Type A† | Type B‡ |

| Major discovery | No major discovery |

Notes: The width of the arrows indicates the relative frequency of the specified outcome. Characteristics in grey tend to be associated with making major discoveries. †Type A laboratories have the following characteristics: 1) Cognitive: High scientific diversity; 2) Social: Well connected to invisible colleges (e.g. networks) in diverse fields; 3) Material resources: Access to new instrumentation and funding for high risk research; 4) Personality of laboratory head: High cognitive complexity, high confidence and motivation; 5) Leadership: Excellent grasp of ways scientific fields might be integrated and ability to move research in that direction. ‡See note in Figure 6.3 about Type B laboratories.

Figure 6.2   Multi-level analysis of major discoveries, panel one

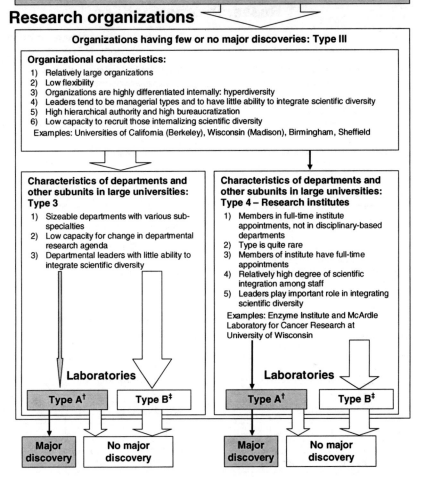

Weak institutional environment

Institutional characteristics: 1) Weak control over personnel; 2) Weak control over scientific disciplines; 3) Weak control over funding for scientific research; 4) Many different types of training systems; 5) Strong normative environment for high risk research

Research organizations

Organizations having few or no major discoveries: Type III

Organizational characteristics:

1) Relatively large organizations
2) Low flexibility
3) Organizations are highly differentiated internally: hyperdiversity
4) Leaders tend to be managerial types and to have little ability to integrate scientific diversity
5) High hierarchical authority and high bureaucratization
6) Low capacity to recruit those internalizing scientific diversity

Examples: Universities of California (Berkeley), Wisconsin (Madison), Birmingham, Sheffield

Characteristics of departments and other subunits in large universities: Type 3

1) Sizeable departments with various sub-specialties
2) Low capacity for change in departmental research agenda
3) Departmental leaders with little ability to integrate scientific diversity

Characteristics of departments and other subunits in large universities: Type 4 – Research institutes

1) Members in full-time institute appointments, not in disciplinary-based departments
2) Type is quite rare
3) Members of institute have full-time appointments
4) Relatively high degree of scientific integration among staff
5) Leaders play important role in integrating scientific diversity

Examples: Enzyme Institute and McArdle Laboratory for Cancer Research at University of Wisconsin

Laboratories

| Type A[†] | Type B[‡] |

Laboratories

| Type A[†] | Type B[‡] |

Major discovery | **No major discovery**

Major discovery | **No major discovery**

Notes: The width of the arrows indicates the relative frequency of the specified outcome. Characteristics in grey tend to be associated with making major discoveries. [†]See note in Figure 6.2 about Type A Laboratories. [‡]Type B laboratories have the following characteristics: 1) Cognitive: Moderately low scientific diversity; 2) Social: Well connected to invisible colleges (e.g. networks) in a single discipline; 3) Material resources: Limited funding for high risk research; 4) Personality of laboratory head: Lack of high cognitive complexity, limited inclination to conduct high risk research; 5) Leadership: Not greatly concerned with integrating scientific fields.

Figure 6.3   Multi-level analysis of major discoveries, panel two

　　　　　　　The evolution of path dependence

Strong institutional environment

Institutional characteristics: 1) Strong control over personnel; 2) Strong control over scientific disciplines; 3) Strong control over funding for scientific research; 4) Few types of training systems; 5) Weak normative environment for high risk research

Research organizations

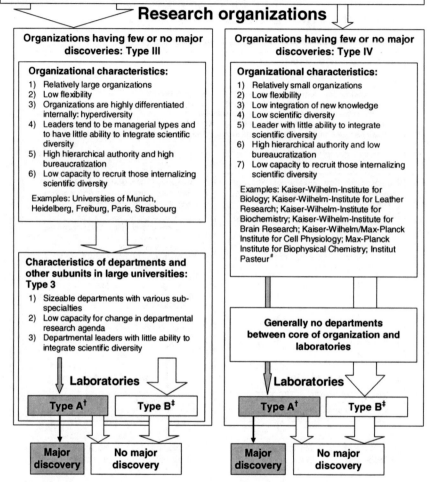

Organizations having few or no major discoveries: Type III

Organizational characteristics:
1) Relatively large organizations
2) Low flexibility
3) Organizations are highly differentiated internally: hyperdiversity
4) Leaders tend to be managerial types and to have little ability to integrate scientific diversity
5) High hierarchical authority and high bureaucratization
6) Low capacity to recruit those internalizing scientific diversity

Examples: Universities of Munich, Heidelberg, Freiburg, Paris, Strasbourg

Characteristics of departments and other subunits in large universities: Type 3
1) Sizeable departments with various sub-specialties
2) Low capacity for change in departmental research agenda
3) Departmental leaders with little ability to integrate scientific diversity

Laboratories

Type A† | Type B‡

Major discovery | No major discovery

Organizations having few or no major discoveries: Type IV

Organizational characteristics:
1) Relatively small organizations
2) Low flexibility
3) Low integration of new knowledge
4) Low scientific diversity
5) Leader with little ability to integrate scientific diversity
6) High hierarchical authority and low bureaucratization
7) Low capacity to recruit those internalizing scientific diversity

Examples: Kaiser-Wilhelm-Institute for Biology; Kaiser-Wilhelm-Institute for Leather Research; Kaiser-Wilhelm-Institute for Biochemistry; Kaiser-Wilhelm-Institute for Brain Research; Kaiser-Wilhelm/Max-Planck Institute for Cell Physiology; Max-Planck Institute for Biophysical Chemistry; Institut Pasteur#

Generally no departments between core of organization and laboratories

Laboratories

Type A† | Type B‡

Major discovery | No major discovery

Notes: The width of the arrows indicates the relative frequency of the specified outcome. Characteristics in grey tend to be associated with making major discoveries. †See note in Figure 6.2 about Type A Laboratories. ‡See note in Figure 6.3 about Type B Laboratories. #Institut Pasteur is a bit of an anomaly within this grouping. For most of its history, it has had relatively few major discoveries. But in the first two decades of the twentieth century and again during the late 1950s and into the 1960s, there were a number of major discoveries there. However, during the years when it had stronger connections with its institutional environment, it had fewer major discoveries.

Figure 6.4　Multi-level analysis of major discoveries, panel three

different scientific fields. Type B laboratories hardly ever have a major discovery (as identified by the criteria in Box 6.1). As Figures 6.2, 6.3 and 6.4 demonstrate, Type B laboratories may exist in almost any kind of research organization, but they are very common in large, highly differentiated organizations having hyper-scientific diversity.

CONCLUDING OBSERVATIONS

Institutions, research organizations and their component parts co-evolve, moving along a historical trajectory which in this chapter is labeled path dependency. Even though this trajectory is important in understanding research organizations and the innovations which take place in them, this is not to suggest that there is some kind of historical determinism. Despite the fact that actors are very much constrained by their environment, those in weak institutional environments have a great deal of latitude in shaping their scientific agenda.

The importance of path dependency for understanding social processes was nicely phrased by Paul David, who is frequently credited as being one of the first to use the concept: 'It is sometimes not possible to uncover the logic (or illogic) of the world around us except by understanding how it got that way' (David, 1985, p. 332). For David, a path-dependent sequence of events was one in which 'important influences upon the eventual outcome can be exerted by temporally remote events, including happenings dominated by chance events' (ibid.; Rycroft and Kash, 2002, pp. 21–2). But as David and others (Arthur, 1994; Rycroft and Kash, 2002) have pointed out, small events may have lasting and important effects – sometimes very modest – and at other times they have major consequences. Path-dependent processes tend to have both direct and indirect effects on innovativeness.

As suggested above, long-term changes in science involve path-dependent processes at multiple levels of society – at the macro institutional level, the meso level (that is, the organization) and the micro level (the laboratory). However, these different levels are intertwined in such a way that they are part of a system with complementary parts integrated into a social system with its own logic. Thus, while every American university and research organization is unique, with its own distinctive culture, when one visits an American research organization for even a short time, one can know very quickly by observing the behavior of actors (language aside) that one is not in a French or German research organization. This system of interdependence is a major characteristic of path-dependent processes. In other words, system interdependency emerges from co-evolutionary processes which are societally specific.

Despite the path-dependent processes operating in the American science system, it is important to make several additional observations. First, although there is a tendency for weak institutional environments to persist across time, changes in those environments are constantly occurring. In the case of the USA, the institutional environment has become somewhat stronger over time, and this alteration has increased the isomorphism among research organizations. This has also been the case in Britain, as research organizations have become increasingly dependent on funds from central government and thus subject to governmental directives.

Second, organizational cultures and structures have a remarkable degree of stability. Hence organizational contexts with the characteristics described in Boxes 6.2 and 6.3 continue over long periods. In short, there is a high degree of organizational path dependency. Figures 6.2, 6.3 and 6.4 suggest that the extent to which organizations make several, few or no major discoveries over time has a distinct pattern. Even so, the structures of laboratories within organizations are somewhat indeterminate. An organization with the characteristics in Box 6.3 may have a Type A laboratory, and even an occasional scientist who makes a major discovery. But there is little likelihood that there will be multiple discoveries in such an organization. Organizations described in terms of Box 6.2 variables have more Type A laboratories, and are more likely to have multiple major discoveries. But even this type of organization also may have Type B laboratories. (Type B laboratories, as previously noted, are unlikely to be places with major discoveries.)

The above analysis points out that innovations such as major discoveries are rare events. We cannot predict where and when they will occur. However, using path dependency, characteristics of institutional environments, organizational isomorphism and resistance to isomorphic pressures, we can begin to address the circumstances under which major discoveries are most, and least, likely to occur.

NOTES

1. I would very much like to acknowledge the help of David Gear, Jerry Hage and Ellen Jane Hollingsworth.
2. On the concept institutional complementarity, see Amable (2000), Hall and Soskice (2001), Crouch (2004), Boyer (2004) and Hollingsworth and Gear (2004).
3. The research project on major discoveries summarized herein is based on a great deal of archival research, many interviews and wide reading in many scientific fields. Archives have been used in the USA (for example, Rockefeller Archive Center, American Philosophical Society, University of Wisconsin, Caltech, University of California Berkeley, University of California San Francisco, University of California San Diego, Harvard Medical School) and in Great Britain and Europe. Over 420 interviews have been conducted with scientists on both sides of the Atlantic.

REFERENCES

Aldrich, H. (1979), *Organization and Environment*, New York: Prentice-Hall.

Aldrich, H., B. McKelvey and D. Ulrich (1984), 'Design strategy from the population perspective', *Journal of Management*, **10**, 67–86.

Allen, M.C. (2004), 'The varieties of capitalism paradigm: not enough variety?', *Socio-Economic Review*, **2**, 87–108.

Amable, B. (2000), 'Institutional complementarity and diversity of social systems of innovation and production', *Review of International Political Economy*, **7** (4), 645–87.

Arthur, B. (1994), *Increasing Returns and Path Dependence in the Economy*, Ann Arbor, MI: University of Michigan Press.

Ash, M.G. (ed.) (1997), *German Universities Past and Future*, Providence, RI: Berghahn.

Astley, W.G. (1985), 'The two ecologies: population and community perspectives on organizational evolution', *Administrative Science Quarterly*, **30**, 224–41.

Baum, J. (1996), 'Organization ecology', in C. Hardy and W. Herds (eds), *The Handbook of Organizational Studies*, London: Sage, pp. 77–114.

Boyer, R. (2004), 'Institutional complementarity: concepts, origins, and methods', unpublished paper presented at 16th Annual Meeting of the Society for the Advancement of Socio-Economics, George Washington University, Washington DC, 10 July.

Clark, B.R. (ed.) (1993), *The Research Foundations of Graduate Education: Germany, Britain, France, United States, Japan*, Berkeley, CA: University of California Press.

Clark, B.R. (1995), *Places of Inquiry: Research and Advanced Education in Modern Universities*, Berkeley, CA: University of California Press.

Crouch, C. (2004), 'Complementarity and innovation', paper prepared for Workshop on Complementarity at Max Plank Institute for Study of Societies, Cologne, Germany, 26–27 March.

Crouch, C. and W. Streeck (eds) (1997), *The Political Economy of Modern Capitalism*, London: Sage Publications.

David, P.A. (1985), 'Clio and the economics of QWERTY', *American Economic Review*, **76**, 332–7.

De Chadarevian, S. (2002), *Designs for Life: Molecular Biology after World War II*, Cambridge: Cambridge University Press.

DiMaggio, P. and W.W. Powell (1983), 'The iron cage revisited: institutional isomorphism and collective rationality in organizational fields', *American Sociological Review*, **48**, 147–60.

Edelman, G. (1994), 'The evolution of somatic selection: the antibody tale', *Genetics*, **138**, 975–81.

Garud, R. and P. Karnøe (eds.) (2001), *Path Dependence and Creation*, Mahwah, NJ: Lawrence Erlbaum Associates.

Geison, G.L. (1978), *Michael Foster and the Cambridge School of Physiology: The Scientific Enterprise in Late Victorian Society*, Princeton, NJ: Princeton University Press.

Gould, S.J. (1980), 'Is a new and general theory of evolution emerging', *Paleobiology*, **6**, 119–30.

Grew, R. (ed.) (1978), *Crises of Political Development in Europe and the United States*, Princeton, NJ: Princeton University Press.

Hage, J. and J.R. Hollingsworth (2000), 'Idea innovation networks: a strategy for integrating organizational and institutional analysis', *Organization Studies*, **21**, 971–1004.

Hall, P.A. and D. Soskice (2001), *Varieties of Capitalism: The Institutional Foundations of Comparative Advantage*, Oxford: Oxford University Press.

Hannan, M. and J. Freeman (1984) 'Structural inertia and organizational change', *American Sociological Review*, **29**, 149–64.

Hannan, M. and J. Freeman (eds) (1989), *Organizational Ecology*, Cambridge, MA: Harvard University Press.

Hawley, A. (1950) *A Theory of Community Structure*, New York: Ronald Press.

Hodgson, G. (2003), 'The mystery of routine: the Darwinian destiny of an evolutionary theory of economic change', *Revue Economique*, **34**, 355–84.

Hollingsworth, E.J. (2009), *Cambridge Scientists: Major Discoveries in Biomedicine and Biology*, forthcoming.

Hollingsworth, J.R. (1986), *A Political Economy of Medicine: Great Britain and the United States*, Baltimore, MO: Johns Hopkins University Press.

Hollingsworth, J.R. (2002), 'Research organizations and major discoveries in twentieth-century science: a case study of excellence in biomedical research', Research Paper 02–003, Berlin: Wissenschaftszentrum Berlin für Sozialforschung.

Hollingsworth, J.R. and R. Boyer (eds) (1997), *Contemporary Capitalism: The Embeddedness of Institutions*, Cambridge and New York: Cambridge University Press.

Hollingsworth, J.R. and D. Gear (2004), 'The "paradoxical nature" of complementarity in the quest for a research agenda on institutional analysis', paper prepared for Workshop on Complementarity at Max Plank Institute for Study of Societies, Cologne, Germany, 26–27 March.

Hollingsworth, J.R., P. Schmitter and W. Streeck (eds) (1994), *Governing Capitalist Economies: Performance and Control of Economic Sectors*, New York: Oxford University Press.

Jacob, F. (1995), *The Statue Within: An Autobiography*, Cold Spring Harbor, NY: Cold Spring Harbor Laboratory Press. This is a re-publication of the 1988 version published in English by Basic Books (translated from the French by Franklin Philip).

Kuhn, T.S. (1962), *The Structure of Scientific Revolutions*, Chicago, IL: University of Chicago Press.

Levi, M. (1997), 'A model, a method, and a map: rational choice in comparative and historical analysis', in M.I. Lichbach and A.S. Zuckerman (eds), *Comparative Politics: Rationality, Culture, and Structure*, Cambridge: Cambridge University Press, pp. 19–41

Mayntz, R. (2001), 'Die Bestimmung von Forschungsthemen in Max-Planck-Instituten im Spannungsfeld wissenschaftlicher und ausserwissenschaftslicher Interessen: Ein Forschungsbericht', Discussion Paper 01/8. Cologne: Max Planck Institute for the Study of Societies.

Mayr, E. (1963), *Animal Species and Evolution*, Cambridge, MA: Harvard University Press.

Mayr, E. (2001), *What Evolution Is*, New York: Basic Books.

McKelvey, B. (1982), *Organizational Systematics: Taxonomy, Evolution, Classification*, Berkeley, CA: University of California Press.

Needham, J. and E. Baldwin (eds) (1949), *Hopkins and Biochemistry, 1861–1947*, Cambridge: W. Heffer and Sons.

Nooteboom, B. (1999), 'Innovation, learning and industrial organization', *Cambridge Journal of Economics*, **23**, 127–50.

Pfeffer, J. (1981), *Power in Organizations*, Marshfield, MA: Pitman.

Pierson, P. (2000), 'Increasing returns, path dependence, and the study of politics', *American Political Science Review*, **94**, 251–67.

Romanelli, E. (1992), 'The evolution of new organizational forms', *Annual Review of Sociology*, **17**, 78–103.

Rizzello, S. and M. Turvani (2002), 'Subjective diversity and social learning: a cognitive perspective for understanding institutional behavior', *Constitutional Political Economy*, **13**, 210–14.

Rycroft, R.W. and D.E. Kash (2002), 'Path dependence in the innovation of complex technologies', *Technology Analysis and Strategic Management*, **14**, 21–35.

Stinchcombe, A. (1965), 'Social structure and organizations', in J. March (ed.), *Handbook of Organizations*, Chicago, IL: Rand McNally, pp. 153–93.

Streeck, W. and K. Yamamura (eds) (2001), *The Origins of Nonliberal Capitalism: Germany and Japan in Comparison*, Ithaca, NY: Cornell University Press.

Tilly, C. (1984), *Big Structures, Large Processes, Huge Comparisons*, New York: Russell Sage Foundation.

Ziman, J. (1987), *Knowing Everything About Nothing*, Cambridge: Cambridge University Press.

7. Path dependence and public policy: lessons from economics

Stephen E. Margolis

INTRODUCTION

Path dependence, as economists have come to use the term, is a condition in which economic outcomes exhibit inertia – they are what they are because they have been what they have been. At this very simple and general level, economies must exhibit path dependence, and lots of it. The houses, roads, factories and offices that we have today must be the ones that were built sometime in the past. In this sense, path dependence is an unavoidable consequence of ordinary durability of many physical assets. Similarly, the production technologies that are available to us today are those that we developed in the past. Knowledge too is a durable investment. Path dependence in this very limited sense is the rule, not the exception.

Economists model individual choices, and therefore aggregate outcomes, as the result of the interplay between what we want and what we can have – our preferences and production possibilities. In turn, production possibilities depend on our endowments, institutions and technologies. Since all three of these depend fundamentally on what has gone on in the past, economic outcomes must depend on history. None of that is new. Durability, broadly defined, has always been a part of economic analysis.

A new twist in this old concern with persistence has appeared in the economic literature since the mid-1980s. This literature expresses a view that economic outcomes depended on the past in more complex and more remote ways than we have ordinarily recognized. The influence of the past is not reflected merely in the resources that we have today. Instead, the past is manifest in the particular choices that we make today from the universe of possibilities. The past does not just govern the opportunity set, it also governs what allocations we choose from that set. I promise to illustrate this, and soon, but first I need to develop some background.

Economists' interest in path dependence, in the sense discussed above, has begun to spread to other fields. These fields include management theory, law and political science. In the following, I present an overview of path dependence that is aimed broadly at the public policy audience. To present that overview, I first discuss some fundamental issues of market performance. Following that, I present the origins and meanings of the contemporary use of path dependence in economics and explore some of the theory and empirical support for path dependence. Finally, I discuss some specific reasons why we should expect to find path dependence in public policies.

Path dependence in economics has been controversial so I should disclose here that I am not exactly a neutral reporter. Much of what follows will draw on work that I have done over the past 15 years with Stan Liebowitz[1] which has clearly put us on one side of the controversy that I will be presenting below. There are nuanced views and subtle distinctions on both sides of the argument, but to set the stage, here is a brutal simplification: the debate over path dependence originates with claims that where path dependence arises, economists' usual confidence in markets is misplaced. As Paul Krugman puts it, under the conditions that suggest path dependence, 'Markets cannot be trusted'.[2] Stan Liebowitz and I have argued that while markets can and do sometimes fail, path dependence does not offer any new brief against markets. Path dependence, in the simple sense of durability, must be all around us. But the logical leap from durability to market failure is long and against the wind.

EFFICIENCY AND EXTERNALITY

Economists' writings on path dependence have been concerned, at least in part, with economic efficiency. In important respects, this debate parallels a more general consideration of externalities. Public policy scholars will certainly be well acquainted with the concept of externality and its implications, but may not have encountered some of the critical perspectives on externality that have appeared in the economics literature. These perspectives are important to our writings on path dependence, so I consider them at some length here.

Economics has always been concerned with what can be called the Adam Smith problem: can the seemingly chaotic actions of individual decision-makers, each seeking his or her own self-interest, be relied upon to yield a desirable arrangement of their economic affairs? Is there any reason that a market outcome – a particular allocation of resources – should be regarded with any respect at all? Is the market allocation likely to be any better than a random draw out of an infinite number of possibilities? Is there any escaping the presumption that a market outcome is inferior to an alternative allocation that might be arranged by a moderately well-informed and well-intentioned social planner? In short, do we need a despot to organize our economic affairs?

Policy-makers inevitably deal with the marginal or incremental version of the Adam Smith problem. What should be the role of government? Economists cannot really get away from it either. In the early 1990s, an interviewer asked Nobel laureate Robert Lucas, 'What subjects do you think are on the economics frontier in the 90s?' He replied, 'In economic policy, the frontier never changes. The issue is always mercantilism and government intervention versus laissez faire and free markets'.[3]

A rough outline of the economists' answer to the Adam Smith question, or at least the answer provided by the economics mainstream, is well known to public policy scholars. In competitive markets, all goods that are worth their cost are produced. That is, markets allow consumers to express their willingness to pay for economic goods. Those who can provide these goods are induced to do so as long as they can produce the goods for less than consumers are willing to pay. Goods that are worth more than they cost to produce are thus produced, where the cost of a good is understood to mean the value of the things that must be given up to produce the good. All potential gains from trade are exploited. Competitive markets are, in a word, efficient.

From such a market equilibrium, we should expect that even well-informed and well-intended rearrangements would not improve things, or to be more precise, such rearrangements would not improve things for people in general. They might make things better for some people and worse for others, but not better for some and no worse for others. Outcomes that cannot be improved upon for people in general are said to be efficient. There are many such efficient outcomes.

That is the very compact version of the theoretical support for economists' presumption that markets are, with certain specific exceptions, efficient. That presumption is why economists take market outcomes as the starting point in public policy considerations. Economic policies – beyond certain market foundations such as the law of property and contract – are a collection of departures from market outcomes. This disposition in favor of markets does incorporate certain normative assumptions, principally that individuals are the relevant judges of their own self-interest and that an action that makes no one better off and some people worse off cannot be judged to make the society better off.

The basic efficiency of markets is the starting point, of course, but it is not where most economists stop. There are categories of allocation problems that markets do not necessarily solve. These categories are identified as externalities and public goods, the so-called market failures. I should emphasize here that when we say these are market failures, we mean that markets do not necessarily solve these allocation problems. They *might* solve some of them, but our theory provides no assurance that markets *necessarily* provide efficient outcomes.

Path dependence is closely related to the familiar problem of externality. An externality is said to exist where a decision-maker does not enjoy the full benefit or suffer the full cost of his or her action. Where some of the benefits of an activity are enjoyed by others, an individual will undertake too little of the activity, that is, less of it than he or she would undertake if somehow he or she enjoyed its full benefit. I don't engage in as much gardening as I might if I gave full consideration to my neighbor's interests. Symmetrically, where some of the costs of an action are borne by others, an individual will undertake too much of the activity. If I bore the full costs of driving my car, I would drive a socially optimal amount – using my car only to the point at which the gains of driving an additional mile equaled all of the costs. But since some of the costs of my driving are borne by others, I drive too much, consuming some miles that have total costs to society, including me, that exceed the benefits to me alone.

The standard teachings on externality move quickly from this presentation to a standard policy framework. Governments, it is argued, can remedy the errors that externalities induce through measures that, one way or another, correct the market allocation. The measures that most directly follow from the definition are taxes or subsidies that align private and social costs. Alternatively, where taxes and subsidies are too costly to administrate, direct regulation can bring about the desired correction.

This brief treatment of externality is often presented as the starting point for policy-oriented courses in economics or economics-oriented courses in public policy. In short, the standard teachings are that markets are good, except for definable categories of market failure. From that conclusion, we carve off large categories of failure that then are treated as suitable matters for public intervention. Environmental regulation is the closest example, where the theoretical foundation is explicitly linked to this analytical framework. Beyond that is a long list of government interventions that can be explained or justified by externality arguments. The list would include zoning, safety regulations, health care, education, workplace safety regulation, and on and on.

The problem with using externality as a platform for government intervention is that not all of the simple interactions that are potential externalities are actually market failures. An externality, by its very nature, confronts people with a real problem. Government remediation of an externality is warranted precisely because it constitutes a loss of wealth that could, in principle, be avoided. That is, some actor is imposing costs that are greater than the benefits that he or she enjoys. All of the parties involved – the harmed and the harmer – could benefit if the inefficiency were undone. By the mere fact that the cost of the externality-bearing activity exceeds the benefits, there is room for a bargain that could yield benefits to both parties. This is part of the contribution of a seminal paper by Ronald Coase (1960). Coase argues that under certain circumstances, transactions among the parties affected by an externality would lead to an efficient allocation of resources.

There are many very practical examples of market actions that internalize would-be externalities, though not all of these are the direct transactions that Coase considers. For example, within a residential area, some land uses impose costs or benefits on others. Investments in the appearance of structures might impose external benefits on owners of nearby structures. While it is not unusual to have government responses to this relationship, typically in the form of architectural standards or zoning, there are market alternatives. A developer of a large parcel of land will internalize all such interactions and will have every incentive to gather together land uses that benefit each other, separate those that harm each other, moderate appropriately any remaining negative effects and efficiently exploit any potential beneficial interactions. Similarly, department stores exist to exploit the potential beneficial interactions among disparate retailing activities. Office parks serve a similar purpose for business activities.

These arrangements are institutional responses that develop through the actions of profit seeking entities – people or companies – that internalize effects that might initially appear, or more importantly actually occur, as externalities. The consequence of such a possibility for economic theory or economic policy is enormous. First, while interactions may be determined by technology or the physical relationships among people, buildings or activities, externalities are not. External effects exist, or not, depending on particular institutional circumstances. Further, some market institutions, that is, institutions that arise from the voluntary actions of independent actors, are created because they solve the problems of interactions that would otherwise be unmediated – externalities. Because such institutions create benefits that exceed their costs, they can be profitable undertakings for their creators.

In principle, the existence of any inefficiency means that there is some possible reallocation that creates benefits that exceeds its costs. Consequently, any inefficiency may constitute a profit opportunity for someone who can figure out a way to solve the problem, unravel the inefficiency and appropriate some of the net benefit. The world of externality is vulnerable to the world of entrepreneurial action.

From this perspective, externality becomes a much less certain condition. It is for this reason that some economists are uneasy with the sometimes glib three-step argument that takes us from interaction to externality to implied public policy measure. This is not to say that there are no externalities that are best dealt with through government action. But it does say that the case for government action is not complete with the mere observation of an interaction that does not appear to be mediated by simple market transactions.

This argument relates closely to one put forward by Harold Demsetz.[4] Demsetz argues that any inefficiency claim implies that the parties affected by the inefficiency are, for some reason, unable to transact to alleviate the implied losses at a cost that is less than the benefit from solving their problem. In effect Demsetz raises the question, if there is some alternative to the status quo that is better for some people and no worse for anyone else (a Pareto improvement), why do the people involved not take the actions necessary to bring about the change? His answer is that the costs of moving to the new allocation – transactions costs, organization costs or whatever we might like to call them – must be prohibitive. There is a better world out there, but the cost of getting from here to there is greater than the benefit. Demsetz's challenge to conventional doctrine on externalities is that these costs do not disappear when governments intervene. The costs may change, but they do not disappear.

In Demsetz's framework, there is still room for public action, and still the possibility that the market outcome is inefficient; inefficient in the sense that there is a feasible alternative that is preferable to market outcomes. But establishing this inefficiency requires that it be demonstrated by a specific policy – literally a policy proposal – for which the benefits exceed the costs, where the costs are defined to include all of the organizational, transactions or administrative costs of the program.

Demsetz's conception of efficiency is a broad condemnation of theoretical welfare economics as it has been practiced. The established welfare economics algorithm is to specify certain economic conditions (tastes, technology and endowments) under some set of market institutions, characterize the ideal outcome, characterize the market outcome and declare the difference to be an inefficiency.

Some critics have incorrectly dismissed Demsetz's stance (and our related arguments) as Panglossian, arguing that it amounts to 'we live in the best of all possible worlds', or 'whatever is, is best'. In fact, it is nothing of the kind. Instead, it is actually a very hard-headed, unromantic and policy-oriented view of the world. It requires that we look for real policies and declare the world to be inefficient only where there are feasible improvements on market outcomes. It is also a view that should feel familiar to public policy scholars. It diminishes somewhat the role of purely theoretical constructions and elevates the role of analysis of actual policies.

All that said, external effects and public goods do remain useful concepts. They direct our attention to circumstances in which there might be a role for collective action. They also may constitute a simple though minimal test of candidates for government intervention. They imply a narrowing of the field for potential efficiency-justified intervention. Of any proposed intervention, it may be asked, is there some reason to think that the decisions of individual producers and consumers cannot be expected to lead to efficient outcomes? Absent an argument that connects the proposal to one of the categories of market failure, the presumption would seem to go against the market intervention. Unfortunately, this hurdle may not be very high, given the ease with which externality may be asserted.

BACK TO THE PAST: PATH DEPENDENCE

Definitions

Thus far, I have referred to path dependence as only a kind of inertia in economic outcomes. That simple characterization does capture the essence of path dependence. A claim that something is path dependent is, for most writers, a claim that in one sense or another, history matters. Here, for example, is Paul David, one of the key advocates for the concept of path dependence: 'A path dependent sequence of economic changes is one of which important influences upon the eventual outcome can be exerted by temporally remote events, including happenings dominated by chance elements rather than systematic forces' (1985, p. 332). For David and some others, an important aspect of path dependence is that small and seemingly remote events can exert a surprising influence on major outcomes. In Brian Arthur's seminal article (1989) on path dependence, titled 'Competing technologies, increasing returns, and lock-in by historical events', he emphasizes the tendency of path-dependent processes to 'lock in' certain economic outcomes. For Arthur, these outcomes are not necessarily chosen by fundamental underlying forces, but rather by 'small events'. Consequently, they are subject to 'nonpredictability' and 'potential inefficiency'.

What sort of things are they talking about? David famously uses the example of the typewriter keyboard, arguing that the QWERTY arrangement was offered at a critical moment in the development of typing technology, became established as the convention and stuck. (More about that later.) Robin Cowan (1990, pp. 542–3) repeats Arthur's story that an outbreak of hoof and mouth disease prompted farmers to leave water troughs empty, which hampered the development of steam automobiles in favor of the internal combustion engine. Cowan offers this episode as a 'small historical event', using Brian Arthur's phrase, that explains, at least in part, how internal combustion came to dominate steam power in automobiles. One more popular tale comes from the standards battle in video-cassette recording between Beta and VHS. As this one is popularly told, Beta was the better standard, but as a result of some fortunate licensing choices, VHS gained an early lead in consumer sales, which resulted in its domination of the field because consumers valued compatibility with one another, and so hopped on an ever-growing VHS bandwagon.

A Taxonomy

The term 'path dependence' has taken on subtly different meanings in different applications. It always incorporates some degree of persistence or memory. But in some instances, path dependence constitutes a 'lock-in' to some regrettable outcome. In other cases, it is just persistence. In our writings (Liebowitz and Margolis, 1995a; 1999), we have defined three types or degrees of path dependence. Two of these are absolutely commonplace and thoroughly incorporated into ordinary reasoning about economic matters. The third is uncommon, and is the type that may have implications for government action.

First-degree path dependence is simple durability. If I build a house with three bedrooms this year; I have a house with three bedrooms next year. There is no error implied by first-degree path dependence. Early on, when I have no children, my house may be a bit larger than would be ideal, given the costs of space. Later, while we have children in the home it may be a bit too small, and still later on when the kids are gone, a bit too large again. All this may be anticipated perfectly well and the house size chosen could well be optimal over the life of a household. Moment to moment the choice could be viewed by an outsider as inefficient, but given the transactions costs of buying and selling a house, or of adding and subtracting from a structure, the arrangement is just fine, something that even an outside observer is likely to understand.

Second-degree path dependence occurs where a decision is made that subsequent events reveal to be inferior to some alternative. This form of path dependence is like the first, except that the durable values chosen at some moment reflect an imperfect forecast. A couple may have chosen a home that would accommodate two children nicely, but then their second pregnancy produces twins. With three children, the house is too small. The couple would act differently if they had it to do over again, yet they may tolerate some crowding, given the costs of adjustment. There is no true error here. The decision-makers made the best use of the available information. After the fact, the resource allocation (the size of the house) is not optimal for the conditions that actually occurred, and an outside observer could not explain the resource allocation without some knowledge of past expectations. Still, while there may be regret under second-degree path dependence, there is no true error, because at the time that it was appropriate to make certain durable commitments, the actors did not have information that would allow them to do better.

Third-degree path dependence, by contrast, involves error. At some moment, an action is taken that can be determined to be inferior to some feasible alternative. This is true error: it is possible to do better, but we have not.

Simple examples like our homebuyers' problems, in which an individual makes a decision that has no external effects, do not offer appealing illustrations of third-degree path dependence. If three bedrooms is not a good choice and they know it, why would they choose three bedrooms? However, when one person's decision can affect the outcomes for someone else at some time in the future, this sort of time-related error becomes a possibility. The Beta–VHS story, which is considered further below, could be made to fit the third-degree definition. If we all preferred the Beta format, but nevertheless all ended up with VHS when we could just as easily have chosen Beta, adoption of VHS as the standard is an error, a market failure and a third-degree form of path dependence.

First- and second-degree path dependences are extremely common. Most actions that we take have some durable consequences, and some consequences of those actions are very long lived. History does matter. Further, history may matter in surprising ways. Durability is not confined to the enduring objects that we ordinarily think of as durable goods. Conventions such as language and measurement systems are also durable. Systems of compatible components are often much more durable than the components themselves. For example, if I once bought a VHS videocassette player, I will end up with a bunch of VHS cassettes, which means that when I replace the player, I will probably buy VHS again. Similarly, banking regulations will prompt financial institutions to grow up in a way that accommodates those regulations, which may make the regulations difficult and possibly unattractive to alter.[5]

The purpose of this taxonomy is to distinguish common instances of path dependence that clearly involve no market failure with the instances of path dependence that do, which Stan Liebowitz and I have argued are uncommon. This is particularly important because some of the economic literature of path dependence has clearly been concerned with market failures. If these claimed market failures are relevant for policy, in the sense that they constitute remediable[6] misallocations, they correspond to our third-degree category. The next section examines these claims.

PATH-DEPENDENT MARKET FAILURE

Consider a simple finger exercise that is motivated by the videocassette standards battle between the Beta and VHS formats. The example does not correspond to the actual Beta–VHS history, but VHS and Beta serve as memorable labels. (I will get to the actual history later.) The videocassette standards battle arises because consumers benefit from being compatible with other consumers. People want to be able to rent movies and lend tapes to friends and family members.

Now suppose that each of us looked at the two formats, Beta and VHS, and we each decided that we preferred the Beta standard. Suppose however, that for some reason, the initial sale or sales of videocassette recorders were VHS format machines. Under that circumstance, new purchasers might buy the VHS format due to their interest in compatibility with other sources of videocassettes. As more and more people adopted VHS, the reason for matching their choices would get stronger and stronger. In the end, we would all end up buying VHS, yet each of us would have been better off if the Beta format had emerged as the standard. Thus it *could* happen that even though the all-Beta equilibrium is preferred and feasible, and each of us knew that we preferred the Beta format, we ended up with VHS. After the fact, we might each applaud our good judgment in avoiding the orphaned Beta format, but we are really not so smart. There is a better world available but we did not find our way to it. The accretion of individually rational decisions did not bring about the outcome that was in our collective interests. This is a market failure.

Though very simple and restricted, this story incorporates the basic structure of a number of formal models of path-dependent market failure. In those models, some initial decision in favor of one standard or technology, perhaps for quite arbitrary reasons, is reinforced by the decisions of many other individuals, each acting in his or her own self-interest in light of the conditions he or she faces.

Now you may well be wondering, if we all like Beta better, why would that first person buy VHS? Or, if we all like Beta better, why would not each of us expect that other people would buy Beta? If we all like Beta better, would not we all see the consumer magazines reporting that Beta is better, causing each of us to expect a Beta avalanche and therefore buy Beta machines? (Might this interest in anticipating the action of the crowd even be one of the reasons for reading consumer magazines?) Would not friends and family be urging each other to join them in Beta paradise? While these considerations lie outside the simple example above, and outside the formal models that correspond to that simple example, they are hardly peripheral matters. We take them up further

Table 7.1   Adoption payoffs

Number of previous adoptions	0	10	20	30	40	50	60	70	80	90	100
Technology A	10	11	12	13	14	15	16	17	18	19	20
Technology B	4	7	10	13	16	19	22	25	28	31	34

below, but first let us look at another example that plays a prominent role in this literature.

One of the seminal articles in the literature of path dependence is Brian Arthur's 1989 paper. An important feature of that paper is a numerical example of a choice between two technologies that each exhibit increasing returns. Arthur's table is reproduced here as Table 7.1. The table shows the payoffs available to adopters of one of two alternative technologies. Notice that as the number of adopters of each technology increases, the payoffs to subsequent adopters increase. For now, assume that an adopter enjoys a benefit according to his or her position in the sequence of adopters, so that the payoffs to early adopters remain smaller than the benefits to later adopters. This payoff structure might occur where later adopters could learn from the trials and errors of early adopters, or could purchase better equipment, or could hire workers who were already trained and experienced. Two features of this numerical example are important. First, it incorporates increasing returns in each technology[7] – payoffs grow as adoptions increase. Second, it assumes that the technology that performs better at high levels of adoption is inferior at low levels. Both features are necessary for the example to work as it does. The first is explicit in Arthur's presentation, the second is not explicitly acknowledged but is a significant restriction.

Arthur's analysis of how this technology adoption would unfold is straightforward. The first adopter would face a choice of payoffs of 10 for technology A or 4 for technology B, and so would choose technology A. The second, third and fourth adopters would do the same, and so on. The eleventh adopter could enjoy a payoff of 11 with technology A, but would still enjoy only 4 as the first adopter of technology B, and would therefore choose technology A. This pattern would continue, with all subsequent decisions reinforcing it, so that with 100 adoptions, additional adopters continue to choose A, enjoying 20, against the alternative, still 4, with B.

The outcome of all this is undesirable, because at high levels of adoption, technology B yields bigger payoffs than technology A. Decentralized decision-making leads inexorably to full adoption of technology A, but technology B ultimately would yield greater benefits. We get, using Arthur's terminology, 'lock-in'.

Indeed, Arthur's numerical example does illustrate a potential for market failure. The payoffs in the table reflect an externality: early adopters do not take into account the potential benefits that they could confer on later adopters, so in principle there is the potential for market failure. But as discussed in the second section, the implied inefficiency suggests a profit opportunity for someone who can figure out how to remedy the problem and appropriate some of the difference between costs and benefits.

If the two technologies in Arthur's example are owned, as would be the case if they were protected by patent, copyright or trade secret, the existence of an actual externality is not at all clear. The owners of each of these technologies can expect to capture a portion of the surpluses that are shown in the table. Clearly, each of the owners would gain from having his or her technology adopted, but if expected adoptions are high, the owner of technology B has more to gain than the owner of technology A. Both owners would be willing to invest something to induce adoption, but the owner of B can expect to recover a larger return from establishing his technology. Each owner would find it in his or her interests to offer discounts and subsidies, to advertise, to provide technical support, to lease rather than sell the technology, to offer money-back guarantees, to grant exclusive licenses, and so on in order to establish his format as the standard. Each of them could use any of a large number of strategies that would, in effect, redistribute the payoffs in the table so as to make the early adopters better off. It is not necessary that the owner be able to appropriate the entire surplus generated. It requires only that the owner of B is not substantially worse than the owner of A at appropriating a portion of the surplus.

Even if the technologies are not owned, adoption of technology A is not inevitable. A very large company, choosing between these technologies, might itself constitute many adoptions. Such a firm might experiment with technology B as an early adopter, then transfer the experience to a large number of other sites or other applications. Again, the potential market failure constitutes a profit opportunity that can be expected to bring forth entrepreneurial efforts. A large firm acting first to adopt technology B will have a cost advantage for a time and will better its competitors further by avoiding the mis-step of adopting technology A.

Arthur's numerical example actually embeds a bigger problem – a more serious potential market failure – than the possibility that A will be chosen over B. As construed, the example offers no mechanism for getting started with either technology. Absent some method of redistributing the payoffs in the table, no party will wish to go first with A *or* B. Instead, each potential adopter will hope to outwait the others, hoping to enjoy the larger payoffs that accrue to later adopters. Absent some auxiliary mechanism for explaining the sequence of adopters, something other than passive reaction to the payoffs available is necessary if either technology is to be adopted in reasonable time, or even adopted at all. Entrepreneurial action to establish these technologies is not a contrived attachment to this example, but a necessary element.

We get a different story altogether if we assume that each adopter of a technology enjoys the same payoff as every other adopter of that technology. That is to say, your payoff depends only on the total number of other adopters, not on your sequence among the adopters. This assumption fits better with a networks or standards adoption than it does with technology adoption. Under this common-payoffs assumption, there is no problem of everyone wanting to go last. In this case, however, if adopters have any foresight, and if they are aware of the basic structure of the payoffs that are shown in the table, they, and we, should not expect that adopters will choose technology A. If large numbers of adoptions are expected (say, we expect that a lot of people will get mobile phones), then adopters will look forward to the payoffs that are available at 100 or more adoptions, and they will simply choose technology B. There is no potential market failure to worry about.

Different results are implied if we assume that the parties involved do not have the information in the payoff table, that the only thing that they can observe is the payoff that is available, at any moment, to the next adopter. If we assume this sort of myopia on the part of all of the parties involved, then indeed the market outcome may well be adoption of technology A, the inferior technology. This, however, would be a peculiar case to identify as a market failure, for the potential Pareto improvement is somehow there, in a theoretical sense, but it is not known to anyone. Neither the owners of the technologies nor the potential consumers are aware of the potential gains of either technology. While it is true that the superior technology B lurks in the background, its capabilities are undetected. In a sense, it is like penicillin before Fleming. It is there, alright, but we are not aware that it might offer us substantial benefits. Of course, the world would be a better place for us if we knew more than we know, but it is not informative to call this condition a market failure.

Arthur's table and the contrived version of the Beta–VHS wars that I presented earlier each raise the possibility of 'lock-in' by historically small and remote events. However, where the resulting lock-in imposes losses, there will be incentives for some of the parties involved to seek ways to avoid the trap; to avoid the implied externality. Where the externality is not internalized, that might be because the costs are too high or the information necessary is unavailable. This does not define away the possibility of relevant market failure or a role for government in remedying such a failure, but it does establish that durability or persistence alone does not establish that market failure is likely. What would be required to establish market failure here is the same as that which is required elsewhere, a demonstration that a feasible improvement is available, even when all of the costs of an actual policy are taken into account.

THE EMPIRICAL CASE FOR PATH-DEPENDENT MARKET FAILURE

Because there are durable assets, the consequences of our decisions can be with us for a long time, even when those decisions turn out to be incorrect. Consequently, we cannot fully explain the allocation of resources by an optimization model that ignores irreversible commitments that were made some time in the past. Examples of first- and second-degree path dependence are abundant. What should be less common is what we have called third-degree path dependence – remediable inefficiencies that are carried into the present by decisions that were made in the past. A portion of the literature of path dependence was concerned with presenting examples of path-dependent market failure. Here, very briefly, are the two cases that are commonly cited in exposition and support of path dependence.

QWERTY–Dvorak

In 'Clio and the economics of QWERTY', Paul David (1985) relates the widely known story of the standards battle in typewriter keyboards to economic theory. According to the standard story, in the 1860s, when Christopher Latham Sholes and his collaborators developed what would become the first commercially successful typewriter, they chose a keyboard arrangement that addressed a mechanical problem of jamming type hammers. That mechanical problem was short lived, but the popularity of Sholes's typewriter, which became the Remington Typewriter, established the 'QWERTY' keyboard arrangement as the standard. In the 1930s, August Dvorak developed a superior keyboard arrangement that was easier to learn and allowed dramatically higher typing speeds. Unfortunately, the story goes, few people have adopted the Dvorak arrangement because machines and training are hard to find, and machines and training are hard to find because so few people have adopted the Dvorak arrangement. Of this, David writes,

> In spite of the presence of the sort of externalities that standard static analysis tells us would interfere with the achievement of the socially optimal degree of systems compatibility, competition in the absence of perfect futures markets

> drove the industry prematurely into standardization *on the wrong system* – where decentralized decision making subsequently has sufficed to hold it. (1985, p. 336, emphasis in the original)

In short, we have a market failure due to the persistence of past decisions. Initial commitments to a standard led us to the wrong system, and decentralized decision-making has kept us there.

The problem with this story is that it is not true. Most of the early studies that established a substantial advantage of Dvorak's patented arrangement were carried out by Dvorak himself. This included one influential study, sometimes called 'The Navy study'[8] that, it turns out, was completed under Dvorak's supervision during the Second World War. The problem is not just a matter of appearance of a conflict of interest. In the Navy study, differences between the experimental treatment of the Dvorak and QWERTY typists repeatedly stack up against QWERTY. Modern experimental and simulation studies that compare the Dvorak and QWERTY arrangements provide mixed results, but show nothing like the enormous advantages that Dvorak claimed and others have echoed. The studies that appear to be the most credible find either no advantage for the Dvorak arrangement or only a very slight one. An experiment performed by Earle Strong for the General Services Administration (GSA) in 1956, which was much anticipated and influential at the time, concluded that the Dvorak keyboard had no advantage at all over the QWERTY keyboard (Strong, 1956). (For a detailed history and discussion, see Liebowitz and Margolis, 1990.)

The QWERTY–Dvorak story has been cited as empirical support in a number of prominent theoretical papers that feature the lock-in property. Even though the QWERTY–Dvorak story is now widely regarded as discredited, some writers continue to use it. Some have even argued that even though the story is not historically correct, it remains a valuable device for illustrating and motivating path dependence. Paul David (1999, p. 3) writes, 'For me the story of the evolution of the QWERTY keyboard format continues to be an instructive and empirically sound heuristic, exhibiting a constellation of generic features to which many episodes in technological and institutional history conform'. In part, this repeats the claim in David's 1985 paper to the effect that QWERTY problems are not uncommon: 'Outcomes of this kind are not so exotic' (p. 336).

Beta–VHS

This standards battle is another favorite illustration of lock-in of an inferior choice, one that has been used by a number of prominent writers including Brian Arthur (1990). The story that is usually told (and here I am following

Arthur closely) is that the market for videocassette recorders started out with two competing formats, VHS and Beta, selling for about the same prices. Because of consumers' interest in compatibility, a small lead for VHS resulting from either luck or some shrewd marketing decisions led to a tipping of the market toward VHS and eventual domination by that format. Arthur notes the claim that Beta is a superior format and argues that if the claim is true, domination by VHS is a lock-in to an inferior choice.

The actual history and technology of this standards battle argue against its continued use as an example of harmful lock-in. The two formats had very similar technology, the result of aborted cooperation between Sony (Beta) and Matsushita (VHS). Tests by the Consumers Union during this standards battle gave a slight edge in picture quality to VHS. The telling difference for most consumers, however, was that the VHS cassette allowed twice the recording time at a given tape speed, so that in early configurations the VHS machines could record for two hours while the Beta machines could record for only one. Beta did have some advantages for editing and special effects, but for most consumers, those advantages were unimportant in comparison with the longer taping time. So the eventual domination by VHS is not a choice of an inferior outcome.[9]

Moreover, the historical feature that most clearly counters the claim that Beta–VHS is an example of path dependence is that Beta had almost a two-year head start on VHS. If path dependence were at work in this case, the established base of Beta machines at the time that VHS arrived should have kept out the new upstart. Instead, consumers made their choices, forcing the market equilibrium rather abruptly off of the Beta path and giving them what they valued – a machine that could record most movies and some sporting events without requiring a change of tapes.

Here again, Stan Liebowitz and I (1999) have written about the VCR wars in much greater detail. We have also discussed allegations of path-dependent market failure concerning the operating systems market, measurement systems and the Japanese Ministry of International Trade and Industry (Liebowitz and Margolis, 1999).[10]

CAUSES OF PATH DEPENDENCE

The examples I have already covered either present or hint at most of the causes of path dependence, but an inventory will illustrate the scope of the path-dependence literature and may suggest some directions for additional research. Most of the literature, including our writing, has been concerned with the potential for path dependence in private actions, particularly in unregulated markets. What has not been explored very much are the origins and consequences of path dependence in public sector actions, a topic that may be of much greater importance to those with interests in public policy. The two lists that follow cannot be exhaustive, nor are the explanations entirely distinct, but I hope they will be illustrative.

Causes of Path Dependence in Private Actions

Durable goods

This is of course the simplest cause, the one that gives us most of the ubiquitous cases of first- and second-degree path dependence. Again, what we have today depends on durable commitments that we made at some time in the past.

Compatible systems

These too are everywhere and can appear with or without interactions between individual agents. Regarding individual actions, compatibility can introduce durability of a system that is greater than the durability of any single component. Consider a shop or factory that could be outfitted with either pneumatic or electric tools. Once the shop is in operation, as individual tools wear out they will be replaced with tools of the same type, because they are compatible with the shop's infrastructure. Similarly, as the infrastructure wears out it will be replaced with the infrastructure of the same type because it is compatible with the stock of tools. In this example, the chain can readily be broken if the choice grows to be inappropriate, but only if the losses are large enough to justify the change. Compatibility that involves many agents can introduce more complicated problems. For example, train tracks of a certain gauge will require carriages of the same gauge. Replacement carriages will have to fit the tracks, and replacement tracks will have to fit the carriages. A single line that did not interconnect with others is much like the pneumatic factory, and change would be straightforward if conditions ever warranted the change. For a system of interconnecting railways, change would require coordination among multiple railways.[11]

Increasing returns

This is a catch-all term in economics that is best understood as bigger is better. Slightly more formally, it means that as we double the scale of an activity, multiplying every input by two, we more than double the output. In the simplest context, this implies that production cost falls as output expands. In the path-dependence literature, increasing returns are used in a more general sense, that the benefits of an activity increase more than in proportion to increases in the scale of the activity. The next three 'causes' can all be understood as instances of increasing returns.

Network effects
Network effects occur where the benefit to any individual from using a particular good depends on the number of other individuals who are using the good. Fax machines and telephones are common examples. Any path dependence originates in the momentum that can build toward the selection of one network in competition with others. Two externalities are alleged, one that may yield the wrong network, following the logic of either the Beta–VHS wars or Arthur's numerical example, and one that yields networks that are too small.[12]

Standards
Standards are conventions that allow individuals to interact efficiently. These include things like languages, measurement systems and operating systems. Standards lead to path dependence because they exhibit network effects. The Beta–VHS example is a standards story. So is competition in operating systems.

Technology development
As experience with a technology grows, the benefits of using the technology often increase and the costs decrease. In competition between technologies, early adoptions may pave the way for later adoptions, so that early decisions can have a lasting effect. Early investments in a technology are irreversible fixed investments that can lend permanence to decisions, for better or worse.

Causes of Path Dependence in Public Actions[13]

Some of the causes of path dependence in private actions will also influence outcomes in the public sector. Simple durability and compatible systems will cause old decisions about public facilities to have lasting influences. The remaining three items in the list above will also appear in the public sector, though the nature of the coordination problems should be different in the public sector.

Concentration of interests
Theories of public choice identify circumstances that allow individual interests to be disproportionately more or less effective in influencing political outcomes. A concentrated interest is more likely to be effective than a diffuse interest – 10 000 people who each have an interest of $1 million are more likely to defend their interest effectively than 10 million people who each have an interest of $1000. The costs of organizing the larger group are simply higher than the cost of organizing the smaller group. In itself,

this asymmetry is not a cause of path dependence, but many public policies create groups of beneficiaries with substantial interests in the policies. Pension policies, tax breaks, subsidies and import protections each create concentrated interests that are likely to be effective in resisting change.

The transitional gains trap[14]

Governments often intervene in markets to blunt competition for one reason or another. Cartelization of agriculture is typically advocated explicitly as a means or raising farmer's incomes, though it is sometimes also supported as necessary to assure stable supplies and prices. Similarly, many city governments restrict the number of taxicab licenses (or medallions), claiming that higher wages for cab drivers will assure higher-quality drivers and better-maintained cabs.

Though these programs often do confer a windfall gain on a group of initial targeted beneficiaries, their benefit is often capitalized into the price of some asset required for entry. In the US tobacco program, for example, owners of 'quota', which is the right to grow tobacco, do earn a return on that asset, but the returns to tobacco farming itself are not elevated over the opportunity costs of farmers. Similarly, a large part of the price of taxicab rides in New York covers the investment costs in the taxi medallions, which now sell for about $300 000 (corporate-owned medallions) and the residual returns to the operators of taxicabs is forced to their opportunity costs. The consequence is that both producers and consumers suffer the monopoly welfare losses, yet current taxicab operators do not enjoy any significant increase in income.

A government could undo this problem by abolishing the supply restrictions, but once the monopoly rents have been capitalized into the cost of entry, abolishing the program has undesired equity effects, quite possibly imposing severe harm on the class of people that the program was intended to help. There is a legitimate equity concern for those who bought medallions at the elevated prices that reflect their scarcity. In principle, the potential winners from removing the output restriction could compensate the potential losers, but typically it will be very difficult to arrange such compensation. The government could buy out the current rights holders, but that too will impose efficiency losses through the deadweight loss of taxation. The consequence is that these restrictions can be quite enduring.[15]

Land use restriction is another important example. It is less obvious, because we do not observe directly the price of a license or quota, but its effects are similar. Some regions place severe restrictions on development of land for residences or other buildings. The resulting rents are capitalized into the prices of buildings and land that is eligible for urban development.

Land is much more densely developed than it would be if land were available to development at its (usually agricultural) opportunity costs, and housing prices are higher. Though it is possible that almost everyone involved would be better if the restrictive land use policy had never been adopted, many people end up with a stake in the system of restrictions. Homeowners and landlords who paid prices that were elevated by land use restrictions could expect to suffer capital losses if the restrictions were ever removed. These parties constitute a formidable interest group favoring the status quo. Asymmetries in the concentration of interests combine with an equity concern for those who bought property at prices that reflect land use restrictions to maintain the status quo.

Kreuger's (1990) study of the history of US policies toward the sugar industry is a detailed illustration of a transitional gains trap. United States tariffs on sugar date back to 1796, however the modern sugar program originated in 1934 as a means of raising the incomes of domestic producers and aiding Cuba. Since then, the program has survived numerous legislative regimes, technology changes and a reversal in the policy objective regarding Cuba. The various incarnations of the sugar program have resulted in higher prices of sugar for US consumers, elevated costs for producers that use sugar or other sweeteners, and for much of the time, substantial budgetary costs. Krueger shows that there were, nevertheless, few benefits to domestic participants. Once instituted, however, the program induced investment in program-specific assets. These investments gave growers, refiners, technical experts and bureaucrats substantial interests in continuation of some program that would maintain domestic prices at levels substantially above the prices in the rest of the world. The concentrated interests of these parties prevailed over the diffused interests of those who would gain from abandoning the program.

In *The Making of Economic Policy*, Dixit (1996) covers closely related themes in his application of Williamson's transactions cost framework to public policy. He observes that policy actions are durable; that once policies are implemented, they are not easily unwound. He cites the vested interests of bureaucrats and the constituencies that gain from a policy as defenders of the new status quo. He also considers those who, while not necessarily the recipients of a wealth transfer, have made irreversible investments as a consequence of the policy – the sugar refiners in Krueger's story of the sugar program. Dixit imports the contract doctrine of 'reliance' as a normative argument for protecting those vested interests: those who have relied on government announcements and made good investments in good faith should not have their investments rendered valueless by a policy reversal (ibid., pp. 22–6). He notes an efficiency argument as well. If governments reverse a policy action and thereby expropriate specific investments induced by those policies, investor responses to subsequent policy actions will be muted.

Of course, if a policy turns out to be misguided, so that the benefits of reversing the policy outweigh the costs, it would be possible in principle for the winners from reversal to compensate the losers while still retaining a surplus. But in the real world of transactions costs that is Dixit's focus, such remedies may not be available. Thus it is not possible to reverse all public policies that turn out to be inferior to some available alternative.

Having made transactions costs a central feature in his analysis of policy-making, Dixit incorporates Williamson's remediability test for inefficiency. Interestingly, he too anticipates the Pangloss criticism:

> This is not a Panglosian assertion that 'everything is for the best in this, the best of all possible worlds'; the best of all possible worlds would not be beset by transactions costs. Rather it is a reminder of how much policy freedom is constrained by transactions costs. It is saying, 'This world is far from being ideal; but a would-be policy innovator would do well to think whether the existing setup is making the best of, or at least coping quite well with, the world's imperfections'. (Dixit, 1996, pp. 146–7)

Dixit's treatment of path dependence draws on Paul David's version of the QWERTY story, noting that path dependence in market behaviour is 'often labeled "the economics of QWERTY." In the same way, the effects discussed above might be called "the politics of QWERTY"' (ibid., p. 28). Maybe 'the politics of taxicabs' would be a better choice.

Diminished competition
There is a potential for inertia in many human activities. People often are most comfortable doing things the way they have done them in the past. Many company histories report that failure or at least a difficult period occurred as the management became resistant to new ideas. In private markets, however, a company that refuses to change, perhaps failing to adopt new technologies, is likely to lose out to new companies or old ones that are less resistant to change. Democratic political processes should play a similar role, dispatching administrations that are unable to adapt to new circumstances, but the competitive pressures are somewhat less intense in the public sector. Candidates and parties constitute bundles of political positions, so that ineffectiveness in any one area may be lost in some larger picture that the voters must evaluate. Still, diminished does not mean absent, and all other things equal, we should expect that under democratic institutions, politicians can survive longer if they can make voters better off.

Limited rewards

Earlier I noted that in markets, some would-be inefficiencies can be remedied through profit-seeking activities that implement efficient changes and yield part of the surplus to the successful entrepreneur. Reward for such activities can be substantial. In the public sector, the compensation of political and civil service employees is highly constrained.[16] Public sector salaries are limited and typically there are no equity shares in government. Again, the distinction is easy to overstate, and entrepreneurship can nevertheless play a role. Politicians may achieve something like an equity share through land or stock holdings, consulting arrangements or other indirect compensation schemes. It is commonly observed that road building enhances the value of land that just happens to be owned by the politicians who managed to get the roads built. Often these outcomes are exposed or condemned as corruption, yet the election and re-election of these politicians suggests that the public either benefit or are not harmed by the practice. If the roads are going to be built, someone will have to assemble the political will to do so. Public sector entrepreneurship, like its private sector counterpart, is a difficult and risky business and is most likely to be undertaken by those with a stake in the outcome.

CONCLUSION

The appeal of path dependence resides in the simple truth that history matters. The debate over path dependence concerns how it matters. Path dependence of a very simple sort – persistence – is intuitively quite appealing and empirically important. There are things, institutions, conventions, practices, relationships and ways of operating that are enduring. Some persistence may not be immediately evident, and discovering that persistence can be important social science.

Path-dependent inefficiency, or lock-in, while theoretically possible, appears to be quite rare. The same forces that act against inefficiencies in 'ordinary' resource allocation also act against inefficiencies where durability is present. Although the conditions that are alleged to give rise to inefficient lock-in are quite common, real-world cases appear to be difficult to find.

Part of our brief has been to advise against confusing simple persistence with inefficient lock-in. The potential for error is extending the intuitive and empirical support for claims about ordinary persistence to the claims of inefficient lock-in. The simple fact of persistence should not be taken to imply a likelihood of inefficiency. Just as policy analysts should not accept the suggestion of remediable market failure at the allegation of externality, they should be skeptical that persistence is likely to enshrine inefficiency.

Public policy scholars may find it particularly interesting to consider sources of path dependence in public sector institutions. Some instances of path dependence may constitute inefficiencies and yet, even in the public sector, there are corrective forces that may mitigate the worst of these.

NOTES

1. Our first paper on this, Liebowitz and Margolis (1990), is a critical examination of the leading historical example on path dependence. Also see Liebowitz and Margolis (1995a; 1999).
2. Krugman (1994, p. 235). The full quote is 'In qwerty worlds, markets cannot be trusted', referring to the leading empirical example of path dependence. In that quote, Krugman is characterizing the path-dependence literature, not necessarily taking a position. In some of his more recent writings, he has expressed skepticism regarding some of the claims in the path-dependence literature.
3. The Federal Reserve Bank of Minneapolis (1993).
4. See Demsetz (1973). Related arguments have been presented by Calebresi (1968), Coase (1964) and Dahlman (1979). Williamson (1993) argues that an allocation that does not fully satisfy the usual efficiency conditions must be *remediable* for it to be properly called inefficient.
5. Mark Roe (1994) provides an extensive discussion of the interrelationships between specific banking regulations and the evolution of financial institutions, arguing in part that these interrelationships have enhanced the persistence of regulations in both Europe and the USA.
6. Our use of remediability in this and other writings follows Williamson (1993), who argues that a conclusion that something is inefficient requires that it be remediable.
7. Usually called 'network effects' in this literature, but in Arthur's telling 'increasing returns' is more appropriate since network effects accrue to old adopters as well as new adopters. I return to this point in a moment.
8. Navy Department (1944).
9. Lardner (1987) provides a detailed history.
10. For some other interesting examples, see Kobayashi and Ribstein (1996) and Van Vleck (1997).
11. Douglas Puffert (2000) provides an extensive study of the history of railroad gauge. Puffert interprets this history as one in which a gauge that was selected largely by chance was perpetuated in subsequent adoptions. In my view, the history that he presents can also be interpreted as one of experimentation of several distinct alternative gauges, with eventual widespread adoption of a choice that was appropriate over a broad range of applications, with survival of non-standard gauges in some local systems where they are particularly well suited. Under either reading, Puffert's history is valuable.
12. Liebowitz and Margolis (1995b) consider both of these. Among other things, we show that ownership of networks overcomes the too-small effect. Katz and Shapiro (1986) and Farrell and Salonor (1985) show various degrees of lock-in resulting from what Katz and Shapiro termed network externalities.
13. Our most complete treatment of path dependence (Liebowitz and Margolis, 1995a), though almost entirely concerned with path dependence in markets, noted that path-dependent inefficiency is more likely in government policies and institutions. The competitive pressures that we argued would act against inefficiencies in private markets are absent or less effective in the public sphere. Recently, political scientists have taken up

path dependence in the public sector and made similar points. See, for example Pierson (2000), who makes a case for path dependence in politics. He agues that increasing returns in the creation and maintenance of institutions, concentrations of power, the 'complexity and opacity of politics' in comparison to markets, and short time horizons induced by the electoral cycle, among other things, can result in path dependence.

14. This term is the title of a paper by Gordon Tullock (1975), which discusses the taxi medallion example that follows here.

15. The differences between markets and government can be overstated. As I am writing, comes news that a proposed buyout of the US tobacco program, which until very recently appeared to be dying in Congress, is now poised to pass. This is, however, somewhat idiosyncratic. John Edwards's candidacy for vice president has made North Carolina a swing state in the presidential election, which in turn has both parties reluctant to oppose this very substantial windfall to North Carolina farmers. Chalk one up, perhaps, for Pierson's 'opacity of politics' and maybe even Brian Arthur's historically small events.

16. Pierson (2000) makes a similar point in comparing our arguments about path dependence in markets with his regarding the public sector. Here again, it is easy to overstate the difference between the public and private sectors.

REFERENCES

Arthur, W.B. (1989), 'Competing technologies, increasing returns, and lock-in by historical events', *Economic Journal*, **97**, 642–65.

Arthur, W.B. (1990), 'Positive feedbacks in the economy', *Scientific American*, **262**, 92–9.

Calebresi, G. (1968), 'Transactions costs, resource allocation and liability rules: a comment', *Journal of Law and Economics*, **11**, 67–74.

Coase, R.H. (1960), 'The problem of social cost', *Journal of Law and Economics*, **3**, 1–44.

Coase, R.H. (1964), 'The regulated industries: discussion', *American Economic Review*, **54**, 194–7.

Cowan, R. (1990), 'Nuclear power reactors: a study of technological lock-in', *Journal of Economic History*, **50**, 541–66.

Dahlman, C. (1979), 'The problem of externality', *Journal of Law and Economics*, **22**, 141–63.

David, P.A. (1985), 'Clio and the economics of QWERTY', *American Economic Review*, **75**, 332–7.

David, P.A. (1999), 'At last, a remedy for chronic QWERTY-skepticism!', discussion paper for the European Summer School in Industrial Dynamics.

Demsetz, H. (1973), 'Information and efficiency: another viewpoint', *Journal of Law and Economics*, **10**, 1–22.

Dixit, A.K. (1996), *The Making of Economic Policy: A Transaction-Cost Politics Perspective*, Cambridge, MA: MIT Press.

Farrell J. and G. Saloner (1985), 'Standardization, compatibility, and innovation', *Rand Journal of Economics*, **16**, 70–83.

Federal Reserve Bank of Minneapolis (1993), 'Interview with Robert E. Lucas', *The Region*, June, available, at: http://www.minneapolisfed.org/publications_papers/pub_display.cfm?id=3727.

Katz, M. and C. Shapiro (1986), 'Technology adoption in the presence of network externalities', *Journal of Political Economy*, **94**, 822–41.

Kobayashi, B. and L. Ribstein (1996), 'Evolutions of spontaneous uniformity: evidence from the evolution of the limited liability company', *Economic Inquiry*, **34**, 464–83.

Krueger, A.O. (1990), 'Political economy of controls: American sugar', in M. Scott and D. Lal (eds), *Public Policy and Economic Development: Essays in Honour of Ian Little*, Oxford: Clarendon Press, pp. 170–216.

Krugman, P. (1994), *Peddling Prosperity*, New York: W.W. Norton.

Lardner, J. (1987), *Fast Forward*, New York: W.W. Norton.

Liebowitz, S.J. and S.E. Margolis (1990), 'The fable of the keys', *Journal of Law and Economics*, **22**, 1–26.

Liebowitz, S.J. and S.E. Margolis (1995a), 'Path dependence, lock-in and history', *Journal of Law, Economics, and Organization*, **11**, 205–26.

Liebowitz, S.J. and S.E. Margolis (1995b), 'Are network externalities a new market failure', *Research in Law and Economics*, **17**, 1–22.

Liebowitz, S.J. and S.E. Margolis (1999), *Winners, Losers and Microsoft: Competition and Antitrust in High Technology*, Oakland, CA: Independent Institute.

Navy Department (1944), *A Practical Experiment in Simplified Keyboard Retraining – A Report of the Retraining of Fourteen Standard Keyboard Typists in the Simplified Keyboard and a Comparison of Typist Improvement from Training on the Standard Keyboard and Retraining in the Simplified Keyboard*, Department of Services, Training Section, Washington, DC: Navy Department, Division of Shore Establishments and Civilian Personnel.

Pierson, P. (2000), 'Increasing returns, path dependence, and the study of politics', *American Political Science Review*, **94**, 251–67.

Puffert, D.J. (2000), 'The standardization of track gauge on North American railways, 1830–1890', *Journal of Economic History*, **60**, 933–60.

Roe, M.J. (1994), *Strong Managers, Weak Owners: The Political Roots of American Corporate Finance*, Princeton, NJ: Princeton University Press.

Strong, E.P. (1956), *A Comparative Experiment in Simplified Keyboard Retraining and Standard Keyboard Supplementary Training*, Washington, DC: US General Services Administration.

Tullock, G. (1975), 'The transitional gains trap', *Bell Journal of Economics*, **6**, 671–8.

Van Vleck, V.N. (1997), 'Delivering coal by road and by rail in Great Britain: the efficiency of the "silly little bobtailed coal wagons"', *Journal of Economic History*, **57**, 139–60.

Williamson, O.E. (1993), 'Transaction cost economics and organization theory', *Industrial and Corporate Change*, **2**, 107–56.

8. Can path dependence explain institutional change? Two approaches applied to welfare state reform[1]

Bernhard Ebbinghaus

INTRODUCTION

Over the past two decades, path dependence has become an increasingly popular concept in institutional theories in economics and other social sciences. Indeed, it has developed into a common 'short hand' to indicate that the past shapes the future – in short, history matters. However, upon closer analysis, we find two distinctly different interpretations of path dependence that I would like to summarize in two metaphors. One common image is the unplanned '*trodden* trail' that emerges through the subsequent repeated use by others of a path spontaneously chosen by an individual. A different illustration is the 'road *juncture*', the branching point at which a person needs to choose one of the available pathways in order to continue the journey. The path-dependence concept thus subsumes two markedly different approaches to understand historical sequencing. The two images of the 'trodden trail' and the 'road juncture' represent different social processes that in my view must be distinguished analytically: a persistent diffusion path and branching pathways. The first model stresses the spontaneous evolution of an institution and its subsequent long-term entrenchment; the second view looks at the interdependent sequence of events that structure the alternatives for future institutional changes.

Nevertheless, common to both approaches is the key idea that in a sequence of events, the latter decisions are not (entirely) independent from those that occurred in the past. In the language of probability theory, this sequential contingency is called path dependence. Path dependence results from non-linear self-reinforcing processes – in economic terms, increasing returns.[2] In a self-exemplifying manner, the adoption of the path-dependence concept in economics since the mid-1980s and somewhat later in the other social sciences demonstrates such a self-reinforcing diffusion process. The astonishingly swift proliferation of the concept must be seen in the context of the revival of institutional theories in economics, political science and sociology.[3] Neo-institutionalists embraced path dependence as empirical proof of the need to study institutions as resulting from dynamic social processes. We can also observe that some (sub-)disciplines, such as political sociology, depart more substantially from the initial use of path dependence in economics. Such recombining and enlarging the concept to be less restrictive or the 'branching out' of different theoretical pathways resembles the second image of path dependence.

Although definitions of institutions abound, they are commonly understood as social rules, norms and ideas (*Leitideen*) that guide, but also restrain, social behavior (Lepsius, 1990; North, 1990). Seen from an anthropological perspective, institutions are imminently functional: as 'taken-for-granted' behavioral routines they ease everyday decision-making; as social norms they regulate social interaction; and as cognitive scripts they reduce uncertainty in a complex world. Since some form of stability is a precondition for institutions to function, most theoretical and empirical analyses have focused thus far on the persistence of institutions (despite the use of 'institutional change' in book titles, for example, Alston et al., 1996; North, 1990). Recently, institutional theorists in various disciplines have pointed out different social mechanisms that stabilize institutions through path-dependent self-reinforcing processes. For the record, it should be noted that the 'old' institutionalists had already alluded to similar processes when referring to 'institutionalization' (Stinchcombe, 1968).

The equally important questions of when and how institutions evolve and why they change have been less often studied by institutionalist researchers. Thus, in this chapter, I raise the question of the degree to which we can explain institutional change with the help of the two mentioned path-dependence approaches. What are the known social mechanisms of path-dependent persistence? Could these also facilitate our explanations of change? To address these questions, I proceed in three steps. First, I sketch the rather deterministic path-dependence model that describes the repetition of one basic decision throughout a network of actors in a process of social diffusion. I discuss this model's shortcomings in explaining institutional change, particularly when it is applied to social institutions. Second, I illustrate the diffusion-like process using examples from my own study of early retirement trends. Third, I introduce the alternative, more open path-dependence concept and locate its potential for studying historical trajectories of institutional change. Fourth, I draw on institutionalist accounts of welfare state reforms to indicate the use of the open pathway concept. Finally, I review the social mechanisms of self-reinforcing processes, discussing their potential use in explaining institutional change – not only institutional inertia.

PATH DEPENDENCE I: 'TRODDEN TRAIL' AND THE DIFFUSION OF AN INSTITUTION

A path-dependent sequence of economic changes is one in which important influences upon the eventual outcome can be exerted by temporarily remote events, including happenings dominated by chance elements rather than systematic forces. (David, 1985, p. 332)

During the early 1980s in the USA, economic historian Paul A. David and system theorist Brian W. Arthur developed the first explicit path-dependence concept.[4] To model path dependence, Arthur used a Polya urn with two differently colored but equally sized sets of balls (Arthur, 1994, ch. 3). Every drawn ball is returned to the urn and doubled by adding a ball of the same color, thus slightly increasing the chances of drawing the same color in the next round. Even though it is always a random process, one color will dominate in the long run due to the positive feedback on already drawn balls of a particular color (the more one color is overrepresented, the more likely it will be drawn in subsequent rounds). Only in the increasingly unlikely event of a balancing out of both colors would there be no long-term positive feedback in either direction. QWERTY is probably the best known example of path dependence applied to technological innovation (David, 1985): the keyboard layout of American typewriters was developed 130 years ago to cope with technical problems of mechanical typewriters, without considering a more efficient keyboard arrangement with respect to typing speed. As users invested in learning this established standard, more optimal alternative keyboards could not later overcome the predominance of QWERTY, even during the fundamental technology-driven switch from mechanical to electric typewriters and then to computer keyboards.[5] The diffusion of this technological standard became a self-reinforcing process: the more people learned to use this design, the less likely it was for competing keyboards to take over.

Even though this prime example is drawn from the history of technological innovations, the path-dependence model based on the increasing return principle has often been applied to social institutions. Instead of the diffusion of a technology, the emphasis in such cases is on the societal acceptance of a social institution, for instance, the spontaneous emergence of a social convention. The time path plays a major role, with the diffusion process occurring slowly and sequentially as some institution diffuses through a social network (see Figure 8.1). Like the image of the trodden

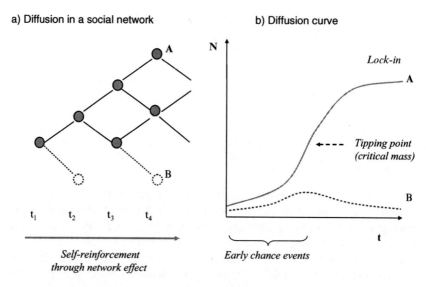

a) Diffusion in a social network   b) Diffusion curve

Figure 8.1   Path dependence I: trodden path

trail, a spontaneous social convention emerges through accidental but repeated use: the more individuals follow suit, the more deeply engrained it becomes. Henceforth, the likelihood that people will divert from it progressively declines. Whatever the reasons for its early success, once a critical mass of individuals has adopted the institution, the positive feedback process will stabilize the 'trodden trail' as ever more people orient their decisions based on the perception that a sufficient number of other people have already done so.

Four conditions are crucial for the 'deterministic'[6] path-dependence theorem (Arthur, 1994, ch. 7; cf. Ackermann, 2001):

1. The path-dependence model assumes an equal starting condition with the same initial probability. Theoretically, there are multiple equilibria possible since which 'path' will be taken depends on chance (tipping more frequently towards one color) during the early stages of the process. For instance, there is no a priori advantage of driving on the right or on the left; however, once a social convention has emerged, it will be very useful for any latecomer to adopt the common practice.

2. Self-reinforcing processes are the social mechanisms that are responsible for one alternative to take a lead over others. The diffusion of an institution occurs in particular through network effects. As more people adopt an innovation, the return on its use will increase. For

example, the more people are already using email, the higher the return for others to also adopt this means of communication.

3. As a consequence of these self-reinforcing processes, the once taken path will stabilize – a phenomenon commonly called 'lock-in'. Its irreversibility derives from the fact that actors have already invested in the dominant path ('sunk costs') and are thus unwilling to switch to an alternate one. Thus, changing from Windows to another operating system such as Linux may be costly, since one would have to learn to use the new system as well as replace all auxiliary software based on the Windows system.

4. According to Arthur, path-dependent processes can thus reinforce inefficient paths. As the model assumes multiple equilibria and early chance events tip the random walk towards one path, a suboptimal path – at least seen *ex post* and for society in general – may thus have emerged as persistent. In the case of keyboards, even a more speed-efficient layout hardly has a chance to replace the old less efficient one since it would require overcoming not only the sunk costs for each individual user but also the coordination problem of getting enough old and new users to switch at the same time.

From the perspective of economics, the inefficiency thesis is the most controversial, given that under unfettered market conditions, the most efficient innovation should prevail. Liebowitz and Margolis (1990; 1995; 1999) take issue with the inefficiency claim of path-dependence theory, both theoretically and empirically.[7] They distinguish three forms of path dependence, only the last version of which they see as contradicting neo-classical economics. As per their definition, first-degree path dependence reflects a process in which an early chance event may have long-term unanticipated consequences without being inefficient (an unproblematic case for both theories). Second-degree path dependence shows *post ante* inefficient long-term consequences, yet individual actors decided rationally on the basis of information available at the time, that is, they would have decided otherwise if they had known. Finally, third-degree path dependence is an inefficient outcome that would have been actually remediable: actors were aware that they deliberately chose a suboptimal solution.

There are two problems with Liebowitz and Margolis's critique (Ackermann, 2001, p. 35). First, they seem to apply a narrow actor-centered perspective – as if the evolution of a path were solely related to the rational decisions of *independent* actors. Yet path dependence is the evolutionary outcome of multi-actor collective interaction, thus an inefficient macro-level outcome (lock-in of a suboptimal institution) can well be the unintended consequence of the interaction of rational micro-level decisions by individual actors. Moreover, by requiring that a once taken path can be switched to remedy inefficiency in their third-degree definition, they assume that which the path-dependence theorem problematizes. The more the path becomes entrenched, the less likely it will be that the technology (or institution) can or will be easily replaced. It should be noted that Arthur and David both stressed that path dependence does not *always* and does not *necessarily* lead to inefficiency. For non-economists, the main concern is not the merits of the inefficiency thesis but the rather deterministic lock-in thesis that denies individual actors' freedom of action and excludes the potential for change.

Since the model assumes that small chance events in the early phase will have crucial long-term effects, both participating individuals and any researcher will find it difficult to predict which path will emerge in the future. Only *ex post* analyses will allow the tracing of paths. Similarly, the necessary critical mass (or tipping point) that has important effects in determining the final outcome of such a non-linear process cannot be pre-determined. It too can only be traced retrospectively through analysis of the diffusion curve. However, the model's main problem is that it excludes the individual actors and their strategies as well as the social contexts in which these processes take place (Crouch and Farrell, 2004): neither unequal resources at the start, nor the strategic action of individuals – who may seek to change course – are taken into account.[8]

The deterministic path-dependence model, in assuming the lasting impact of chance events at the beginning of but not later in the process, necessarily claims the inflexibility of institutions. But such 'lock-in' of a path seems to be a rather unrealistic assumption since it rules out even gradual adaptations of an institution to the environment that may be necessary for its long-term survival. Indeed, the Polya urn model is a closed system with an internal feedback mechanism that increases the number of balls of the winning color. An end to the 'lock-in' would only be possible through exogenous intervening factors, which are certainly outside the theoretical model. Thus, this 'deterministic' model can only explain those hyper-stable cases of path dependence that follow the assumption of stochastic events and unobstructed self-reinforcing processes.

PATH DEPENDENCE EXAMPLE I: UNINTENDED CONSEQUENCES OF EARLY RETIREMENT

Let me illustrate the process of path-dependent diffusion with an example from welfare state research (see Figure 8.2), showing the self-reinforcing path dependence in the case of early retirement (Ebbinghaus, 2006). Early

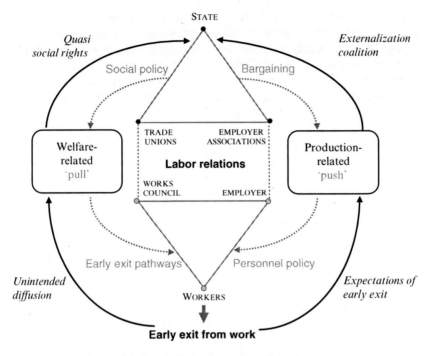

Figure 8.2   Example of path dependence I: early retirement

exit from work has become a common social practice for employers to shed labor and for older workers to seek early retirement, particularly since the onset of mass unemployment in the 1970s (Esping-Andersen, 1996). Although public policies advanced by the state and social partners in the national arena provided multiple pathways into early retirement, the expansion of such programs was largely an unintended consequence of policies not implemented with the explicit purpose of ever earlier withdrawal from the labor force. Instead, two actor constellations in and across workplaces have promoted the proliferation of this 'social innovation': the older workers (and workplace representatives) support early exits and the employers (and workplace representatives) use it for their own purposes.

As early as the 1930s, sociologist Robert K. Merton delineated several social mechanisms for such unintended consequences as a result of diffusion processes (Merton, 1936). His well-known example delineates how the rumor of bankruptcy can lead to a self-fulfilling prophecy: as panicked depositors withdraw their funds, the bank indeed falls into insolvency. Moreover, Merton also pointed out the impact of social comparison (with peers) and social expectations as social mechanisms that have large-scale consequences (Merton, 1967). Both processes play a role in explaining the expansion of early retirement and the subsequent difficulties to reverse its course, particularly in continental Europe (Ebbinghaus, 2000). While there are welfare-related 'pull' factors that explain the effects on labor supply (the decision of ever more workers to withdraw early from work) there are also 'push' factors that account for labor demand problems, especially the tendency of firms to shed older workers.

On the 'pull' side, public policies provided unintended pathways to retire early (Kohli et al., 1991), for instance, disability rules were increasingly used over time for shedding older workers from work. Moreover, many arrangements set up for particular circumstances became generalized through peer comparisons and public expectations to all sectors and conditions: early retirement programs that had started in particular sectors became a quasi-social right for all. In fact, once a particular cohort had retired earlier; the following cohorts claimed the right to do the same. This holds true particularly in pay-as-you-go systems: workers perceive that they have already paid into a scheme from which their former colleagues went on early retirement and that they have thus earned the same right when they reach the same age. However, this originally unintended diffusion of early exit has had the perverse effect that welfare state expenditures increased and social security contributions had to be raised, leading to further pressures on the labor market (Esping-Andersen, 1996). Once the quasi-social right was firmly entrenched, it became very difficult for governments to reverse such policies, or even control the ongoing early exit regimes, not least because there are also 'push' factors at work. This self-reinforcing diffusion process of a quasi-social right of early withdrawal in which programs largely intended for other purposes are generalized exemplifies the first type of path-dependent processes, the 'trodden trail' metaphor.

On the 'push' side, employers (or personnel departments) also have good reasons to collude with worker representatives in shedding older workers during a phase of downsizing and/or to maintain a high-skill internal labor market (Ebbinghaus, 2001). This is particularly the case when (1) public policies provide possibilities to off-load the costs and (2) early retirement benefits are socially acceptable to workplace representatives. Yet there is also a mechanism of deterministic path dependence at work that leads to unintended consequences (in Merton's terminology, a self-fulfilling prophecy). Employers defend early retirement by suggesting that older workers are less productive, although empirical evidence has not confirmed this belief (Casey, 1997). Regardless of the true productivity rates, once employers assume that workers are leaving earlier, they stop investing in continuing education or retraining measures for workers as their early retirement age approaches. This leads to an ever earlier out-dating of older workers' skill profiles, which then serves as proof of their lower productivity – a genuine self-fulfilling prophecy. Reversing early exit trends would therefore also require the altering of firm-level actors' expectations. Thus, the largely unfounded belief of employers about age-related productivity declines of older workers – in combination with firms' use of early retirement for socially accepted restructuring – leads to a self-reinforcing, self-fulfilling prophecy with long-term negative effects on welfare states.

PATH DEPENDENCE II: BRANCHING PATHWAYS AND THE STRUCTURING OF ALTERNATIVES

> Path-dependence is a way to narrow conceptually the choice set and link deci-sion making through time. It is not a story of inevitability in which the past predicts the future. (North, 1990, pp. 98–9)

In historical-institutionalist studies, the concept of path dependence has been used in a broader, non-deterministic sense: the concept 'path' is not primarily used to describe the emergence and persistence of an (unchanged) institution by repeated uniform basic decisions of individual actors, but the long-term developmental pathway of an institution, or complex insti-tutional arrangement, shaped by and then further adapted by collective actors. Actors are rarely in a situation in which they can ignore the past and decide *de novo*; their decisions are bound by past and current institutions. The main question here is, what are the consequences of path dependence for the further development of an institution? In other words, how much do past decisions shape the available alternatives for future ones? The emphasis here is on the *timing* and *sequence* of events (Pierson, 2004).

A seminal application of the developmental concept was undertaken by Douglass C. North, who won the Nobel prize in economics in 1993 for his work in economic history. North posed the question, why have some societies maintained less efficient developmental paths (North, 1990, p. 7)? Indeed, neoclassical competition theory and international trade theory are challenged by the puzzle of less efficient economic systems that are neither negatively selected nor converge towards a more productive institutional arrangement. According to North, there are three main causes that may explain the persistence of a suboptimal economic pathway (North, 1990):

- *Transaction costs* are high due to non-competitive markets – the adaptive mechanisms of prizes do not work properly (cf. North and Thomas, 1973).

- *Political factors* obstruct the institutionalization of property rights in such a way that competitive markets cannot operate properly (cf. North, 1981).
- The once established institutions become *locked-in* through path-dependent self-reinforcement (cf. North, 1990).

North, as many other social scientists with a historical approach, uses path dependence in the double sense used in this chapter as he refers both to the deterministic path dependence (I) of institutional lock-in due to micro-level diffusion processes as well as to the open developmental path dependence (II) as a sequence of macro-level institutional changes that are shaped by the lower level lock-in. Economic history is only one of many disciplines in the social sciences that have increasingly used the more open path-dependence concept to describe institutional development. In fact, comparative historical studies of the development of modern societies have continually used path dependence as a concept to claim that history matters. Beginning in the 1960s, prominent political sociologists Seymour Martin Lipset and Stein Rokkan adopted such a path-dependence view *avant la lettre* to explain the genesis and freezing of modern party systems in Western Europe (Lipset and Rokkan, 1967).[9] While the freezing thesis – that the post-war party system was highly institutionalized – seems to rest on a deterministic inertia claim, their diachronical approach was very sensitive to variance in the timing and sequences in social and political cleavages giving rise to distinct party formations across Western Europe prior to the 1960s (Flora, 1999).

Three features stand out as common themes in the older and newer historical analyses of developmental pathways (see Figure 8.3):

1. An institution emerges at a *critical juncture* at which collective actors establish new rules. The selection of a pathway is the result of political conflicts and power relations (Knight, 1992) during a window of opportunity for action, often opened up through a societal crisis situation (Stinchcombe, 1975).
2. A second element is the subsequent process of *institutionalization* through self-reinforcing processes, similar to those described by Arthur and David. Here, positive feedback allows for the societal acceptance of a newly established institution, providing legitimacy and objectivation (Berger and Luckmann, 1977).
3. The third feature is a wider understanding of path dependence in the sense of the *sequence* of contingent decisions. Earlier decisions, once institutionalized, 'structure the alternatives' (Rokkan, 1999) of later ones.

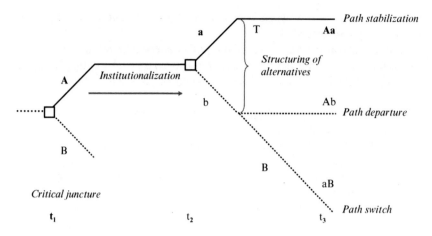

Figure 8.3   Path dependence II: branching pathways

An example of path dependence as narrowing the choice set is the juridical principle of precedence (and *stare decisis*) in the English common law tradition: courts are bound by past judgments and cannot divert without special reasons, thus reinforcing the traditional interpretation of law over long periods of time (Hathaway, 2000). The broader concept of path dependence thus reflects the metaphor of branching pathways, of sequential junctures at which collective actors decide which of the available alternative pathways they will follow. The claim is that, depending on the timing of previous institutions, their subsequent degree of institutionalization, and particular circumstances of the juncture, the alternatives are structured, with more fundamental changes more costly than gradual ones.

In contrast to the deterministic path-dependence theorem that assumes chance events will have long-term consequences, the developmental approach focuses on the particular historical origins of institutions.[10] Historical institutionalists see institutions emerging from more or less conscious choices by collective actors at critical junctures. Even if it is often impossible to precisely predict a critical juncture, for instance the fall of the Berlin wall in 1989, retrospective analysis can reveal the factors leading to the emergence of a new institution as the result of the interactions of collective action by individual and corporate actors in a given historical situation. However, this does not imply that the institution was necessarily planned or intended to operate in the way it actually emerged. The critical juncture model serves first and foremost as a working hypothesis that needs to be studied in historical comparative research. For instance, was the First World War a break, a catalyst or the continuation of long-term trends in modern societies?

In comparison to the deterministic path-dependence model, the developmental view allows for more openness to change. Analytically, three scenarios of institutional transformation can be distinguished:

(a) path *stabilization*: marginal adaptation to environmental changes without changing core principles;
(b) path *departure*: gradual adaptation through *partial* renewal of institutional arrangements and limited redirection of core principles;
(c) path *cessation or switching*: intervention that ends the self-reinforcement of an established institution and may give way to a new institution in its place.

If an institution is severely entrenched, we can expect path stability through marginal adaptation to changing environmental conditions to be the most likely scenario. Long-term stability results not only due to self-reinforcing processes that lead to 'lock-in' (according to deterministic path dependence), but also through successful gradual adaptation, often stated under the motto *plus ça change, plus c'est la même chose*. However, it remains an empirical question whether such adaptations are sufficient to stabilize the institution or whether institutional inertia inhibits necessary changes that may facilitate a path departure or even a systemic break.

A path departure becomes increasingly likely when more significant changes in the environment occur and the self-reinforcing mechanism provides sufficient resources for gradual adaptation. Here, the most relevant idea is of open path dependence, in which earlier decisions narrow the choice set but do not determine the next adaptive step. Path departure lies between locked-in inertia, when nothing effectively changes the basic foundation, and radical system change, when everything is built *de novo*. Yet between these extremes, path departure also entails various forms and often occurs through a variety of simultaneous processes:

- Long-term *gradual changes* that sum up over time to important reorientations (Pierson, 2000b).
- A *functional transformation* through which the same institution serves a different purpose than initially intended (Thelen, 2003).
- Institutional *layering* occurs through the addition of (new) institutional arrangements with divergent orientation (Thelen, 2003).

Further taxonomies of institutional change have been proposed (Streeck and Thelen, 2005), though we need to go beyond only describing different processes of change and establish the underlying mechanisms behind such processes as well as the conditions under which they are likely to occur.

The third and least likely possibility is radical transformation – path cessation or path switching. As in the case of the emergence of institutions, here we would examine the critical juncture at which a change in the opportunity structure led to a freeing-up of societal resources (Stinchcombe, 1965) and allowed a shift in the path, not least through the actions of political entrepreneurs. In such cases, it becomes necessary to explain why the self-reinforcing processes have ended and how a new institution could be established in its stead. A voluminous literature in political sociology has investigated the conditions necessary for revolutionary change (see Goldstone, 2003) and the conditions for a paradigm change (third-order change) in state policies (Hall, 1993).

In general, we can conclude that the more open developmental perspective can in principle be used to analyse the different forms of institutional inertia and change. However, when we attempt to explain these different forms of institutional change, we need to go beyond the heuristics of the path-dependence metaphor and study the actual processes of change (Thelen, 2003). In addition, we need a theoretical underpinning and empirical tests of the social mechanisms that lead to self-reinforcement or may even lead to deinstitutionalization. In the final section, I turn to these 'social mechanisms' (Hedström and Swedberg, 1998), that is, middle-range theories that help to explain recurrent social processes such as self-reinforcing feedback.

PATH DEPENDENCE EXAMPLE II: MULTIPLE PATHWAYS OF WELFARE REFORM

To give an application of the open path-dependence approach, I briefly discuss multiple pathways of current welfare state reform (see Figure 8.4). Esping-Andersen's important study *Three Worlds of Welfare Capitalism* (Esping-Andersen, 1990) assumes long-term historical political forces that shape welfare regimes, that is, the redistributive principles and institutional mix of social policies. At critical junctures in the formation of welfare states, new political alliances led to systemic reforms of policies dealing with new social risks in industrial societies (Flora and Alber, 1981). Other historical alternatives were not taken – they became 'suppressed historical alternatives' (Moore, 1978). Thus, the road towards universal citizenship pensions was foreclosed in Germany through the institutionalization of the social insurance for workers under Bismarck in 1889 and again after the Second World War when the Adenauer government's pension reform of 1957 introduced a full pay-as-you-go system.

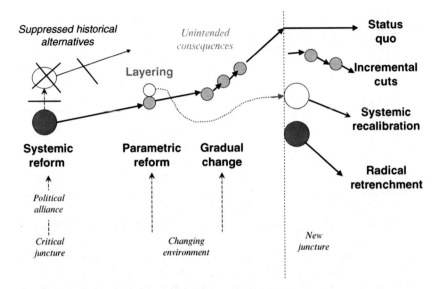

Figure 8.4   Path dependence II: pension reform

For Esping-Andersen, societal forces and historical legacies have led to entrenched regimes or frozen institutional landscapes from which they can hardly escape, even when they result in perverse effects. For instance, the continental European welfare states (Esping-Andersen, 1996; Scharpf, 2001) are locked into the 'welfare state without work' problem. They suffer the continental dilemma: as passive labor market policies are used to take workers out of work to alleviate labor market disequilibria, the higher the social security cost pressures that in turn lead to higher labor costs and thus yet more pressure to shed labor. Although smaller parametric reforms have been implemented in an attempt to shift the costs of social security between different insurance systems, these reforms did not change the status quo. Arguments in favor of path persistence pointed to the difficulties of altering a pay-as-you-go system due to the double-payer problem: the current working generation would have to pay for the acquired rights of pensioners and save for their own future pensions (Pierson, 1997). Because the benefits of a system change would be diffused and can only be received in the future, welfare retrenchment would lead to immediate and concentrated cuts – a change in social policy that is politically difficult to achieve, particularly given the blame avoidance of office-seeking politicians (Myles and Pierson, 2001). The pay-as-you-go principle in social insurance is certainly a strong self-reinforcing process, resembling the deterministic path-dependence theorem.

Nevertheless, several welfare states that were said to be frozen land-scapes (Esping-Andersen, 1996) have been able to adopt substantial reforms (Hinrichs, 2000; Palier, 2000; Reynaud, 2000; Taylor-Gooby, 1999). Some welfare states have been able to make up for missed oppor-tunities and reintroduce 'suppressed historical alternatives' in particular situations of crisis and then expand upon them. Thus, the Dutch pension system introduced a basic pension system after the Second World War, after emergency measures had temporarily set the ground and private occu-pational pensions had in the meantime filled the void of earnings-related supplements (Haverland, 2001). Those pension systems that already had institutional arrangements, like a private second tier, would not have to introduce such a scheme from scratch but could use these 'dormant' his-torical alternatives to start a gradual process of transforming an old-age security system from public towards private provisions. Moreover, minor changes in the past could lead to a long-term gradual transformation, increasing the share of private pensions through a gradual decline in ben-efits from the pay-as-you-go public system. Gradual changes could thus lead to long-term systemic recalibration of a system (that is, path depar-ture); these may also be more acceptable politically, not least because the changes are at first unobservable or too complicated to understand (Myles and Pierson, 2001). Grandfathering rules that exempt current pensioners from retrenchment at the expense of cuts for future beneficiaries have been a common device in welfare reforms negotiated by governments with trade unions, as the core union membership is exempted or less affected by changes (Ebbinghaus and Hassel, 2000; Brugiavini et al., 2001). Hence, there does exist a large variety of intermediate changes (path departure) in between the extreme cases of status quo maintenance (path stabilization) claimed by political scientists and radical system change (path switch) often advocated by economists.

INSTITUTIONAL THEORIES AND SELF-REINFORCING MECHANISMS

Both perspectives on path dependence share the assumption that self-reinforcing processes foster the stabilization of institutions. Long before the path-dependence debate, these processes have been examined as various social science theories studied processes labeled 'institutionaliza-tion' (Berger and Luckmann, 1977). Economists, sociologists, political sci-entists and historians have made various contributions to account for the underlying social mechanisms leading to institutional inertia. I group the different institutional theories and the specific mechanisms they emphasize

(3) FUNCTIONALIST SYSTEM THEORY

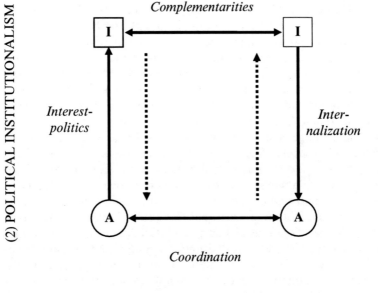

Figure 8.5   Mechanisms of self-reinforcement

into four analytical types (Ackermann, 2001; Mahoney, 2000). Using this schema (see Figure 8.5), I locate the four different social mechanisms by separating the level of interaction between actors (micro-level) from the system level of institutions (macro-level), as well as the interaction between these two levels. I discuss these four modes of self-reinforcing mechanisms that are used to explain institutional inertia, utilizing the theoretical approaches closest to them, and will then turn them upside down to explain institutional change. James Mahoney (2000) distinguishes utilitarian, functionalist, power-related and legitimacy oriented approaches, while Rolf Ackermann (2001) delineates three mechanisms: coordination effects, complementarities and interdependence between the regulative and action levels. In my schema, I combine each theoretical paradigm with the social mechanism most prominently associated with its approach. I separate the interdependencies between actor and institutional realm in interest politics (aggregation of interests from the micro- to macro-level) and internalization (the impact of institutions on actors' beliefs and actions).[11]

(I) *Utilitarian theories* (institutional economics and rational choice theory in sociology) start from the assumption of rational behavior and focus on coordination problems among individuals.[12] In this micro-level perspective, the emergence and stability of social institutions is seen as a collective action problem (Olson, 1965). A social convention only develops spontaneously when enough actors see sufficient personal utility in it and are willing to contribute to produce a public good. A coordination effect may derive from the network economies of scale: the more users in a network that participate, the more everyone (old and new users) will profit from it. An example from geography is the agglomeration effect (Arthur, 1994, chs 4, 6). For a variety of reasons, the first computer software firms started up near Stanford University, but with increased numbers in Silicon Valley the regional concentration became a positive location factor, attracting ever more computer firms.

(II) *Political institutionalists* in political science focus on the role of political institutions and intermediary interest organizations (cf. Hall and Taylor, 1996; Thelen, 1999).[13] On the one hand, social groupings have vested sectionalist interests that they seek to pursue in politics. On the other hand, political institutions and politics shape the opportunity structure and strategic preferences for political action in society. Path dependence in politics may thus result from policy feedbacks through which political institutions shape the interest groupings that are in favor of maintaining a particular status quo (Pierson, 1993). A historical example is the German pension insurance for white-collar employees that helped to reinforce and maintain status differences for a century and also led to the separate trade union organization of white-collar interests (Kocka, 1981; see also Esping-Andersen and Korpi, 1984).

(III) *Functionalist system theory* (Parsons and Smelser, 1956) but also more implicitly the new political economy (Hall and Soskice, 2001) explain the endurance of institutions through their 'embedding' into the overall institutional landscape (Granovetter, 1985).[14] Complementary institutions are interconnected and mutually support each other (Milgrom and Roberts, 1994; Schmidt and Spindler, 2002). An example of such complementarities is the German dual vocational training system and the diversified quality production system it supports (Soskice, 1999). The two systems are functionally interdependent: the vocational training system provides the supply and the production system the demand for highly skilled workers. Even though we should avoid the functionalist pitfall of reading the origins of institutions into their later function (Stinchcombe, 1968), once complementarities emerge interdependent institutions do tend to persist (Thelen and Kume, 2001).

(IV) *Sociological institutionalism* has focused since Emile Durkheim on the normative function of institutions. In addition, cognitive dimensions of institutionalization (internalization) may also reinforce path-dependent persistence: dominant behavioral norms in societies are internalized as cognitive schemata and are socialized as taken-for-granted routines that are no longer questioned (Zucker, 1977). The new institutionalism in organizational sociology stresses socially accepted routines (Powell and DiMaggio, 1991). Organizations adopt institutional isomorphism by copying institutions not for efficiency reasons, but because they are perceived to be legitimate and appropriate (DiMaggio and Powell, 1983). An example of isomorphism is the transplantation of the Western German model of university structures to Eastern German tertiary education after the fall of the socialist regime. The Eastern state's adoption of an established institutional form, despite being increasingly criticized in the West, provided the necessary legitimacy to attract academics, students and resources.

From quite different theoretical standpoints, institutional theories use these four social mechanisms to explain institutionalization, leading to an institution's persistence. Yet, we need further empirical studies to test whether and which of these social mechanisms are actually at work and if they indeed are causal in stabilizing a particular institution. Only if such self-reinforcing mechanisms are shown to exist, can institutional theories claim to explain the observed path dependence of institutions.

A central avenue for future research will be to examine whether the processes of institutional change can be explained with the same self-reinforcing social mechanisms simply by turning them upside down. While the chances for path departure may increase with the long-term erosion of self-reinforcing processes (deinstitutionalization), institutional change may also occur suddenly due to historically contingent events that provoke a path cessation or even path switch. Mirroring the discussion of the four social mechanisms used to explain institutional inertia above, the arguments may be turned around to address the cases of path departure and even path cessation.

1. In the case of *coordination* effects, path departure could occur through declining economies of scale or through a transformation of the purpose of an existing network. For instance, in the example

of agglomeration effects, there could be limits to growth through overcrowding. Moreover, political entrepreneurs in other locations may consciously seek to build a competing network with similar scale effects through policies sponsoring relocation.

2. Shifts in *power relations* and new interest groupings are potential causes for politically induced institutional change (Stinchcombe, 1968). However, the opportunity costs for political action are differently structured depending upon the institutional context (Immergut, 1991): there are often multiple veto points in political decision-making structures that provide leverage to block reforms. Changes in the institutional power structure and the decline in mobilizing power would thus alter the political conditions for a status quo coalition. For instance, the decline in union membership and government-induced reforms of the social partners' self-administration in social insurance schemes increased the possibilities for reform (Visser and Hemerijck, 1997).

3. Path departure could occur under conditions of institutional inter-dependence when *complementarities* wane. While the interlocking between institutions may loosen, an institution may be also endangered through tight coupling with another institution if this complementary institution can no longer provide or has changed its function due to external changes. Thus, the increasing erosion of the voluntary dual vocational training system due to externally induced reasons can have major long-term repercussions on the skill profiles of German firms.

4. *Deinstitutionalization* may occur through a change in normative or cognitive processes. This could happen through the delegitimation of an institution, if the script becomes less and less appropriate to real world contexts. New ideas may also lead to paradigm shifts that call taken-for-granted routines into question (Lieberman, 2002). Thus, postmodern value-changes and new lifestyles have led to the erosion of traditional social norms without necessarily replacing them by new commonly held norms.

The study of the social mechanisms of institutional change is certainly still at its beginning (Thelen, 2002), partly because the theoretical and empirical work on institutions has thus far concentrated on resistance to change. The deterministic conception of path dependence (I) based on studies of technological innovation has led to a narrow conception of institutional change as non-change (or inertia). The Polya urn, given its parsimonious but closed system view, has shaped our understanding of path dependence in a limiting way. The model as such is only an illustration and can neither predict the timing and outcome of the tipping-point, nor does it explain the self-reinforcement process. Increasing attention to the social mechanisms underlying processes of institutionalization has provided more insights into the possible factors contributing to institutional inertia. However, it is the more open path-dependence (II) approach delineated above that leads to an increasing attention to institutional change. Adherents to the second perspective study a wider range of long-term institutional evolutionary processes and thus provide ample evidence for a variety of forms in path developments: path continuation, departure, switching or cessation. Although a variety of examples was presented here, the taxonomy of such changes is still being developed, and the social mechanisms and conditions for the different forms have not yet been clearly delineated.

CONCLUSION

In conclusion, I would like to sum up my arguments concerning path dependence and institutional change in four main points (see Table 8.1). First, path dependence is a concept with at least two established meanings in institutional research that refer to distinct phenomena: micro-level diffusion processes in social networks and macro-level institutional arrangements that shape subsequent (political) decision-making. The first model is fitted to repeated decisions that reinforce each other, given sunk costs, coordination effects, cognitive schemas and vested interests. The empirical examples of the entrenchment of early retirement policies indicate that such processes may lead to unintended consequences, yet that reform is very difficult given institutional lock-in. Second, the deterministic path-dependence theorem can only model the persistence of diffusion processes under relatively restrictive conditions, that is, unabated self-reinforcement without external intervention. It can explain neither the emergence nor the change of institutions, since it leaves the former to chance (stochastic tipping-point) and rules out the latter (no endogenous capacity for change). Third, the more open developmental approach has thus far served largely as a heuristic for historical research that is flexible enough to describe institutional persistence and change. Certainly, we need to theoretically specify and empirically confirm the social mechanisms of institutionalization and later changes in historical process analyses. Research on welfare state reform has provided new insights into the openness and variety of path-dependent changes. Fourth, if institutional path dependence structures the alternatives of subsequent decisions, then it should be possible to systematically study the varying impact of institutional configurations on institutional change and persistence using cross-national comparative

Table 8.1   Two models of path dependence

	Path dependence I	Path dependence II
Metaphor	*Trodden trail*	*Road juncture*
Process	**Diffusion of social norm**	**Structuring of alternatives**
Model	Polya urn (see Figure 8.1)	Decision tree (see Figure 8.3)
Events	Repetition of basic decision	Sequence of institutional changes
Level	Social network of individuals (micro-level)	Collective or corporate actors (macro-level)
Beginning	Small chance events	Major critical juncture
Momentum	'Tipping point': critical mass of innovators	Later junctures: full, partial or no institutional persistence
Outcome	Deterministic persistence (inertia) through self-reinforcement	Open process of institutional change
Self-reinforcement mechanisms	Coordination (network effects) Vested interests (sunk costs) Institutional complementarities (system effects) Internalization (taken-for-granted)	
Institutional change	External to model (inertia only)	Varying: path stabilization, departure, switch or cessation
Factors of change	Only exogenous	Endogenous (e.g. deinstitutionalization) and exogenous (e.g. revolution)

analysis. To do just that in the future, we need to develop middle-range theories of institutional change that go beyond a crude fixation on path dependence as persistence and instead help us to explore the potential for path departure that is institutional change in its proper sense (Streeck and Thelen, 2005). This chapter indicates the need for and potential of such an endeavor.

NOTES

1. A previous version of the paper was published as MPIfG disscussion paper 2005 at the Max Planck Institute, Cologne; the author is grateful to Justin Powell (WZ Berlin), Raymund Werle (MPIfG, Cologne) and Sigrid Quack (MPIfG, Cologne) for their detailed comments.
2. In probability theory, 'path *in*dependence' refers to the independence of two subsequent events: throwing a dice for a second time is unrelated to the first outcome, thus the probability that a double six will be drawn is: $1/36 = 1/6 \times 1/6$. In contrast, 'path

dependence' describes cases in which the probability of a subsequent event *is* related to earlier events. In the case of a lottery, when we draw 6 out of 48 balls, the chances to get a particular number at first is 1/48, but at the second draw the chance is 1/47 since one ball has already been removed, and so on.

3. As an introduction to institutional economics see (Eggertsson, 1996; Sjöstrand, 1993), in organizational sociology (DiMaggio and Powell, 1991; Nee, 1998) and political science (Hall and Taylor, 1996; Immergut, 1998; Thelen, 1999).

4. Brian W. Arthur and Paul A. David both taught at Stanford University during the mid-1980s and had exchanged ideas on path dependence (see Arthur, 1994, preface). In 1983, Arthur published his working paper on 'increasing returns' with the International Institute for Applied System Analysis in Vienna, which was first published in an academic journal *(Economic Journal)* as late as 1989 (Arthur, 1994, ch. 2). His article in *Scientific American* of February 1990 popularized 'positive feedbacks'. Paul A. David's six-page QWERTY paper (David, 1985) soon became a *locus classicus* for path-dependence theory.

5. David (1985) explained the path-dependent self-reinforcement with three mechanisms: system interdependency between *hardware* (QWERTY keyboard) and *software* (speed of typing skills). Due to economies of scale, firms would buy QWERTY typewriters since ever more secretaries had learned that new keyboard. Moreover, for individual secretaries the investment in learning QWERTY became a sunk cost; they were hardly willing to learn another new keyboard, especially as their employers were unwilling to pay for such training due to fear of poaching by other employers.

6. Following Mahoney (2000), who argues 'that path dependence characterizes specifically those historical sequences in which contingent events set into motion institutional patterns or event chains that have deterministic properties' (p. 507), I call this approach 'deterministic'.

7. David's QWERTY story was criticized by Liebowitz and Margolis as a 'fable' (Liebowitz and Margolis, 1990; 1995; 1996), and they question whether there were indeed more (efficient) alternatives to QWERTY and whether its initial rise was such a chance event. Liebowitz and Margolis extended their criticisms to other common examples for path dependence in technology (VHS versus Betamax) and raised doubts about the case of Microsoft (Liebowitz and Margolis, 1999).

8. In business administration studies, the active creative role of (Schumpeterian) entrepreneurs and innovators is stressed and technological change occurs through *path creation* (but see also for Austrian institutional economics: Fu-Lai Yu, 2001; Garud and Karnøe, 2001). Policy analyses and organizational sociology similarly sometimes assume political entrepreneurs to play a crucial role (Beckert, 1999).

9. Not only S.M. Lipset and Stein Rokkan but also Reinhard Bendix (1964), Barrington Moore (1966) and Immanuel Wallerstein (1979) developed such developmental perspectives, however, the comparison of these trajectories served very different methodological purposes (Skocpol, 1984; Tilly, 1984): stressing similarities, uniqueness or variations on the 'road to modernity'.

10. The stochastic path-dependence theorem of Arthur's Polya urn model (named after George Polya) led many theorists of path dependence to make chance events at the beginning a *precondition* for path dependence (Goldstone, 1998; Mahoney, 2000). Even if *critical junctures* are contingent events that could be started by historical coincidence or *Cournot effects* (Boudon, 1984, p. 168), macro-social change is nevertheless the result of action by collective actors and hardly of 'small chance events'. For instance, the fall of the Berlin wall may have been triggered by mistakes of the regime, but it still took a mass protest movement before and after 9 November 1989 to accomplish regime change and political transformation.

11. Ackermann (2001, p. 91), an economist, excludes power-based explanations (rent-seeking) from his analysis of institutional 'inflexibility', disregarding the factors that North (1981; 1990) and many others embraced in their institutional analyses. He claims that in these cases a direct intervention takes place and no self-reinforcing mechanism

is at work (Ackermann, 2001, p. 91). In contrast, I follow Mahoney's sociological perspective and include the power-based explanations of path dependence here because of its importance in institution building (see also Shalev, 2001) that has been most prominent in the *old* institutionalism in sociology (Stinchcombe, 1997) and in the *new* politics institutionalism (Pierson, 2000a).

12. Institutional economics subsumes a variety of theories looking at property-rights, transaction costs and principal–agent relations (Erlei et al., 1999; Furubotn and Richter, 2000; Martiensen, 2000). Rational choice (RC) theories assume rational action of individual actors and explain institutions as rational coordination games; RC theory is promient in American political institutional analysis (Weingast, 1996) and sociological studies of collective action (Elster, 2000; Hechter and Kanazawa, 1997), following in the tradition of Olson (1965).

13. While this approach is known in political science as 'New Institutionalism' and historical institutionalism (cf. Steinmo et al., 1992; Hall and Taylor, 1996; Immergut, 1998; Thelen, 1999), it should not be confused with the neo-institutionalism in organizational analysis (see below).

14. For functionalist system theory, see Parsons and Smelser (1956); Parsons (1991) and Stinchcombe (1968). The comparative political economy approach (Aoki, 2001; Crouch and Streeck, 1997; Hall and Soskice, 2001; Hollingsworth and Boyer, 1997) stresses the institutional embedding of production systems and analyzes their institutional complementarities (for a discussion of its underlying functionalism see Lütz, 2003)

REFERENCES

Ackermann, Rolf (2001), *Pfadabhängigkeit, Institutionen und Regelreform*, Tübingen: Mohr Siebeck.

Alston, Lee J., Thráinn Eggertsson and Douglass C. North (eds) (1996), *Empirical Studies in Institutional Change*, Cambridge: Cambridge University Press.

Aoki, Mashaiko (2001), *Towards a Comparative Institutional Analysis*, Cambridge, MA: MIT Press.

Arthur, W. Brian (1994), *Increasing Returns and Path Dependence in the Economy*, Ann Arbor, MI: University of Michigan Press.

Beckert, Jens (1999), 'Agency, entrepreneurs, and institutional change: the role of strategic choice and institutionalized practices in organizations', *Organization Studies*, **20** (5), 777–99.

Bendix, Reinhard (1964), *Nation-Building and Citizenship: Studies of our Changing Social Order*, Berkeley, CA: University of California Press, new enlarged edn, 1977.

Berger, Peter L. and Thomas Luckmann (1977), *Die gesellschaftliche Konstruktion der Wirklichkeit. Eine Theorie der Wissenssoziologie (5. Auflage)*, Frankfurt a.M.: Fischer. First published 1969.

Boudon, Raymond (1984), *La place du désordre. Critiques des théories du changement social*, Paris: Presse Universitaire France.

Brugiavini, Agar, Bernhard Ebbinghaus, Richard Freeman, Pietro Garibaldi, Bertil Holmund, Martin Schludi and Thierry Verdier (2001), 'Part II: What Do Unions Do to the Welfare States?', in T. Boeri, A. Brugiavini and L. Calmfors (eds), *The Role of Unions in the Twenty-First Century: A Report to the Fondazione Rodolfo Debenedetti*, Oxford: Oxford University Press, pp. 157–277.

Casey, Bernard (1997), 'Incentives and disincentives to early and late retirement', ILO Conference, Geneva, September.

Crouch, Colin and Henry Farrell (2004), 'Breaking the path of institutional development? Alternatives to the new determinism', *Rationality and Society*, **16** (1), 5–43.

Crouch, Colin and Wolfgang Streeck (eds) (1997), *Political Economy of Modern Capitalism. Mapping Convergence and Diversity*, London: Sage.

David, Paul A. (1985), 'Clio and the economics of QWERTY', *American Economic Review*, **75** (2), 332–7.

DiMaggio, Paul J. and Walter W. Powell (1983), 'The iron cage revisited: institutional isomorphism and collective rationality in organizational fields', *American Sociological Review*, **48** (2), 147–60.

DiMaggio, Paul J. and Walter W. Powell (1991), 'Introduction', in W.W. Powell and P.J. DiMaggio (eds), *The New Institutionalism in Organizational Analysis*, Chicago, IL: University of Chicago, pp. 1–38.

Ebbinghaus, Bernhard (2000), 'Any way out of "exit from work"? Reversing the entrenched pathways of early retirement', in F.W. Scharpf and V. Schmidt (eds), *Welfare and Work in the Open Economy Vol II*, Oxford: Oxford University Press, pp. 511–33.

Ebbinghaus, Bernhard (2001), 'When labour and capital collude: the political economy of early retirement in Europe, Japan and the USA', in B. Ebbinghaus and P. Manow (eds), *Comparing Welfare Capitalism: Social Policy and Political Economy in Europe, Japan and the USA*, London: Routledge, pp. 76–101.

Ebbinghaus, Bernhard (2006), *Reforming Early Retirement in Europe, Japan and the USA*, Oxford: Oxford University Press.

Ebbinghaus, Bernhard and Anke Hassel (2000), 'Striking deals: concertation in the reform of continental European welfare states', *Journal of European Public Policy*, **7** (1), 44–62.

Eggertsson, Thráinn (1996), 'A note on the economics of institutions', in L.J. Alston, T. Eggertsson and D.C. North (eds), *Empirical Studies in Institutional Change*, Cambridge: Cambridge University Press, pp. 6–24.

Elster, Jon (2000), 'Rational choice history: a case of excessive ambition', *American Political Science Review*, (3), 685–702.

Erlei, Mathias, Martin Leschke and Dirk Sauerland (1999), *Neue Institutionenökonomik*, Stuttgart: Schäffer-Poeschel Verlag.

Esping-Andersen, Gøsta (1990), *Three Worlds of Welfare Capitalism*, Princeton, NJ: Princeton University Press.

Esping-Andersen, Gøsta (1996), 'Welfare states without work: the impasse of labour shedding and familialism in continental European social policy', in G. Esping-Andersen (ed.), *Welfare States in Transition: National Adaptations in Global Economies*, London: Sage, pp. 66–87.

Esping-Andersen, Gøsta and Walter Korpi (1984), 'Social policy as class politics in post-war capitalism: Scandinavia, Austria and Germany', in J.H. Goldthorpe (ed.), *Order and Conflict in Contemporary Capitalism*, Oxford: Clarendon Press, pp. 179–208.

Flora, Peter (1999), 'Introduction', in P. Flora, S. Kuhnle and D. Urwin (eds), *State Formation, Nation-Building and Mass Politics in Europe. The Theory of Stein Rokkan*, Oxford: Oxford University Press, pp. 244–5.

Flora, Peter and Jens Alber (1981), 'Modernization, democratization, and the development of welfare states in Western Europe', in P. Flora and A.J. Heidenheimer (eds), *The Development of Welfare States in Europe and America*, New Brunswick, NJ: Transaction Books, pp. 37–80.

Fu-Lai Yu, Tony (2001), 'An entrepreneurial perspective of institutional change', *Constitutional Political Economy*, **12** (3), 217–36.

Furubotn, Eirik G. and Rudolf Richter (2000), *Institutions and Economic Theory. The Contribution of the New Institutional Economics*, Ann Arbor, MI: University of Michigan Press.

Garud, Raghu and Peter Karnøe (eds) (2001), *Path Dependence and Creation*, Mahwah, NJ, London: Lawrence Erlbaum Associates.

Goldstone, Jack A. (1998), 'Initial conditions, general laws, path dependence, and explanation in historical sociology', *American Journal of Sociology*, **104** (3), 829–45.

Goldstone, Jack A. (2003), 'Comparative historical analysis and knowledge accumulation in the study of revolutions', in J. Mahoney and D. Rueschemeyer (eds), *Comparative Historical Analysis in the Social Sciences*, New York: Cambridge University Press, pp. 41–90.

Granovetter, Mark (1985), 'Economic action and social structures: the problem of embeddedness', *American Journal of Sociology*, **91** (3), 481–510.

Hall, Peter A. (1993), 'Policy paradigms, social learning, and the state. The case of economic policymaking in Britain', *Comparative Politics*, **25**, 275–97.

Hall, Peter A. and David Soskice (eds) (2001), *Varieties of Capitalism: The Institutional Foundations of Comparative Advantage*, New York: Oxford University Press.

Hall, Peter A. and Rosemary C.R. Taylor (1996), 'Political science and the three new institutionalisms', *Political Studies*, **44**, 936–57.

Hathaway, Oona A. (2000), 'Path dependence in the law: the course and pattern of legal change in a common law system', *Working Paper Series, Law & Economics, Boston University* (00–06).

Haverland, Markus (2001), 'Another Dutch miracle? Explaining Dutch and German pension trajectories', *Journal of European Social Policy*, **11** (4), 308–23.

Hechter, Michael and Satosht Kanazawa (1997), 'Sociological rational choice theory', *Annual Review of Sociology*, **23**, 191–214.

Hedström, Peter and Richard Swedberg (eds) (1998), *Social Mechanisms: An Analytical Approach to Social Theory*, Cambridge: Cambridge University Press.

Hinrichs, Karl (2000), 'Elephants on the move: patterns of public pension reform in OECD countries', *European Review*, **8** (3), 353–78.

Hollingsworth, J. Rogers and Robert Boyer (eds) (1997), *Contemporary Capitalism: The Embeddedness of Institutions*, New York: Cambridge University Press.

Immergut, Ellen M. (1991), 'Institutions, veto points, and policy results: a comparative analysis of health care', *Journal of Public Policy*, **10** (4), 391–416.

Immergut, Ellen M. (1998), 'The theoretical core of the new institutionalism', *Politics and Society*, **26** (1), 5–34.

Knight, Jack (1992), *Institutions and Social Conflict*, New York: Cambridge University.

Kocka, Jürgen (1981), *Die Angestellten in der deutschen Geschichte 1850–1980*, Göttingen: Vandenhoeck & Ruprecht.

Kohli, Martin, Martin Rein, Anne-Marie Guillemard and Herman van Gunsteren (eds) (1991), *Time for Retirement: Comparative Studies on Early Exit from the Labor Force*, New York: Cambridge University Press.

Lepsius, M. Rainer (1990), *Interessen, Ideen und Institutionen*, Opladen: Westdeutscher.

Lieberman, Robert C. (2002), 'Ideas, institutions, and political order: explaining political change', *American Political Science Review*, **96** (4), 697–712.

Liebowitz, Stan J. and Stephen E. Margolis (1990), 'The fable of the keys', *Journal of Law and Economics*, **33**, 1–25.

Liebowitz, Stan J. and Stephen E. Margolis (1995), 'Path dependence, lock-in, and history', *Journal of Law, Economics and Organization*, **11** (1), 205–26.

Liebowitz, Stan J. and Stephen E. Margolis (1996), 'Typing Errors', *Reason Online*, Junc, available at: http://www.reason.com/9606/Fe.QWERTY.html.

Liebowitz, Stan J. and Stephen E. Margolis (1999), *Winners, Losers & Microsoft: Competition and Antitrust in High Techology*, Oakland, CA: Independent Institute.

Lipset, Seymour Martin and Stein Rokkan (1967), 'Cleavage structures, party systems, and voter alignments: an introduction', in S.M. Lipset and S. Rokkan (eds), *Party Systems and Voter Alignments: Cross-National Perspectives*, New York: Free Press, pp. 1–64.

Lütz, Susanne (2003), 'Governance in der politischen Ökonomie', *MPIfG Discussion Paper*, 03(5).

Mahoney, James (2000), 'Path dependence in historical sociology', *Theory and Society*, **29** (4), 507–48.

Martiensen, Jörn (2000), *Institutionenökonomik*, München: Verlag Franz Vahlen.

Merton, Robert K. (1936), 'The unanticipated consequences of purposive social action', *American Sociological Review*, **1** (6), 894–904.

Merton, Robert K. (1967), *On Theoretical Sociology. Five Essays, Old and New*, New York: Free Press.

Milgrom, Paul and John Roberts (1994), 'Complementarities and systems: understanding Japanese economic organization', *Estudios Economicos*, **9**, 3–42.

Moore, Barrington, Jr (1966), *Social Origins of Dictatorship and Democracy. Lord and Peasant in the Making of the Modern World*, Boston, MA: Beacon Press.

Moore, Barrington, Jr (1978), *Injustice. The Social Bases of Obedience and Revolt*, New York: M.E. Sharpe.

Myles, John and Paul Pierson (2001), 'The comparative political economy of pension reform', in P. Pierson (ed.), *The New Politics of the Welfare State*, New York: Oxford University Press, pp. 305–33.

Nee, Victor (1998), 'Sources of the new institutionalism', in M.C. Brinton and V. Nee (eds), *The New Institutionalism in Sociology*, New York: Russell Sage Foundation, pp. 1–16.

North, Douglass C. (1981), *Structure and Change in Economic History*, New York: W.W. Norton.

North, Douglass C. (1990), *Institutions, Institutional Change and Economic Performance*, Cambridge: Cambridge University.

North, Douglass C. and Robert P. Thomas (1973), *The Rise of the Western World: A New Economic History*, Cambridge: Cambridge University Press.

Olson, Mancur (1965), *The Logic of Collective Action: Public Goods and the Theory of Groups*, 2nd edn, Cambridge, MA: Harvard University.

Palier, Bruno (2000), '"Defrosting" the French welfare state', *West European Politics*, **23** (2), 113–36.

Parsons, Talcott (1991), *The Social System (with a new preface by Bryan S. Turner)*, London: Routledge, First published 1951.

Parsons, Talcott and Neil J. Smelser (1956), *Economy and Society. A Study in the Integration of Economic and Social Theory*, London: Routledge & Kegan.

Pierson, Paul (1993), 'When effect becomes cause: policy feedback and political change', *World Politics*, **45** (4), 595–628.

Pierson, Paul (1997), 'The politics of pension reform', in K.G. Banting and R. Boadway (eds), *Reform of Retirement Income Policy*, Kingston/Ontario: School of Policy Studies, pp. 273–93.

Pierson, Paul (2000a), 'Increasing returns, path dependence, and the study of politics', *American Political Science Review*, **94** (2), 251–67.

Pierson, Paul (2000b), 'Not just what, but when: timing and sequence in political processes', *Studies of American Political Development*, **14** (Spring): 72–92.

Pierson, Paul (2004), *Politics in Time. History, Institutions, and Social Analysis*, Princeton, NJ: Princeton University Press.

Powell, Walter W. and Paul J. DiMaggio (eds) (1991), *The New Institutionalism in Organizational Analysis*, Chicago, IL: University of Chicago.

Reynaud, Emmanuel (ed.) (2000), *Social Dialogue and Pension Reform: United Kingdom, United States, Germany, Japan, Sweden, Italy, Spain*, Geneva: International Labour Office.

Rokkan, Stein (1999), *State Formation, Nation-Building and Mass Politics in Europe. The Theory of Stein Rokkan*, Oxford: Oxford University Press.

Scharpf, Fritz W. (2001), 'Employment and the welfare state: a continental dilemma', in B. Ebbinghaus and P. Manow (eds), *Comparing Welfare Capitalism: Social Policy and Political Economy in Europe, Japan and the USA*, London: Routledge, pp. 270–83.

Schmidt, Reinhard H. and Gerald Spindler (2002), 'Path dependence, corporate governance and complementarity', *International Finance*, **5** (3), 311–33.

Shalev, Michael (2001), 'The politics of elective affinities: a commentary', in B. Ebbinghaus and P. Manow (eds), *Comparing Welfare Capitalism: Social Policy and Political Economy in Europe, Japan and the USA*, London: Routledge, pp. 287–303.

Sjöstrand, Sven-Erik (1993), 'On institutional thought in the social and economic sciences', in S.-E. Sjöstrand (ed.) *Institutional Change: Theory and Empirical Findings*, Armonk, NY: M.E. Sharpe, pp. 3–31.

Skocpol, Theda (ed.) (1984), *Vision and Method in Historical Sociology*, Cambridge: Cambridge University.

Soskice, David (1999), 'Divergent production regimes: coordinated and uncoordinated market economies in the 1980s and 1990s', in H. Kitschelt, P. Lange, G. Marks and J. Stephens (eds), *Continuity and Change in Contemporary Capitalism*, New York: Cambridge University Press, pp. 101–34.

Steinmo, Sven, Kathleen Thelen and Frank Longstreth (eds) (1992), *Structuring Politics. Historical Institutionalism in Comparative Analysis*, New York: Cambridge University Press.

Stinchcombe, Arthur L. (1965), 'Social structure and organizations', in J.G. March (ed.), *Handbook of Organizations*, Chicago, IL: R. McNally, pp. 142–93.

Stinchcombe, Arthur L. (1968), *Constructing Social Theories*, New York: Harcourt, Brace and World.

Stinchcombe, Arthur L. (1975), 'Social structure and politics', in F.I. Greenstein and N.W. Polsby (eds), *Macropolitical Theory*, Reading, MA: Addison-Wesley, pp. 557–622.

Stinchcombe, Arthur L. (1997), 'On the virtues of the old institutionalism', *Annual Review of Sociology*, **23**, 1–18.

Streeck, Wolfgang and Kathleen Thelen (2005), 'Introduction: institutional change in advanced political economies', in W. Streeck and K. Thelen (eds), *Beyond Continuity Institutional Change in Advanced Political Economies*, Oxford: Oxford University Press, pp. 1–39.

Taylor-Gooby, Peter (1999), 'Policy change at a time of retrenchment: recent pension reform in France, Germany, Italy and the UK', *Social Policy & Administration*, **33** (1), 1–19.

Thelen, Kathleen (1999), 'Historical institutionalism in comparative politics', *Annual Review of Political Science*, **2**, 369–404.

Thelen, Kathleen (2002), 'The explanatory power of historical institutionalism', in R. Mayntz (ed.), *Akteure – Mechanismen – Modelle: Zur Theoriefähigkeit makro-sozialer Analysen*, Frankfurt: Campus, pp. 91–107.

Thelen, Kathleen (2003), 'How institutions evolve: insights form comparative-historical analysis', in J. Mahoney and D. Rueschemeyer (eds), *Comparative-Historical Analysis: Innovations in Theory and Method*, New York: Cambridge University Press, pp. 208–40.

Thelen, Kathleen and Ikuo Kume (2001), 'The rise of nonliberal training regimes: Germany and Japan compared', in W. Streeck and K. Yamamura (eds), *The Origins of Nonliberal Capitalism: Germany and Japan in Comparison*, Ithaca, NY: Cornell University Press, pp. 200–227.

Tilly, Charles (1984), *Big Structures, Large Processes, Huge Comparisons*, New York: Russell Sage.

Visser, Jelle and Anton Hemerijck (1997), *'A Dutch Miracle': Job Growth, Welfare Reform, and Corporatism in the Netherlands*, Amsterdam: Amsterdam University Press.

Wallerstein, Immanuel (1979), *The Capitalist World-Economy*, Cambridge: Cambridge University.

Weingast, Barry R. (1996), 'Political institutions: rational choice perspectives', in R.E. Goodin and H.-D. Klingemann (eds), *A New Handbook of Political Science*, Oxford: Oxford University Press, pp. 167–90.

Zucker, Lynne G (1977), 'The role of institutionalization in cultural perspective', *American Sociological Review*, **42**, 726–43.

Index

Ackermann, Rolf 206
actor-network theory (ANT) 72
actors
    path evolution 195–6
    political processes 112–16, 118, 120,
        132
    self-reinforcement 206
adaptation 89
administrative corporatism 123–7
administrative systems 110–11
agentiality 36
agglomeration 90, 91–4, 97–9, 207,
    209
Agricultural Adjustment
    Administration (AAA) 55, 56
agriculture
    cartelization 184
    Dust Bowl 44, 61–3, 65
    farm size 50, 53, 58–61, 62–3
    Great Plains 47–52, 53–63, 65–6
Aldcroft, Derek H. 76
Amable, B. 9
Americanization 23, 36
Andersson-Skog, Lena 14
Angel of History, The (Klee) 19, 39
Antonelli, C. 3
aridity (Great Plains) 43–4, 48–50,
    51–2, 65
Arrow, Kenneth 2
Arthur, W. Brian
    increasing returns 5–6, 88–90, 93,
        176, 193
    technology lock-in effects 3, 45, 172,
        180–81, 195, 196
asset erosion 101–2
Astley, W.G. 144, 146
Atkinson, A.B. 3
autonomy 150

bankruptcy 197
beneficiaries of public policy 183–4

Benjamin, Walter 19
Bennet, A. 113
Berlin Wall 201
Betamax 6, 7, 45, 173, 174, 175,
    180–81, 183
Bijker, W. 2
biomedical science
    characteristics facilitating radical
        innovation 149, 157–61, 162
    constraints on radical innovation
        153, 157–61, 162
    indicators of radical innovation 147,
        148
    and institutional environments 139,
        141–3
    organizational isomorphism 143–6,
        154–6
    and path dependence 156–62
    radical innovation in 139, 146–54
Birmingham University 159
Blomqvist, P. 123
bottlenecks 73
bounded rationality 115–16
Boyer, R. 9
branching pathways 191, 199–205,
    210–11
Branting, Hjalmar 33
Britain
    coal industry 2
    democracy 22
    institutional environments 157, 162
    radical innovations in biomedical
        science 139
    railways 76–7, 79, 80
    telephone networks 82
    universities 142, 144, 152, 155, 156,
        158, 159
    see also United Kingdom (UK)
Brown, M. 56
bureaucratic systems 110–11, 153, 158,
    159, 160

California, University of 143, 158, 159
California Institute of Technology 143
Cambridge University 152, 155, 156,
  158
Canada 78
capital 47
capitalism 9, 111, 143
Carnegie Institution 146
causal chain model 117
Chandler, Alfred 77
change patterns 15, 117–20
Chicago, University of 143
Clapham, John 13
class identity 29–30, 32–3
Clawson, M. 55
clustering
  competitive advantage 95–9
  in economic geography 90, 91–7
  and history 97–102
  and path dependence 102–4
coal industry 2
Coase, Ronald 170
Cochrane, W.W. 53
collective action 61–3, 207
Colorado 43, 50, 54, 55, 56, 58, 60, 61
communication 149, 150
community culture 37
compatible systems 182
compensation 187
competition 96–7, 186
competitive advantage 95–7, 99–102
competitive markets 167–72
complementarities 206, 209, 211
Confederation of Swedish Enterprise
  123–31
consolidation of Great Plains farms
  58–61
contingency, historical 73
Cooper, M.R. 62
coordinated market economies (CMEs)
  111
coordination
  agglomeration 93
  path dependence 89, 112
  self-reinforcement 206, 208–9, 211
Copley Medal 148
corporate structure 30
corporatism 116, 123–7
costs 89, 92–3, 112
Cournot, A.A. 2

Cowan, Robin 172–3
Crafoord prize 148
crisis
  concept of 24–7
  points of 27–30, 31
  solutions in Germany and Sweden
    30–36
  as tool of analysis 37–40
critical junctures
  and path dependence 116–20,
    200–201, 203, 211
  in political processes 109, 116–20,
    132–3
  Swedish model 120–31
  see also road junctures
critical mass 194, 196, 211
critique, and crisis 24–7
culture 37–9, 94
cumulative model 117

David, Paul
  path dependence 3–5, 90, 161,
    196
  QWERTY keyboard 71–2, 172,
    179–80, 186, 193
  technology and history 2, 45
decision tree 201, 211
deinstitutionalization 206, 209, 211
demand, sophistication of 96
democracy 22–3
Demsetz, Harold 171
Denzau, A.T. 8
deterministic path dependence 194–6,
  210–11
developmental pathways 199–205,
  210–11
diamond model 96
differentiation 153
diffusion 191, 193–9, 210–11
DiMaggio, P. 144
diminished competition 186
diversity, scientific 149–50, 151, 153,
  156, 157, 158, 159, 160
Dixit, A.K. 9–10, 185–6
Dobbin, Frank 80
drought 43–4, 48–50, 51–2, 65
Dunlavy, Colleen A. 80–81
durability 173–4, 182
Durkheim, Emile 208
Dust Bowl 44, 61–3, 65

Dvorak keyboard 179–80
Dylan, Bob 104

early developments 70, 76, 90, 109
early retirement 196–9
Ebbinghaus, Bernhard 14
economic geography
  and path dependence 87–91, 102–4
  spatial clustering 90, 91–7
economic growth 12, 75–8
economics
  efficiency 45–7, 167–72, 185–6,
    195–6, 199–200
  externalities 167–72
  and history 20
  inefficient economic systems 199–200
  and path dependence 1–13, 75,
    166–7, 173–4, 195
economies of scale 207, 208–9
efficiency 45–7, 167–72, 185–6, 195–6,
    199–200
Eliasson, G. 96
Elman, C. 113
Elster, Jon 115
Elvander, Nils 129
employers 127–31
employers' organizations 35–6, 123–31
Enlightenment 19
environmental regulation 169
Esping-Andersen, G. 111–12, 203–4
European railways 75–6, 77, 79
evolution of organizations 144, 146
externalities 61–3, 167–72, 177–81

factor conditions 96
Farm Security Administration 55
farming
  cartelization 184
  Dust Bowl 44, 61–3, 65
  farm size 50, 53, 58–61, 62–3
  Great Plains 47–52, 53–63, 65–6
Federal Emergency Recovery
  Administration (FEMA) 55
financial support, settlement of the
  Great Plains 55–6, 57, 58
Finland 76
first-degree path dependence
  durability 173, 174, 182
  economic growth 12
  and efficiency 195

Great Plains 47
  nature of 46, 173, 174
  and rational choice 6–7
  relevance of 11
flexibility 150, 151, 158, 159, 160
Fogel, R.W. 76
folk (*volk*) concept 32–6
Foreman-Peck, James 79, 82
Foucault, Michel 35, 38
France 22, 29, 80, 139, 144
Frankel, M. 2
Freiburg, University of 160
French Revolution 25
functional transformation 202
functionalist system theory 206, 207–8
funding, of research 157
future shock 25

Gartland, M.P. 1
Gemeinschaft 34
Germany
  capitalism type 111
  crisis response 30–36
  economic growth 76
  National Socialism 29, 30–36
  radical innovations in biomedical
    science 139
  railways 81
  Sonderweg thesis 21–2
  universities 142, 143, 144, 160, 208
  welfare state 111, 203–4, 207–8, 209
Gesellschaft 34
Gillette, J.M. 56–7
Gourvish, Terry 79
governance 12, 123–7
government
  and externalities 167–72
  and path dependence 183–7
  support for Great Plains farms 54
  systems of 110–11
gradual change 202
Great Plains
  aridity 43–4, 48–50, 51–2, 65
  collective action, failure of 61–3
  farm failure and path dependence
    53–63, 65–6
  location 43, 49
  population 44
  settlement effects of path
    dependence 47–52

Great Plains Committee 62
growth 12, 75–8

Halcrow, H. 53
Hallberg Adu, Kajsa 14
Hansen, Z.K. 51, 52, 53–4, 61, 62, 63
Hanssom, Per-Albin 33
hard path dependency 24
Harvard 143, 152, 155, 156, 158
Hegel, Georg W.F. 19
Heidelberg, University of 160
Heiner, R.A. 8
hierarchical authority 153
Hippocrates 26
historical contingency 73
historical institutionalism 109–10, 114, 118, 201
historical sociology 20, 21–3
historicity 36
historism 20
history
    durability 174
    and economic geography 88, 90
    and economics 1–2
    organizational development 141
    and path dependence 1–2, 10, 19–21, 103, 140
    path-breaking crises 31
    political processes 108–12
    spatial clustering 97–102
    and technology 2, 45
Hitler, Adolf 31, 32
Hodgson, G.M. 1, 4, 144
Hollingsworth, Rogers 14
Hollywood 95
Homestead Act 48, 50, 51, 54
Hughes, Thomas P. 2, 72–3
hyperdiversity 153, 159, 160

idiographic explanations of history 19–21
Illinois, University of 143
illness 26
imperfect markets 74–5
increasing returns
    institutional change 74–5
    non-increasing returns 113
    and path dependence 88–91, 109, 182–3
    railway policy 78–9

and technology 5–6, 89–91
    see also self-reinforcement
incremental change 8–9
Indiana University 143
industrialization 27–8
inefficiency 167–72, 195–6, 199–200
inertia 98, 99, 166, 186, 206–10, 211
information 6–8, 50–51
infrastructure 92–3
Innis, Harold 78
innovation
    characteristics facilitating 149, 157–61, 162
    constraints on 153, 157–61, 162
    indicators 147, 148
    and institutional environments 139, 141–3
    organizational isomorphism 143–6, 154–6
    and path dependence 72, 139, 146–54, 156–62
    studies 13
innovative milieu 94
insolvency 197
Institut Pasteur 160
institutional change
    increasing returns 74–5, 113
    and path dependence 192, 210–11
    political influence 74–5, 206, 209
    road junctures 199–205
    self-reinforcement 205–10
    trodden trail 193–9
institutional environments
    organizational isomorphism 143–6, 152, 154–6, 162, 208
    and organizations 139, 156–62
    radical innovation in organizations 146–54
    and research organizations 139, 141–3
    universities 142–3, 144, 151–2, 158, 159, 160
institutional layering 202
institutional theory 8–10, 11–12, 205–10
institutionalization 192, 200–201, 205–10
institutions
    historical institutionalism 109–10, 114, 118, 201

institutional endowment 100
meaning of 192
and path dependence 70–75, 78–83, 90, 192
and path-breaking crises 37–9
political actors 112–16
political processes 117–20
property rights in the Great Plains 48–52
railways 77–8
self-reinforcement 205–10
interests, influence of 183–4
internal combustion engine 172–3
internalization 206, 211
Italy 29

Japan 36
Jefferson, Thomas 48
Johansson, Joakim 124–6
Johns Hopkins University 143, 147
Johnson, Vance 61

Kaijser, Arne 81
Kaiser Wilhelm Institutes 151, 160
Kansas 43, 50, 54, 55, 56, 57, 58, 60
Katz, M.L. 45
Katznelson, I. 117–18
Kay, Adrian 113
Kindleberger, C.P. 2
Kjellén, Rudolf 32–3
Klee, Paul 19
knowledge 50–51, 94, 100, 103
Kocka, Jürgen 22
Koselleck, Reinhart 24–5, 26, 39
Kreuger, A.O. 10, 185
Krugman, Paul 87, 89, 167
Kuhn, Thomas 147

laboratories 157–61
Laboratory of Molecular Biology (LMB) 156
labour 93, 127–31
Lagerholm, Magnus 14
Lamprecht, Karl 20
land policy 47–52
land use 170, 184–5, 187
Landauer, Gustav 32
language 23, 37–9
large technical system approach (LTS) 72–3

Lasker Awards 148
law 201
leadership 149, 151–2, 156, 157, 158, 159, 160
learning 89, 94, 100, 112
Lebergott, S. 56
Levi, Margaret 140
Libecap, Gary D. 14, 51, 52, 53–4, 61, 62, 63
liberal market economies (LMEs) 111
Liebowitz, S.J. 6–8, 10, 45–6, 72, 167, 174, 181, 195
Lipartito, Kenneth 73
Lipset, Seymour Martin 200
LO (Landsorganisationen i Sverige, Swedish Trade Union Confederation) 122, 127–31
local rivalry 96–7
localization economies 92–4
localized capabilities 99–102
lock-in effects
inefficient economic systems 200
loss of competitive advantage 100–102
path dependence 4, 91, 140, 187–8
railways 78
self-reinforcement 195, 196
technology 3, 5–6, 45, 101, 172–3, 176–81, 195, 196
long-term change 202
loosely coupled systems 73
Louisa Gross Horwitz prize 148
Lucas, Robert 168
Lundvall, B.-Å 94
Lunn, Eugene 32

Maginnis, Martin 52
Magnusson, Lars 2, 3, 6, 9, 10, 115, 119
Mahoney, J. 8, 109, 113, 206
Malmberg, Anders 14, 101
Margolis, Stephen E. 6–8, 10, 14, 45–6, 72, 167, 174, 181, 195
markets
and crises 27
externalities 167–72
failures 168–72, 175–81
imperfect markets 74–5
labour 93
railways 77–8
sophistication of 96

Marshall, Alfred 87, 93
Martin, R. 3, 7, 101
Marx, Karl 19, 26
Maskell, P. 101
Massachusetts Institute of Technology
    143
Matthew, Gospel of St 104
Max Planck Institutes 142, 151, 160
McKelvey, B. 144
mechanization 56
Merton, Robert K. 197–8
Michigan, University of 143
Midwest (USA) 43, 60, 61
migration 44, 56–8, 59, 63
milieu 94
Millward, Robert 79, 82
Minnesota, University of 143
mitarbeiter 29–30
modernity 36–7
modernization 22–3, 36
momentum 72–3
Montana 43, 50, 52, 53–4, 56, 58,
    60
Moore, Barrington 22
Mosse, George 32
Munich, University of 160
Mussolini, Benito 29
Myrdal, G. 90

National Institute of Health
    (Maryland) 147
national socialism 32–3
National Socialism (Germany) 29,
    30–36
nationalism 28
nationalization 79
Nebraska 43, 44, 50, 54, 56, 58, 60
Nelson, Richard R. 8, 12, 88
neoclassical economic theory
    crisis 26–7
    origins 20
    and path dependence 6–8, 10–11, 75,
        173–4, 195
    persistence of suboptimal pathways
        199–200
neo-institutionalism 192
Netherlands 111, 205
network effects 5, 78–9, 176, 183, 211
New Deal 29, 55
new institutionalism 109, 114

New Mexico 56, 58, 60
new political economy 207
New York University 143
Nobel Prize 148, 152, 199
nomothetic explanations of history
    19–21, 24
non-increasing returns 113
North, Douglass 8–9, 11, 12, 74, 90,
    199–200
North Dakota 43, 44, 50, 54, 56, 58,
    60

Öberg, PerOla 14
Oklahoma 44, 54, 55, 56, 60
open path dependence 202, 203–5,
    210–11
organizational isomorphism 143–6,
    152, 154–6, 162, 208
organizations
    characteristics facilitating radical
        innovation 149, 157–61, 162
    constraints on radical innovation
        153, 157–61, 162
    and history 141
    and institutional environments 139,
        141–3, 156–62
    organizational isomorphism 143–6,
        152, 154–6, 162, 208
    path dependence within 139, 146–54,
        156–62
organized labour 122, 125–6, 127–31
Ottosson, Jan 6, 9, 10, 115, 119
Oxford University 158

Paine, Thomas 26
Paris, University of 160
path cessation 202, 203, 208, 211
path departure 202, 208, 211
path dependence
    causes 181–7
    coordination 89, 112
    critical junctures 116–20, 200–201,
        203, 211
    definition 4, 15, 172–3
    degrees of 6–7, 140
    deterministic path dependence
        194–6, 210–11
    diffusion 191, 193–9, 210–11
    Dust Bowl 61–3
    early developments 70

and economic geography 87–91,
    102–4
and economics 1–13, 75, 166–7,
    173–4, 195
and efficiency 45–7
externalities 169–72
governance 12
and government 183–7
Great Plains 47–52, 53–63, 65–6
historical institutionalism 118
historical sociology 21–3
and history 1–2, 10, 19–21, 103, 140
increasing returns 88–91, 109, 182–3
and institutional change 192, 210–11
institutional theory 8–10, 11–12
and institutions 70–75, 78–83, 90,
    192
lock-in effects 4, 91, 140, 187–8
and market failure 168–72, 175–81
within organizations 156–62
origins 1–2
patterns of change 15
and political processes 108–12,
    113–14, 131–3, 188–9
and radical innovation 139, 146–54,
    156–62
and railways 71–5, 78–83
regulations 12, 78–82
road junctures 191, 199–205, 210–11
spatial clustering 102–4
strong 2
Swedish model 120–31
taxonomy 173–4
technology 2, 3–6, 70–75, 82, 183,
    193
trodden trail 191, 193–9, 210–11
types 191
weak 2
path diffusion 191, 193–9, 210–11
path stabilization 202, 211
path switching 202, 203, 208, 211
path-breaking crises
    concept of 24–7
    points of 27–30
    solutions in Germany and Sweden
        30–36
    as tool of analysis 37–40
pensions 123, 196–9, 203–5, 207
Perrow, Charles 73
persistence 166–7, 187–8

Pierson, Paul 9, 13, 74, 108, 113–14,
    116, 118, 140
Polanyi, Karl 27
political economy 14, 20
political influence
    inefficient economic systems 200
    institutional change 74–5, 206, 209
    railways 78, 79–82
    settlement of the Great Plains 47,
        51, 54–5
political institutionalism 206, 207
political processes
    actors 112–16, 118, 120, 132
    compensation 187
    critical junctures 109, 116–20, 132–3
    diminished competition 186
    and markets 27
    and path dependence 108–12,
        113–14, 131–3, 188–9
    Swedish model 120–31
political transaction costs 9–10, 46
Polya urn 88–9, 193, 196, 209, 211
Pontusson, Jonas 128
Porter, Michael E. 93, 95–6
poverty 28
Powell, John Wesley 43, 48, 50, 51, 65
Powell, W.W. 144
power relations 206, 209
precedence (in law) 201
Princeton 143
private ownership 79–82
property rights 47–52, 199
proximity, and path dependence 103
Prussia 81
public ownership 79–82
public policy 167–72, 183–7
Puffert, Douglas 2, 45, 77
punctuated equilibrium 8, 13, 118, 119
Putnam, Robert 109

QWERTY keyboard 3, 7, 45, 71–2,
    172, 179–80, 186, 193

radical innovation
    characteristics facilitating 149,
        157–61, 162
    constraints on 153, 157–61, 162
    indicators 147, 148
    and institutional environments 139,
        141–3

organizational isomorphism 143–6,
     154–6
and path dependence 139, 146–54,
     156–62
railways
  and growth 75–8
  and path dependence 71–5, 78–83
  standardized gauges 45, 77, 182, 188
random effects 5–6
rational choice 6–7, 115–16
rationality 10–11
rationalization 35–6
reactive sequences 113
recruitment 149, 158, 159, 160
reflexivity 36
regulation 12, 78–82
reliance 185
relocation 98
remediable inefficiencies 46–7, 174,
     179, 186
Renne, Roland 62
research organizations
  characteristics facilitating radical
     innovation 149, 157–61, 162
  constraints on radical innovation
     153, 157–61, 162
  and institutional environments 139,
     141–3
  organizational isomorphism 143–6,
     154–6
  path dependence within 139, 146–54,
     156–62
Resettlement Administration 54, 55
resources 92–3
retirement 196–9
reverse salients 73
rewards 187
Rice University 143
road junctures 191, 199–205, 210–11;
     see also critical junctures
Rockefeller, John D., Sr 152
Rockefeller University 143, 146, 151–2,
     158
Rokkan, Stein 200
Roosevelt, Franklin D. 29
Rosenberg, Nathan 2, 72
Ross, E.A. 98
Rothstein, Bo 116, 124
Rousseau, Jean Jacques 26
routines 12

rule-following 11
Rutherford, M. 7

salience 73
Salk Institute 146, 158
Saxenian, A. 94
Scandinavia 29
Schumpeter, Joseph A. 1–2
scientists 152
Scott, Peter 2, 76
Scripps Research Institute 143, 147,
     158
second-degree path dependence
  durability 173–4, 182
  economic growth 12
  and efficiency 195
  Great Plains 47
  nature of 46
  and rational choice 6–7
  relevance of 11
self-fulfilling prophecies 198–9
self-reinforcement
  developmental pathways 200–201
  diffusion 194–5, 196
  institutions 205–10, 211
  see also increasing returns
sequence of decisions 200–201
Shapiro, C. 45
Sheffield University 159
Sholes, Christopher Latham 179
Silicon Valley 94, 95, 207
Skocpol, T. 114
small events
  increasing returns 74
  path dependence 140, 161
  regional development 90
  technology lock-in effects 5–6, 172–3
  trodden trail 211
Smith, Adam 167–8
social construction of technology
     (SCOT) 72
social democracy 30–36
Social Democratic Party (Sweden)
     30–36, 121–3
social integration
  crisis points 27–30, 31
  scientific community 149, 150, 151,
     157
social learning 72
social networks 193–9, 207

social policy 111–12
social responsibility 29
social sciences 20
sociological institutionalism 206, 208
sociology 13, 20, 21–3
socio-technical systems 72
soft path dependency 24, 39
soil erosion 61–3
Sonderweg thesis 21–2
South Dakota 43, 44, 50, 54, 56, 58, 60
spatial clustering
    competitive advantage 95–9
    in economic geography 90, 91–7
    and history 97–102
    and path dependence 102–4
spatial dimensions and organizational
    structure 77–8
stabilization 202, 211
standards 183
Stanford University 143, 207
state ownership 79–82
steam power 172–3
Stiglitz, J.E. 3
Stinchcombe, Arthur 109, 145, 147
Strasbourg, University of 160
Stråth, Bo 14
Streeck, W. 9
Strong, Earle 180
subsidy 55–6, 57, 58
substitution 102
sugar 185
sunk costs 211
Sunley, P. 3, 7
Svensson, Torsten 121–2, 123
Sweden
    capitalism type 111
    corporatism 116, 124–7
    crisis response (1930s) 30–36
    railways 76, 79–80, 81
    Social Democratic Party 30–36,
        121–3
    wage-bargaining 127–31
    welfare state 112, 121–3
Swedish Employers' Confederation
    (SAF) 123–31
Swedish model 120–31
Swenson, Peter 128

tacit knowledge 94, 100, 103
Taeuber, C. 55

taxicabs 184
Taylor, C.C. 55
technology
    adoption 175–81, 183
    and growth 75–8
    and history 2, 45
    increasing returns 5–6, 89–91
    lock-in effects 3, 5–6, 45, 101, 172–3,
        176–81, 195, 196
    and path dependence 2, 3–6, 70–75,
        82, 183, 193
telephone networks 81–2
Texas 54, 55, 56, 58, 60
Thelen, Kathleen A. 8, 9, 74, 112, 114,
    118–20, 128, 132
third-degree path dependence
    and efficiency 195–6
    market failure 174, 175–81
    nature of 46
    and rational choice 6–7
Thomas, M. 4
Thornthwaite, Warren 54
threshold model 117
Thucydides 26
tightly coupled systems 73, 82
Tilly, C. 141
time horizons 116–20
tipping point 194, 196, 211
tobacco 184, 189
Törnqvist, Christer 128
trade unions 122, 125–6, 127–31
Trägårdh, Lars 32, 34
transaction costs
    agglomeration effects 93
    externalities 171
    inefficient economic systems 199
    political transaction costs 9–10, 46
    remediability 186
transitional gains trap 184–6
trodden trail 191, 193–9, 210–11

ubiquitification 102
unemployment 28, 29
United Kingdom (UK) 76–7, 111; *see
    also* Britain
United States of America (USA)
    and Canada 78
    capitalism type 111
    democracy 22
    institutional environments 157, 162

radical innovations in biomedical
science 139, 146–7
railways 76, 79, 80, 81
social responsibility 29
sugar 185
taxicabs 184
tobacco 184, 189
universities 143, 144, 146, 151–2,
158, 159, 207
welfare state 112
see also Great Plains
universities
agglomeration 207
institutional environments 142–3,
144, 151–2, 158, 159, 160
organizational isomorphism 146,
154–6, 208
University College London 158
urbanization economies 92
utilitarian theories 206, 207

Vanberg, V. 7
Vanderbilt University 143
varieties of capitalism 9, 111, 143
Veblen, Thorstein 2, 76
vested interests 211
veto points 81, 82
VHS 6, 7, 45, 173, 174, 175, 180–81,
183
videocassette recorders (VCRs) 6, 7,
173, 174, 175, 180–81, 183

Visser, Jelle 131
volk (*folk*) concept 32–6
Vromen, J.J. 7

wage-bargaining 127–31
Washington, University of 158
weather, Great Plains 43–4, 48–50,
51–2
Webb, J.N. 56
Weber, Max 38, 39
welfare economics 171
welfare state
Germany 111, 203–4, 207–8,
209
group labels 111–12
open path dependence 203–5
path-dependent diffusion 196–9
rise of 13
Sweden 112, 121–3
Swedish model 120–31
Western democracy 22–3
Williamson, O.E. 186
wind erosion 61–3
Windows 195
Winter, Sidney G. 8, 12, 88
Wisconsin, University of 143, 159
Witt, U. 7
workers' organizations 35–6
Works Progress Administration
55
Worster, Donald 55